Joseph Schmuller

SAMS
Teach Yourself
UML

in 24 Hours

SECOND EDITION

SAMS

201 West 103rd St., Indianapolis, Indiana 46290 USA

Sams Teach Yourself UML in 24 Hours, Second Edition

Copyright ©2002 by Sams Publishing

International Standard Book Number: 0-672-32238-2

Library of Congress Catalog Card Number: 2001089207

Printed in the United States of America

First Printing: August 2001

03   02   4   3   2

Trademarks

Warning and Disclaimer

EXECUTIVE EDITOR
Michael Stephens

DEVELOPMENT EDITOR
Christy A. Franklin

MANAGING EDITOR
Matt Purcell

PROJECT EDITOR
Andy Beaster

PRODUCTION EDITOR
Matt Wynalda

INDEXER
Sandra Henselmeier

TECHNICAL EDITOR
Paul Gustavson

INTERIOR DESIGN
Gary Adair

COVER DESIGN
Aren Howell

LAYOUT TECHNICIAN
Cheryl Lynch

Contents at a Glance

Contents

Contents

About the Author

JOSEPH SCHMULLER is a Functional Analyst with Convergys. From 1991 through 1997, he was Editor in Chief of *PC AI* Magazine. He has written numerous articles and reviews on advanced computing technology, and is the author of *ActiveX No experience required* and *Dynamic HTML Master the Essentials*. Holder of a Ph.D. from the University of Wisconsin, he is an Adjunct Professor at the University of North Florida.

Dedication

To my wonderful mother, Sara Riba Schmuller,

Who taught me how to teach myself.

Acknowledgments

Writing a book is an arduous process. Happily, the world-class team at Sams Publishing has made it a lot easier. It's a pleasure to acknowledge their contributions. For the first edition, Acquisitions Editor Chris Webb and Development Editor Matt Purcell helped turn my thoughts into readable prose. Above and beyond their considerable editorial skills, I thank them for their encouragement, patience, and support. Technical Editors Bill Rowe and Michael Tobler made sure the content was technically sound, and I'm grateful to them for it. Senior Editor Susan Moore and the outstanding artists and Production Staff turned the manuscript and its numerous diagrams into the book you're reading. For the second edition, Executive Editor Michael Stephens, Development Editor Christy Franklin, Production Editor Matt Wynalda, and Technical Editor Paul Gustavson did an exemplary job from start to finish. Their patience, wisdom, and editorial skills have strengthened the book.

My thanks to David Fugate of Waterside Productions for putting me in another rewarding project.

When I wrote the first edition, I was privileged to work every day with a group of excellent professionals at Bank of America's Consumer Finance Technologies (CFT) Division—specifically, as a member of the Reusable Objects and Components group. My colleagues provided empathy and cooperation. In particular, conversations with Keith Barrett and Rob Warner helped clarify my thinking on a number of issues. Sadly, the time of my involvement with the first edition marked the untimely passing of our Division Director, Tom Williamson. Tom was the heart and soul of CFT, and was an advisor, mentor, colleague, and friend.

As I completed the second edition, I began working with a wonderful group of new colleagues at Convergys.

I thank my dearest friends, the Spragues of Madison, Wisconsin, in whose neighborhood I happened to be when I started writing the first edition and again when I finished it. I thank my mother and my brother David for their love and for always being there for me, and Kathryn (LOML and GOMD) for always being everything to me.

Tell Us What You Think!

As the reader of this book, *you* are our most important critic and commentator. We value your opinion and want to know what we're doing right, what we could do better, what areas you'd like to see us publish in, and any other words of wisdom you're willing to pass our way.

As an Executive Editor for Sams Publishing, I welcome your comments. You can fax, e-mail, or write me directly to let me know what you did or didn't like about this book—as well as what we can do to make our books stronger.

Please note that I cannot help you with technical problems related to the topic of this book, and that due to the high volume of mail I receive, I might not be able to reply to every message.

When you write, please be sure to include this book's title and author as well as your name and phone or fax number. I will carefully review your comments and share them with the author and editors who worked on the book.

Fax: 317-581-4770

E-mail: feedback@samspublishing.com

Mail: Michael Stephens
          Executive Editor
          Sams Publishing
          201 West 103rd Street
          Indianapolis, IN 46290 USA

Introduction

It's all about vision. A complex system comes into being when someone has a vision of how technology can make things better. Developers have to fully understand the vision and keep it firmly in mind as they create the system that realizes the vision.

System development projects are successful to the extent that they bridge the gap between visionary and developer. The Unified Modeling Language (UML) is a tool for building the bridge. It helps you capture the vision for a system, and then enables you to communicate the vision to anyone who has a stake in the system. It does this via a set of symbols and diagrams. Each diagram plays a different role within the development process.

The goal of this book—for both the first and second editions—is to give you a firm foundation in the UML in 24 hours of study. Each hour presents examples to strengthen your understanding, and most of the hours provide exercises that enable you to put your new-found knowledge to use.

In preparing this edition I went through the original and tightened up the prose, adding and updating material where necessary. I've refined some of the models and diagrams, and added quiz questions and exercises. Along the way, I eliminated errors and inconsistencies that a number of readers were kind enough to point out. I've divided the book into three parts. Part I, "Getting Started," gives an overview of the UML and then moves into object-orientation, which forms the foundation concepts for diagramming objects and classes. I examine the *use case*—a construct for showing how a system looks to a user, and then show how to diagram use cases. I spend extra time on the concepts behind object-orientation and use cases, as these two ideas form the basis for the parts of the UML you're most likely to use most of the time. The remaining hours in Part I get you working with the rest of the UML diagrams.

Part II, "A Case Study," presents a simplified methodology for development along with a fictional case study. Thus, the hours in Part II show how the UML fits into the context of a development project. You'll see how the elements of the UML work together in a model of a system.

In Part III, "Looking Ahead," we apply the UML to design patterns and embedded systems, and then examine its application in a couple of other areas.

Several vendors provide packages that enable you to create UML diagrams and coordinate them into a model. The best known package is Rational Rose. Another is Select Enterprise. Visual UML is a worthy contender. So are GDPro and the modeling tool from TogetherSoft.

Microsoft has licensed Rational's technology and offers Visual Modeler, a subset of Rational Rose that Visual Studio developers can incorporate into their work. Just after the first edition of this book was published, Microsoft acquired Visio, and the higher-level editions of the Microsoft Visio diagramming tool provide UML capabilities.

For this book, however, all you'll need are pencil and paper to draw the diagrams, and a healthy curiosity about the state of the art in system design.

Let's get started!

Conventions Used in This Book

A Note presents interesting pieces of information related to the surrounding discussion.

 New Term icons highlight clear definitions of new, essential terms. The terms appear in italic.

PART I
Getting Started

Hour

HOUR 1

Introducing the UML

The Unified Modeling Language (UML) is one of the most exciting tools in the world of object-oriented system development today. Why? The UML provides a visual modeling language that enables system builders to create blueprints that capture their visions in a standard, easy-to-understand way, and provides a mechanism to effectively share and communicate these designs with others.

In this hour, you'll learn

- Why the UML is necessary
- How the UML came to be
- The diagrams of the UML
- Why it's important to use a number of different types of diagrams

Communicating the vision is of utmost importance. Before the advent of the UML, system development was often a hit-or-miss proposition. System analysts would try to assess the needs of their clients, generate a requirements analysis in some notation that the analyst understood (but not always the client), give that analysis to a programmer or team of programmers, and hope that the final product was the system the client wanted.

> **Some Terms**
>
> Throughout this book, consider a *system* to be a combination of software and hardware that provides a solution for a business problem. *System development* is the creation of a system for a *client*, the person who has the problem to be solved. An *analyst* documents the client's problem and relays it to *developers*, programmers who build the software that solve the problem and deploy the software on computer hardware.

Because system development is a human activity, the potential for error lurked at every stage of the process. The analyst might have misunderstood the client. The analyst might have produced a document the client couldn't comprehend. The results of the analysis might not have been clear to the programmers, who subsequently might have created a program that was difficult to use and not a solution to the client's original problem.

Is it any wonder that many of the long-standing systems in use today are clunky, cumbersome, and hard to use?

Adding a Method to the Madness

In the early days of computing, few programmers relied on in-depth analyses of the problem at hand. If they did any analysis at all, it was typically on the back of a napkin. They often wrote programs from the ground up, creating code as they went along. Although this added an aura of romance and daring to the process, it's proved to be inappropriate in today's high-stakes business world.

Today, a well-thought-out plan is crucial. A client has to understand what a development team is going to do, and must be able to indicate changes if the team hasn't fully grasped the client's needs (or if the client changes his or her mind along the way). Also, development is typically a team-oriented effort, so each member of the team has to know where his or her work fits into the big picture (and what that big picture is).

As the world becomes more complex, the computer-based systems that inhabit the world also must increase in complexity. They often involve multiple pieces of hardware and software, networked across great distances, linked to databases that contain mountains of information. If you want to create successful systems, how do you get your hands around the complexity?

The key is to organize the design process in a way that analysts, clients, programmers, and others involved in system development can understand and agree on. The UML provides the organization.

Just as you wouldn't build a complex structure like an office building without first creating a detailed blueprint, you wouldn't build a complex system to inhabit that office building without first creating a detailed design plan. The plan should be one that you could show a client just as surely as an architect shows a blueprint to the person who's paying for a building. That design plan should result from a careful analysis of the client's needs.

Short timeframes for development are another feature of the contemporary system development landscape. When the deadlines fall on top of one another, a solid design is an absolute necessity.

Still another aspect of modern life necessitates solid design: corporate takeovers. When one company acquires another, the new organization might change important aspects of an in-progress development project (the implementation tool, the coding language, and more). A bulletproof project blueprint will facilitate the changeover. If the design is solid, a change in implementation can proceed smoothly.

The need for solid designs has brought about a need for a design notation that analysts, developers, and clients will accept as a standard—just as the notation in schematic diagrams of circuits serves as a standard for electronics engineers and the notation in Feynman diagrams serves as a standard for physicists. The UML is that notation.

How the UML Came to Be

The UML is the brainchild of Grady Booch, James Rumbaugh, and Ivar Jacobson. Dubbed "the Three Amigos," these gentlemen worked in separate organizations through the '80s and early '90s, each devising his own methodology for object-oriented analysis and design. Their methodologies achieved preeminence over those of numerous competitors. By the mid '90s, they began to borrow ideas from each other, so they decided to evolve their work together.

> Hours 2, "Understanding Object-Orientation," and 4, "Working with Relationships," deal with object-orientation. Object-oriented concepts play major roles throughout the book.

In 1994, Rumbaugh joined Rational Software Corporation, where Booch was already working. Jacobson enlisted at Rational a year later.

The rest, as they say, is history. Draft versions of the UML began to circulate throughout the software industry and the resulting feedback brought substantial changes. As many corporations felt the UML would serve their strategic purposes, a UML consortium sprung up.

Members included DEC, Hewlett-Packard, Intellicorp, Microsoft, Oracle, Texas Instruments, Rational, and others. In 1997, the consortium produced version 1.0 of the UML and submitted it to the Object Management Group (OMG) in response to the OMG's request for a proposal for a standard modeling language.

The consortium expanded, generated version 1.1, and submitted it to the OMG, who adopted it in late 1997. The OMG took over the maintenance of the UML and produced two more revisions in 1998. The UML has become a de facto standard in the software industry, and it continues to evolve. It's currently in version 1.3, with version 2.0 expected sometime in 2002.

The Components of the UML

The UML consists of a number of graphical elements that combine to form diagrams. Because it's a language, the UML has rules for combining these elements. Rather than tell you about these elements and rules, let's jump right into the diagrams because they're what you'll use to do system analysis.

> This approach is analogous to learning a foreign language by using it, instead of by learning its grammar and conjugating its verbs. After you've spent some time using a foreign language it's easier to understand the grammatical rules and verb conjugations anyway.

NEW TERM   The purpose of the diagrams is to present multiple views of a system; this set of multiple views is called a *model*. A UML model of a system is something like a scale model of a building along with an artist's rendition of the building. It's important to note that a UML model describes *what* a system is supposed to do. It doesn't tell *how* to implement the system.

The subsections that follow briefly describe the most common diagrams of the UML and the concepts they represent. Later in Part I, you'll examine each one much more closely. Bear in mind that hybrids of these diagrams are possible, and that the UML provides ways for you to organize and extend its diagrams.

Models

The concept of a model is useful throughout the scientific and engineering fields. In the most general sense, when you create a model you're using something that you know a great deal about to help you understand something you know very little about. In some fields, a model is a set of equations. In others, a model is a computer simulation. Many types of models are possible.

1

> For our purposes, a model is a set of UML diagrams that we can examine, assess, and modify in order to understand and develop a system.

Class Diagram

Think about the things in the world around you. (A pretty broad request, admittedly, but try it anyway!) It's probably the case that most of them have attributes (properties) and that they behave in a certain way. We can think of these behaviors as a set of operations.

NEW TERM You'll also see that things naturally fall into categories (automobiles, furniture, washing machines...). We refer to these categories as classes. A *class* is a category or group of things that have similar attributes and common behaviors. Here's an example. Anything in the class of washing machines has attributes such as brand name, model, serial number, and capacity. Behaviors for things in this class include the operations "add clothes," "add detergent," "turn on," and "remove clothes."

Figure 1.1 shows an example of the UML notation that captures these attributes and behaviors of a washing machine. A rectangle is the icon that represents the class. It's divided into three areas. The uppermost area contains the name, the middle area holds the attributes, and the lowest area the operations. A class diagram consists of a number of these rectangles connected by lines that show how the classes relate to one another.

FIGURE **1.1**

The UML class icon.

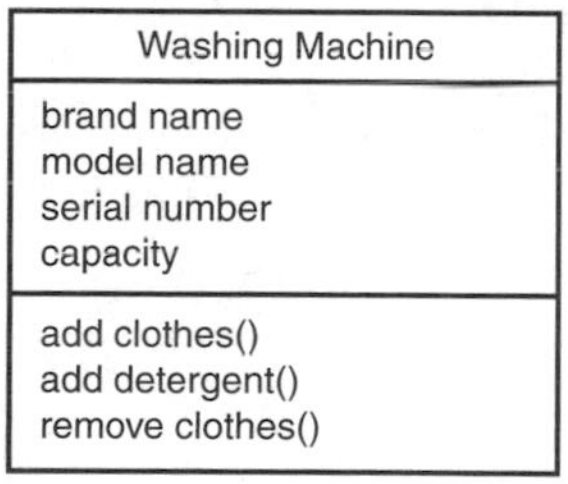

Washing Machine
brand name model name serial number capacity
add clothes() add detergent() remove clothes()

Why bother to think about classes of things and their attributes and behaviors? In order to interact with our complex world, most modern software simulates some aspect of the world. Decades of experience suggest that it's easiest to develop software that does this when the software represents classes of real-world things. Class diagrams provide the representations that developers work from.

Class diagrams help on the analysis side, too. They enable analysts to talk to clients in the clients' terminology and thus stimulate the clients to reveal important details about the problem they want solved.

Object Diagram

NEW TERM An *object* is an instance of a class—a specific thing that has specific values of the attributes and behavior. Your washer, for example, might have the brand name Laundatorium, the model name Washmeister, a serial number of GL57774, and a capacity of 16 pounds.

Figure 1.2 shows how the UML represents an object. Note that the icon is a rectangle, just like the class icon, but the name is underlined. The name of the specific instance is on the left side of a colon, and the name of the class is on the right side of the colon.

FIGURE 1.2
The UML object icon.

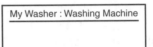

Use Case Diagram

NEW TERM A *use case* is a description of a system's behavior from a user's standpoint. For system developers, this is a valuable tool: it's a tried-and-true technique for gathering system requirements from a user's point of view. That's important if the goal is to build a system that real people (and not just computerphiles) can use.

We'll discuss use cases in greater detail later. For now, here's a quick example. You use a washing machine, obviously, to wash your clothes. Figure 1.3 shows how you'd represent this in a UML use case diagram.

FIGURE 1.3
The UML use case diagram.

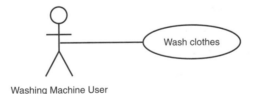

Washing Machine User

NEW TERM The little stick figure that corresponds to the washing machine user is called an *actor*. The ellipse represents the use case. Note that the actor—the entity that initiates the use case—can be a person or another system.

State Diagram

At any given time, an object is in a particular state. A person can be a newborn, infant, child, adolescent, teenager, or adult. An elevator is either moving upward, stopped, or moving downward. A washing machine can be either in the soak, wash, rinse, spin, or off state.

The UML state diagram, shown in Figure 1.4, captures this bit of reality. The figure shows that the washing machine transitions from one state to the next.

FIGURE 1.4

The UML state diagram.

The symbol at the top of the figure represents the start state and the symbol at the bottom represents the end state.

Sequence Diagram

Class diagrams and object diagrams represent static information. In a functioning system, however, objects interact with one another, and these interactions occur over time. The UML sequence diagram shows the time-based dynamics of the interaction.

Continuing with the washing machine example, the components of the machine include a water pipe (for fresh water input), a drum (the part that holds the clothes), and a drain. These, of course, are also objects. (As you'll see, an object can consist of other objects.)

What happens when you invoke the Wash clothes use case? Assuming you've completed the "add clothes," "add detergent," and "turn on" operations, the sequence of steps goes something like this:

1. Water enters the drum via the water pipe
2. The drum remains stationary for five minutes
3. Water stops entering
4. The drum rotates back and forth for fifteen minutes
5. Soapy water leaves via the drain
6. Water entry restarts

7. The drum continues rotating back and forth

8. Water entry stops

9. Rinse water exits via the drain

10. The drum rotation becomes unidirectional and increases in speed for five minutes

11. The drum rotation stops, and the wash is done

Figure 1.5 shows a sequence diagram that captures the interactions among the water supply, drum, and drain (represented as rectangles at the top of the diagram) that take place over time. Time, in this diagram, proceeds from top to bottom.

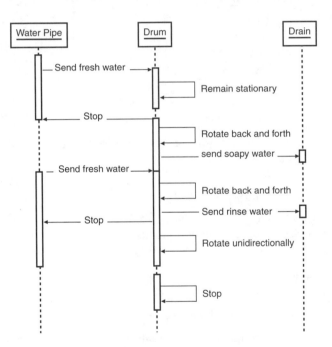

By the way, getting back to the ideas about states, we can characterize steps 1 and 2 as the soak state, 3 and 4 as the wash state, 5 through 7 as the rinse state, and 8 through 10 as the spin state.

Activity Diagram

The activities that occur within a use case or within an object's behavior typically occur in a sequence, as in the eleven steps of the preceding subsection. Figure 1.6 shows how the UML activity diagram represents steps 4 through 6 of that sequence.

FIGURE 1.6
The UML activity diagram.

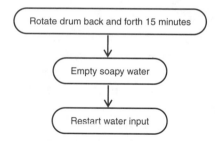

Collaboration Diagram

The elements of a system work together to accomplish the system's objectives, and a modeling language must have a way of representing this. The UML collaboration diagram, designed for this purpose, is shown in Figure 1.7. This example adds an internal timer to the set of classes that constitute a washing machine. After a certain amount of time, the timer stops the flow of water and starts the drum rotating back and forth.

FIGURE 1.7
The UML collaboration diagram.

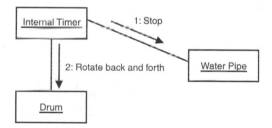

Component Diagram

This diagram and the next one move away from the world of washing machines because the component diagram and the deployment diagram are geared expressly toward computer systems.

Modern software development proceeds via components, which is particularly important in team-based development efforts. Without elaborating too much at this point, Figure 1.8 shows how the UML represents a software component.

FIGURE 1.8
The UML component diagram.

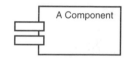

Deployment Diagram

The UML deployment diagram shows the physical architecture of a computer-based system. It can depict the computers and devices, show their connections with one another, and show the software that sits on each machine. Each computer is represented by a cube, with interconnections between computers drawn as lines connecting the cubes. Figure 1.9 presents an example.

FIGURE **1.9**
The UML deployment diagram.

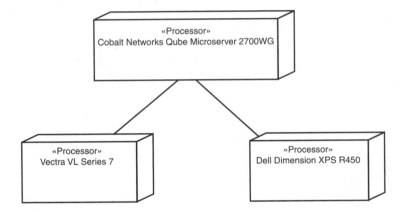

Some Other Features

Earlier, I mentioned that the UML provides features that enable you to organize and extend the diagrams.

Packages

NEW TERM   Sometimes, you'll find the need to organize the elements of a diagram into a group. You might want to show that a number of classes or components are part of a particular subsystem. To do this, you group them into a *package*, represented by a tabbed folder, as in Figure 1.10.

FIGURE **1.10**
The UML package allows you to group the elements of a diagram.

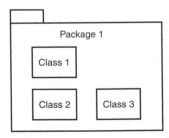

Notes

NEW TERM It often happens that one part of a diagram doesn't present an unambiguous explanation of why it's there or how to work with it. When that's the case, the UML *note* is helpful. Think of a note as the graphic equivalent of a yellow sticky. Its icon is a rectangle with a folded corner. Inside the rectangle is explanatory text. Figure 1.11 shows an example. You attach the note to a diagram element by connecting a dashed line from the element to the note.

FIGURE 1.11

In any diagram, you can add explanatory comments by attaching a note.

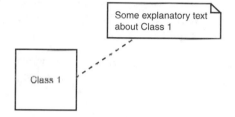

Stereotypes

NEW TERM The UML provides a number of useful items, but it's not an exhaustive set. Every now and then, you'll be designing a system that needs some tailor-made items. *Stereotypes* enable you to take existing UML elements and turn them into new ones. It's sort of like buying a suit off the rack and having it altered to fit your particular measurements (as opposed to creating one out of a bolt of cloth). Think of a stereotype as just this kind of alteration. You represent it as a name enclosed in two pairs of angle brackets called *guillemets* and then you apply that name appropriately.

NEW TERM The concept of an interface provides a good example. An *interface* is a class that just has operations and has no attributes. It's a set of behaviors that you might want to use again and again throughout your model. Instead of inventing a new element to represent an interface, you can use a class icon with «Interface» situated just above the class name. Figure 1.12 shows you how.

FIGURE 1.12

A stereotype allows you to create new elements from existing ones.

Why So Many Diagrams?

As you can see, the UML's diagrams make it possible to examine a system from a number of viewpoints. It's important to note that not all the diagrams must appear in every UML model. Most UML models, in fact, contain a subset of the diagrams I listed.

NEW TERM Why is it necessary to have numerous views of a system? Typically, a system has a number of different *stakeholders*—people who have interests in different aspects of the system. Let's return to the washing machine example. If you're designing a washing machine's motor, you have one view of the system. If you're writing the operating instructions, you have another. If you're designing the machine's overall shape, you see the system in a totally different way than if you just want to wash your clothes.

Conscientious system design involves all the possible viewpoints, and each UML diagram gives you a way of incorporating a particular view. The objective is to satisfy every type of stakeholder.

Summary

System development is a human activity. Without an easy-to-understand notation system, the development process has great potential for error.

The UML is a notation system that has become a standard in the system development world. It's the result of work done by Grady Booch, James Rumbaugh, and Ivar Jacobson. Consisting of a set of diagrams, the UML provides a standard that enables the system analyst to build a multifaceted blueprint that's comprehensible to clients, programmers, and everyone involved in the development process. It's necessary to have all these diagrams because each one speaks to a different stakeholder in the system.

A UML model tells *what* a system is supposed to do. It doesn't tell *how* the system is supposed to do it.

Q&A

Q I've seen the Unified Modeling Language referred to as "UML" and also as "the UML." Which is correct?

A The creators of the language prefer "the UML."

Q **You've made the point that the UML is a great tool for analysts. The deployment diagram, however, doesn't seem like something that would be all that useful in the analysis stage of system development. Isn't it more appropriate for a later stage?**

A It's really never too early to start thinking about deployment (or other issues traditionally left for later in development). Although it's true that the analyst is concerned with talking to clients and users, early in the process an analyst might think about the computers and components that will make up the system hardware. Sometimes the client dictates this. Sometimes the client wants a recommendation from the development team. Certainly a system architect will find the deployment diagram useful.

Q **You mentioned that hybrid diagrams are possible. Does UML, excuse me, *the* UML impose limitations on which elements you can combine with which on a diagram?**

A No. The UML sets no limits. It's usually the case, however, that a diagram contains one kind of element. You could put class icons on a deployment diagram, but that might not be very useful.

Workshop

You've jumped into the UML. Now it's time to firm up your knowledge of this great tool by answering some questions and going through some exercises. The answers appear in Appendix A, "Quiz Answers."

Quiz

1. Why is it necessary to have a variety of diagrams in a model of a system?

2. Which diagrams give a static view of a system?

3. Which diagrams provide a dynamic view of a system (that is, show change over time)?

Exercises

1. Suppose you're building a computer-based system that plays chess with a user. Which UML diagrams would be useful in designing the system? Why?

2. For the system in the exercise you just completed, list the questions you would ask a potential user and why you would ask them.

HOUR 2

Understanding Object-Orientation

In this hour, you'll learn about object-orientation, the foundation of much of the modeling you'll do. Specifically, you'll learn these important object-oriented concepts:

- Abstraction
- Inheritance
- Polymorphism
- Encapsulation
- Message sending
- Associations
- Aggregation

Object-orientation has taken the software world by storm, and rightfully so. As a way of creating programs, it has a number of advantages. It fosters a component-based approach to software development so that you first create a system by creating a set of classes. Then, you can expand the system by adding capabilities to components you've already built or by adding new components.

Finally, you can reuse the classes you created when you build a new system, cutting down substantially on system development time.

The UML plays into all this by allowing you to build easy-to-use and easy-to-understand models of objects so that programmers can create them in software.

Object-orientation is a mindset—a mindset that depends on a few fundamental principles. In this hour, you'll learn those principles. You'll find out what makes objects tick and how to use them in analysis and design. In the next hour, you'll begin to apply UML to these principles.

Objects, Objects Everywhere

Objects, concrete and otherwise, are all around us. They make up our world. As I pointed out in the previous hour, modern software typically simulates the world—or a small slice of it—so programs usually mimic the objects in the world. If you understand some essentials of objects, you'll comprehend what has to go into the software representations of them.

NEW TERM   First and foremost, an object is an instance of a class (a category). You and I, for example, are instances of the person class. An object has *structure*. That is, it has attributes (properties) and behavior. An object's behavior consists of the *operations* it carries out. Attributes and operations taken together are called *features*.

As objects in the person class, you and I each have these attributes: height, weight, and age. (You can imagine a number of others.) We also perform these operations: eat, sleep, read, write, speak, go to work, and more. If we were to create a system that deals with information on people—say, a payroll system or a system for a human resources department—we would likely incorporate some of these attributes and some of these operations in our software.

In the world of object-orientation, a class serves another purpose in addition to categorization. A class is a template for making objects. Think of it as a cookie cutter that stamps out new objects. (Some might argue that this is the same as categorization, but let's avoid that debate.)

Let's go back to the washing machine example. If the washing machine class is specified as having the attributes brand name, model name, serial number, and capacity—along with the operations add clothes, add detergent, and remove clothes—you have a mechanism for turning out new instances of the washing machine class. That is, you can create new objects based on this class (see Figure 2.1).

This is particularly important in the world of object-oriented software development. Although this book won't focus on programming, it helps your understanding of object-orientation if you know that classes in object-oriented programs can create new instances.

In Hour 3, "Working with Object-Orientation," you'll see that class names like *washing machine* are written as WashingMachine and feature names like *serial number* are written as serialNumber. During this hour we're discussing object-orientation in English rather than in the UML, so I'll stick to the way you normally see names in print.

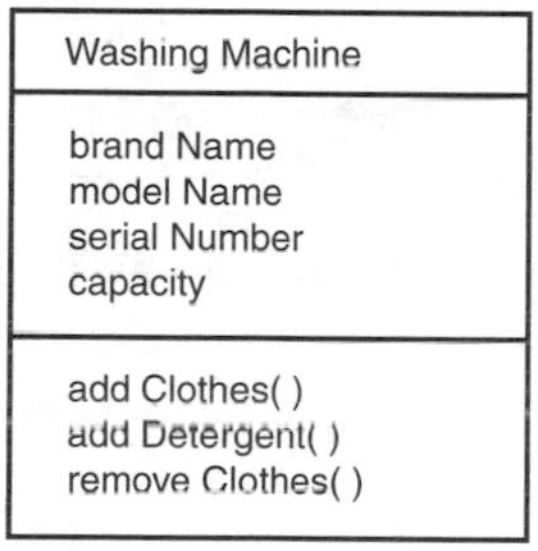

FIGURE 2.1

The washing machine class—the original model of a washing machine—is a template for creating new instances of washing machines.

Washing Machine
brand Name model Name serial Number capacity
add Clothes( ) add Detergent( ) remove Clothes( )

Here's something else to be aware of. Remember that the purpose of object-orientation is to develop software that reflects (that is, "models") a particular slice of the world. The more attributes and behaviors you take into account, the more your model will be in tune with reality. In the washing machine example, you'll have a potentially more accurate model if you include the attributes drum volume, internal timer, trap, motor, and motor speed. You might also increase the accuracy of the model if you include the operations add bleach, time the soak, time the wash, time the rinse, and time the spin (see Figure 2.2).

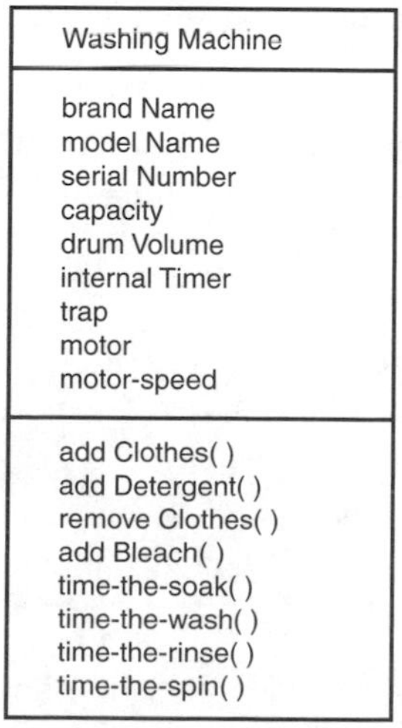

FIGURE 2.2

Adding attributes and operations brings the model closer to reality.

Washing Machine
brand Name model Name serial Number capacity drum Volume internal Timer trap motor motor-speed
add Clothes( ) add Detergent( ) remove Clothes( ) add Bleach( ) time-the-soak( ) time-the-wash( ) time-the-rinse( ) time-the-spin( )

Some Concepts

Object-orientation goes beyond just modeling attributes and behavior. It considers other aspects of objects as well. These aspects are called *abstraction*, *inheritance*, *polymorphism*, and *encapsulation*. Three other important parts of object-orientation are *message sending*, *associations*, and *aggregation*. Let's examine each of these concepts.

Abstraction

 Abstraction means, simply, to filter out an object's properties and operations until just the ones you need are left. What does "just the ones you need" mean?

Different types of problems require different amounts of information, even if those problems are in the same general area. In the second pass at building a washing machine class, more attributes and operations emerged than in the first pass. Was it worth it?

If you're part of a development team that's ultimately going to create a computer program that simulates exactly how a washing machine does what it does, it's definitely worth it. A computer program like that (which might be useful to design engineers who are actually building a washing machine) has to have enough in it to make accurate predictions about what will happen when the washing machine is built, fully functioning, and washing clothes. For this kind of program, in fact, you can filter out the serial number attribute because it's probably not going to be very helpful.

If, on the other hand, you're going to create software to track the transactions in a laundry that has a number of washing machines, it's probably not worth it. In this program, you might not need all the detailed attributes and operations mentioned in the preceding section. You might, however, want to include the serial number of each washing machine object.

In any case, what you're left with, after you've made your decisions about what to include and what to exclude, is an abstraction of a washing machine.

Inheritance

 A class, as I previously mentioned, is a category of objects (and, in the software world, a template for creating new objects). An object is an instance of a class. This idea has an important consequence: As an instance of a class, an object has all the characteristics of its class. This is called *inheritance*. Whatever attributes and operations you decide on for the washing machine class, each object in that class will inherit those attributes and operations.

Not only can an object inherit from a class, a class can inherit from another class. Washing machines, refrigerators, microwave ovens, toasters, dishwashers, radios, waffle makers, blenders, and irons are all classes. They're also members of a more general class: appliances.

An appliance has the attributes on-off switch and electric wire, and the operations turn-on and turn-off. Each of the appliance classes inherits those attributes as well. Thus, if you know something is an appliance, you know immediately that it has the appliance class's attributes and operations.

NEW TERM Another way to say this is that washing machine, refrigerator, microwave oven, and so on are all *subclasses* of the appliance class. The appliance class, in turn, is a *superclass* of all those others. Figure 2.3 shows the superclass-subclass relationship.

FIGURE 2.3

Appliances inherit the attributes and operations of the appliance class. Each appliance is a subclass of the appliance class. The appliance class is a superclass of each subclass.

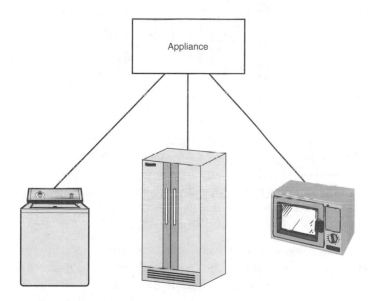

Inheritance doesn't have to stop there. Appliance, for example, is a subclass of the household item class. Furniture is another subclass of household item, as Figure 2.4 shows. Furniture, of course, has its own subclasses.

FIGURE 2.4

Superclasses can also be subclasses, and inherit from other superclasses.

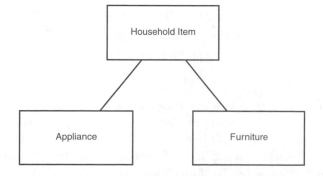

Polymorphism

NEW TERM Sometimes an operation has the same name in different classes. For example, you can open a door, you can open a window, you can open a newspaper, a present, a bank account, or a conversation. In each case, you're performing a different operation. In object-orientation, each class "knows" how that operation is supposed to take place. This is *polymorphism* (see Figure 2.5).

FIGURE 2.5

In polymorphism, an operation can have the same name in different classes, and proceed differently in each class.

At first look, it would seem that this concept is more important to software developers than to modelers. After all, software developers have to create the software that implements these methods in computer programs, and they have to be aware of important differences among operations that might have the same name. And they can build software classes that "know" what they're supposed to do.

But polymorphism is important to modelers, too. It allows the modeler to speak to the client (who's familiar with the slice of the world to be modeled) in the client's own words and terminology. Sometimes that terminology naturally leads to operation words (like "open") that can have more than one meaning. Polymorphism enables the modeler to maintain that terminology without having to make up artificial words to maintain an unnecessary uniqueness of terms.

Encapsulation

In a TV commercial that aired a few years ago, two people discuss all the money they'll save if they dial a particular 7-digit prefix before dialing a long-distance phone call.

One of them asks, incredulously, "How does that work?"

The other replies: "How does popcorn pop? Who cares?"

NEW TERM That's the essence of *encapsulation*: When an object carries out its operations, those operations are hidden (see Figure 2.6). When most people watch a television show, they usually don't know or care about the complex electronics that sits in back of the TV screen and all the many operations that have to occur in order to paint the image on the screen. The TV does what it does and hides the process from us. Most other appliances work that way, too. (Thankfully!)

FIGURE 2.6

Objects encapsulate what they do. That is, they hide the inner workings of their operations from the outside world and from other objects.

The TV hides its operations from the person watching it.

Why is this important? In the software world, encapsulation helps cut down on the potential for bad things to happen. In a system that consists of objects, the objects depend on each other in various ways. If one of them happens to malfunction and software engineers have to change it in some way, hiding its operations from other objects means that it probably won't be necessary to change those other objects.

Turning from software to reality, you see the importance of encapsulation in the objects you work with, too. Your computer monitor, in a sense, hides its operations from your computer's CPU. When something goes wrong with your monitor, you either fix or replace it. You probably won't have to fix or replace the CPU along with it.

NEW TERM   While we're on the subject, here's a related concept. An object hides what it does from other objects and from the outside world. (For this reason, encapsulation is also called *information hiding*.) But an object does have to present a "face" to the outside world so you can initiate those operations. The TV, for example, has a set of buttons either on the TV itself or on a remote. A washing machine has a set of dials that enable you to set temperature and water level. The TV's buttons and the washing machine's dials are called *interfaces*.

Message Sending

I've mentioned that in a system, objects work together. They do this by sending messages to one another. One object sends another a message to perform an operation, and the receiving object performs that operation.

A TV and a remote present a nice intuitive example from the world around us. When you want to watch a TV show, you hunt around for the remote, settle into your favorite chair, and push the On button. What happens? The remote-object sends a message (literally!) to the TV-object to turn itself on. The TV-object receives this message, knows how to perform the turn-on operation, and turns itself on. When you want to watch a different channel, you click the appropriate button on the remote, and the remote-object sends a different message—change channel—to the TV-object. The remote can also communicate with the TV via other messages for changing the volume, muting the volume, and setting up closed captioning.

Let's go back to interfaces for a moment. Most of the things you do from the remote, you can also do by getting out of the chair, going to the TV, and clicking buttons on the TV. (You might actually try that sometime!) The interface the TV presents to you (the set of buttons) is obviously not the same interface it presents to the remote (an infrared receiver). Figure 2.7 illustrates this.

FIGURE 2.7

An example of message sending from one object to another. The remote-object sends a message to the TV-object to turn itself on. The TV-object receives the message through its interface, an infrared receiver.

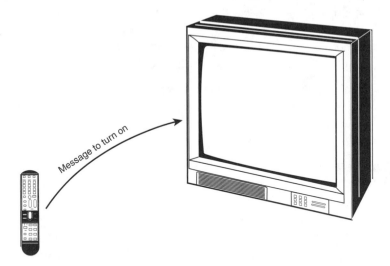

Message to turn on

Associations

Another common occurrence is that objects are typically related to one another in some fashion. For example, when you turn on your TV, in object-oriented terms, you're in an *association* with your TV.

The "turn-on" association is unidirectional (one-way), as in Figure 2.8. That is, you turn your TV on. Unless you watch way too much television, however, it doesn't return the favor. Other associations, like "is married to," are bidirectional.

FIGURE 2.8

Objects are often associated with each other in some way. When you turn on your TV, you're in a unidirectional association with it.

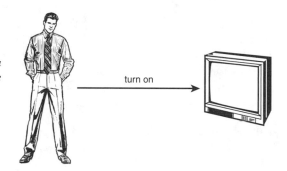

turn on

Sometimes an object might be associated with another in more than one way. If you and your coworker are friends, that's an example. You're in an "is the friend of" association, as well as an "is the coworker of" association, as Figure 2.9 shows.

FIGURE 2.9

Objects are sometimes associated with each other in more than one way.

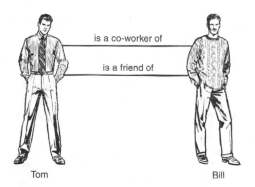

is a co-worker of

is a friend of

Tom   Bill

A class can be associated with more than one other class. A person can ride in a car, and a person can also ride in a bus (see Figure 2.10).

FIGURE 2.10

A class can associate with more than one other class.

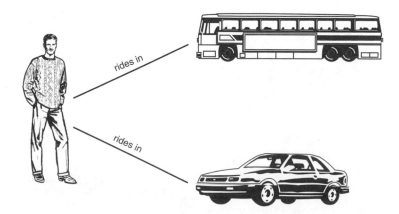

rides in

rides in

NEW TERM   *Multiplicity* is an important aspect of associations among objects. It tells the number of objects in one class that relate to a single object of the associated class. For example, in a typical college course, the course is taught by a single instructor. The course and the instructor are in a one-to-one association. In a proseminar, however, several instructors might teach the course throughout the semester. In that case, the course and the instructor are in a one-to-many association.

You can find all kinds of multiplicities if you look hard enough. A bicycle rides on two tires (a one-to-two multiplicity), a tricycle rides on three, and an eighteen-wheeler on eighteen.

Aggregation

Think about your computer system. It consists of a CPU box, a keyboard, a mouse, a monitor, a CD-ROM drive, one or more hard drives, a modem, a disk drive, a printer, and possibly some speakers. Inside the CPU box, along with the aforementioned drives, you have a CPU, a graphics card, a sound card, and some other elements you would undoubtedly find it hard to live without.

NEW TERM   Your computer is an *aggregation*, another kind of association among objects. Like many other things worth having, the computer is made from a number of different types of components (see Figure 2.11). You can probably come up with numerous examples of aggregations.

FIGURE 2.11

A typical computer system is an example of an aggregation—an object that's made up of a combination of a number of different types of objects.

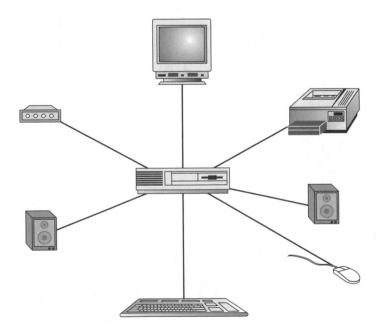

NEW TERM   One form of aggregation involves a strong relationship between an aggregate object and its component objects. This is called *composition*. The key to composition is that the component exists as a component only within the composite object. For example, a shirt is a composite of a body, a collar, sleeves, buttons, buttonholes, and cuffs. Do away with the shirt and the collar becomes useless.

Sometimes, a component in a composite doesn't last as long as the composite itself. The leaves on a tree can die out before the tree does. If you destroy the tree, the leaves also die (see Figure 2.12).

FIGURE 2.12

In a composition, a component can sometimes die out before the composite does. If you destroy the composite, you destroy the component as well.

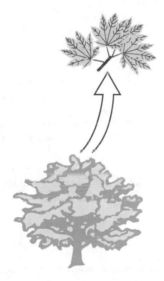

Aggregation and composition are important because they reflect extremely common occurrences, and thus help you create models that closely resemble reality.

The Payoff

Objects and their associations form the backbone of functioning systems. In order to model those systems, you have to understand what those associations are. If you're aware of the possible types of associations, you'll have a well-stocked bag of tricks when you talk to clients about their needs, gather their requirements, and create models of the systems that help them meet their business challenges.

NEW TERM   The important thing is to use the concepts of object-orientation to help you understand the client's area of knowledge (his or her *domain*), and to illustrate your understanding to the client in terms that he or she understands.

That's where the UML comes in. In the next three hours, you'll learn how to apply the UML to visualize the concepts you learned in this hour.

Summary

Object-orientation is a mindset that depends on a few fundamental principles. An object is an instance of a class. A class is a general category of objects that have the same attributes and operations. When you create an object, the problem area you're working in determines how many of the attributes and operations to consider.

Inheritance is an important aspect of object-orientation: An object inherits the attributes and operations of its class. A class can also inherit attributes and operations from another class.

Polymorphism is another important aspect. It specifies that an operation can have the same name in different classes, and each class will perform the operation in a different way.

Objects hide the performance of their operations from other objects and from the outside world. Each object presents an interface so that other objects (and people) can get it to perform its operations.

Objects work together by sending messages to one another. The messages are requests to perform operations.

Objects are typically associated with one another. The association can take a variety of forms. An object in one class may associate with any number of objects in another.

Aggregation is a type of association. An aggregate object consists of a set of component objects. A composition is a special kind of aggregation. In a composite object, the components exist only as part of the composite.

Q&A

Q **You said that object-orientation has taken the software world by storm. Aren't some important applications non-object-oriented?**

A Yes. The ones that aren't object-oriented are often called "legacy" systems—programs that in many cases are starting to show their age. Object-orientation offers numerous advantages, such as reusability and fast development time. For these reasons, you're likely to see new applications (and rewritten versions of many legacy applications) written the object-oriented way.

Workshop

To review what you've learned about object-orientation, try your hand at these quiz questions. You'll find the quiz answers in Appendix A. This is a theoretical hour, so I haven't included any exercises. You'll see quite a few in the hours to come, however!

Quiz

1. What is an object?
2. How do objects work together?
3. What does multiplicity indicate?
4. Can two objects associate with one another in more than one way?

2

Hour 3

Working with Object-Orientation

Now it's time to put the UML together with the object-oriented concepts you learned in the last hour. In this hour, you'll firm up your knowledge of object-orientation as you learn more about the UML. You'll learn about

- Visualizing a class
- Attributes
- Operations
- Responsibilities and constraints
- Discovering classes

Visualizing a Class

As I pointed out in the first hour, a rectangle is the icon that represents a class in the UML. The name of the class is, by convention, a word with an initial uppercase letter. It appears near the top of the rectangle. If your class has a two-word name, join the two words together and capitalize the first letter of the second word (as in WashingMachine in Figure 3.1).

FIGURE 3.1
The UML class icon.

WashingMachine

Another UML construct, the package, can play a role in the name of a class. As I pointed out in Hour 1, "Introducing the UML," a package is the UML's way of organizing a diagram's elements. As you might recall, the UML represents a package as a tabbed folder whose name is a text string (see Figure 3.2).

FIGURE 3.2
A UML package.

Household Appliances

NEW TERM   If the WashingMachine class is part of a package called Household Appliances, you can give it the name Household appliances::WashingMachine. The double colons separate the package name on the left from the class name on the right. This type of class name is called a *pathname* (see Figure 3.3).

FIGURE 3.3
A class with a path-name.

Household Appliances::WashingMachine

Attributes

NEW TERM   An *attribute* is a property of a class. It describes a range of values that the property may hold in objects (that is, in "instances") of that class. A class may have zero or more attributes. By convention, a one-word attribute name is written in lowercase letters. If the name consists of more than one word, the words are joined and each word other than the first word begins with an uppercase letter. The list of attribute names begins below a line separating them from the class name, as Figure 3.4 shows.

Every object of the class has a specific value for every attribute. Figure 3.5 presents an example. Note that an object's name begins with a lowercase letter, precedes a colon that precedes the class name, and the whole name is underlined.

FIGURE 3.4

A class and its attributes.

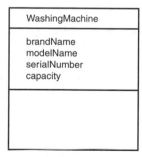

WashingMachine
brandName modelName serialNumber capacity

The name myWasher:WashingMachine is a *named instance*. It's also possible to have an *anonymous instance* like :WashingMachine.

FIGURE 3.5

An object has a specific value for every one of its class's attributes.

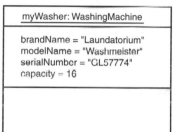

myWasher: WashingMachine
brandName = "Laundatorium" modelName = "Washmeister" serialNumber = "GL57774" capacity = 16

The UML gives you the option of indicating additional information for attributes. In the icon for the class, you can specify a type for each attribute's value. Possible types include string, floating-point number, integer, and Boolean (and other enumerated types). To indicate a type, use a colon to separate the attribute-name from the type. You can also indicate a default value for an attribute. Figure 3.6 shows these ways of specifying attributes.

FIGURE 3.6

An attribute can show its type as well as a default value.

WashingMachine
brandName: String = "Laundatorium" modelName: String serialNumber: String capacity: Integer

An *enumerated type* is a data type defined by a list of named values. Boolean, for instance, is an enumerated type because it consists of the values "true" and "false." You can define your own enumerated types like State, which consists of the values "solid," "liquid," and "gas."

Operations

NEW TERM An *operation* is something that a class can do, or that you (or another class) can do to a class. Like an attribute-name, an operation's name is all in lowercase if it's one word. If the name consists of more than one word, join the words and begin all words after the first with an uppercase letter. The list of operations begins below a line that separates the operations from the attributes, as in Figure 3.7.

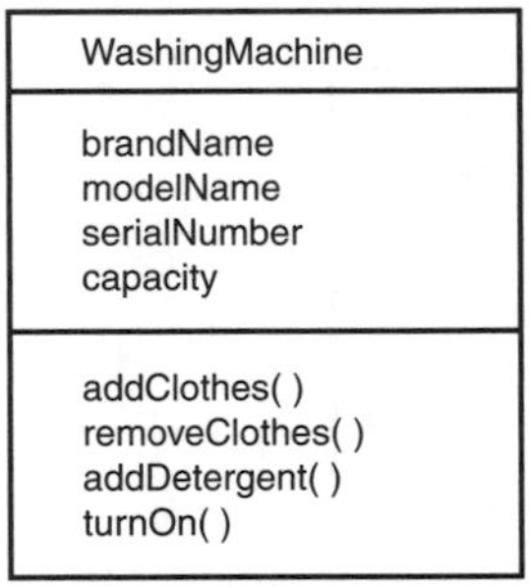

FIGURE 3.7

The list of a class's operations appears below a line that separates them from the class's attributes.

WashingMachine
brandName modelName serialNumber capacity
addClothes( ) removeClothes( ) addDetergent( ) turnOn( )

NEW TERM Just as you can indicate additional information for attributes, you can indicate additional information for operations. In the parentheses that follow an operation name, you can show the parameter that the operation works on, along with that parameter's type. One kind of operation, the *function*, returns a value after it finishes doing its work. For a function, you can show the value it returns and that value's type.

NEW TERM These pieces of information about an operation are called the operation's *signature*. Figure 3.8 shows how you represent the signature.

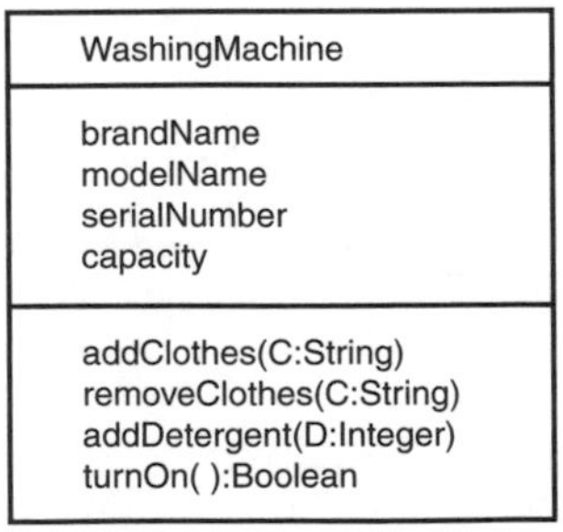

FIGURE 3.8

The signature for an operation.

WashingMachine
brandName modelName serialNumber capacity
addClothes(C:String) removeClothes(C:String) addDetergent(D:Integer) turnOn( ):Boolean

Attributes, Operations, and Visualization

We've been dealing with classes in isolation thus far, and showing all the attributes and operations of a class. In practice, however, you'll show more than one class at a time. When you do that, it's typically not useful to always display all the attributes and operations. To do so would make the diagram way too busy. Instead, you can just show the class name and leave either the attribute area or the operation area empty (or leave them both empty), as Figure 3.9 shows.

FIGURE 3.9

In practice, you don't always show all of a class's attributes and operations.

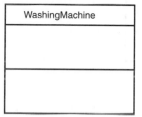

Sometimes it might be helpful to show some (but not all) of the attributes or operations. To indicate that you've only shown some of them, you follow the list of the ones you've shown with three dots "...". This is called an *ellipsis*, and omitting some or all of the attributes or operations is called *eliding* a class. Figure 3.10 shows the use of an ellipsis.

FIGURE 3.10

An ellipsis indicates that the displayed attributes or operations aren't the whole set.

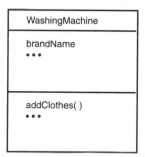

If you have a long list of attributes or operations, you can use a stereotype to organize in ways that will make the list comprehensible. A stereotype is the UML's way of enabling you to extend it: It allows you to create new elements that are specific to the particular problem you're trying to solve. As I mentioned in Hour 1, you show a stereotype as a name enclosed inside two pairs of small angle brackets called *guillemets*. For an attribute list, you can use a stereotype as a heading for a subset of the attributes, as in Figure 3.11.

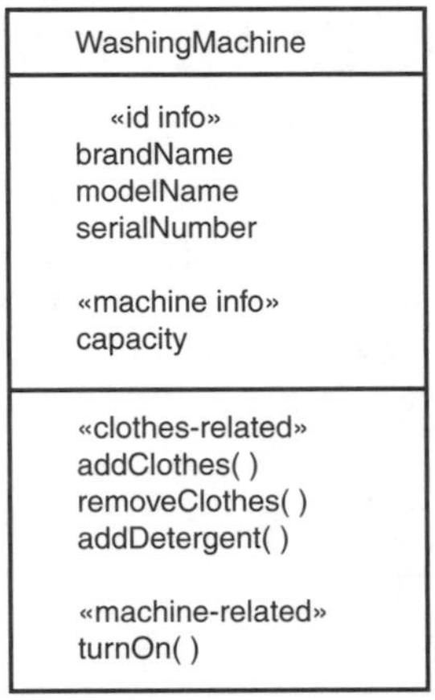

FIGURE 3.11

You can use a stereo-type to organize a list of attributes or opera-tions.

WashingMachine
«id info» brandName modelName serialNumber «machine info» capacity
«clothes-related» addClothes( ) removeClothes( ) addDetergent( ) «machine-related» turnOn( )

The stereotype is a flexible construct. You can use it in many different ways. For example, you can use it above the name of a class in a class icon to indicate something about the role that class plays. I'll have more to say about stereotypes in Hour 14, "Understanding the Foundations of the UML."

Responsibilities and Constraints

NEW TERM The class icon enables you to specify still another type of information about a class. In an area below the operations list, you can show the class's responsibility. The *responsibility* is a description of what the class has to do—that is, what its attributes and operations are trying to accomplish. A washing machine, for example, has the responsibility of taking dirty clothes as input and producing clean clothes as output.

In the icon, you indicate responsibilities in an area below the area that contains the operations (see Figure 3.12).

The idea here is to include enough information to describe a class in an unambiguous way. Indicating the class's responsibilities is an informal way to eliminate ambiguity.

NEW TERM A slightly more formal way is to add a *constraint*, a free-form text enclosed in curly brackets. The bracketed text specifies one or more rules the class follows. For example, suppose in the WashingMachine class you wanted to specify that the capacity of a washer can only be 16, 18, or 20 pounds (and thus "constrain" the WashingMachine class's capacity attribute). You would write {capacity = 16 or 18 or 20 lbs} near the WashingMachine class icon. Figure 3.13 shows how to do it.

FIGURE 3.12

In a class icon, you write the class's responsibilities in an area below the operations list area.

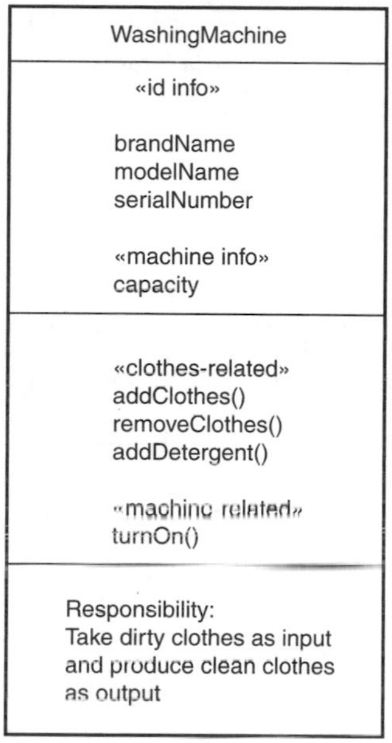

WashingMachine
«id info»
brandName modelName serialNumber
«machine info» capacity
«clothes-related» addClothes() removeClothes() addDetergent()
«machine related» turnOn()
Responsibility: Take dirty clothes as input and produce clean clothes as output

FIGURE 3.13

The rule in curly brackets constrains the capacity attribute to be one of three possible values.

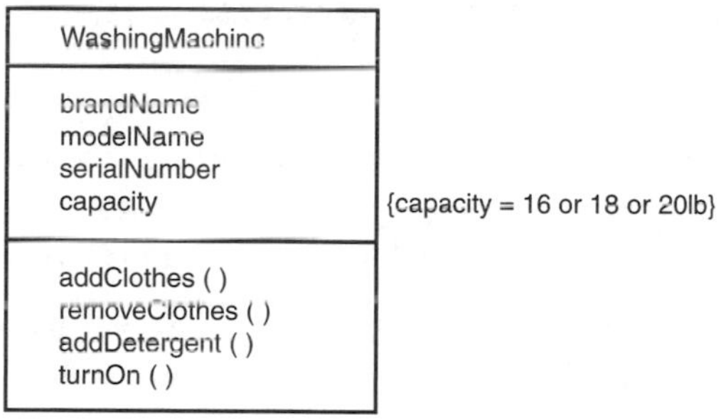

WashingMachine
brandName modelName serialNumber capacity
addClothes ( ) removeClothes ( ) addDetergent ( ) turnOn ( )

{capacity = 16 or 18 or 20lb}

The UML works with still another—and much more formal—way of adding constraints that make definitions more explicit. It's an entire language called *Object Constraint Language* (OCL). An advanced and sometimes useful tool, OCL has its own set of rules, terms, and operators.

Attached Notes

Above and beyond attributes, operations, responsibilities, and constraints, you can add still more information to a class in the form of notes attached to the class.

You'll usually add a note to an attribute or operation. Figure 3.14 shows a note referring to a government standard that tells where to find out how serial numbers are generated for objects in the WashingMachine class.

FIGURE **3.14**

An attached note pro-vides further informa-tion about the class.

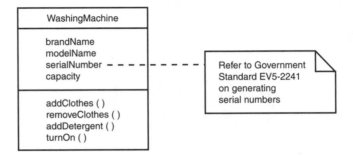

 A note can contain a graphic as well as text.

Classes—What They Do and How to Find Them

Classes are the vocabulary and terminology of an area of knowledge. As you talk with clients, analyze their area of knowledge, and design computer systems that solve prob-lems in that area, you learn the terminology and model the terms as classes in the UML.

In your conversations with clients, be alert to the nouns they use to describe the entities in their business. Those nouns will become the classes in your model. Be alert also to the verbs that you hear because these will constitute the operations in those classes. The attributes will emerge as nouns related to the class nouns. After you have a core list of classes, question the clients as to what each class is supposed to do within the business. Their answers will tell you the class responsibilities.

Suppose you're an analyst building a model of the game of basketball, and you're inter-viewing a coach in order to understand the game. The conversation might go something like this:

Analyst: "Coach, what's basketball all about?"

Coach: "The goal of the game is to shoot the ball through the basket and score more points than your opponent. Each team consists of five players: two guards, two forwards, and a center. Each team advances the ball toward the basket with the objective of ulti-mately shooting the ball through the basket."

Analyst: "How does it advance the ball?"

Coach: "By dribbling and passing. But the team has to take a shot at the basket before the shot clock expires."

Analyst: "Shot clock?"

Coach: "Yes. That's 24 seconds in the pros, 30 seconds in international play, and 35 seconds in college to take a shot after a team gets possession of the ball."

Analyst: "How does the scoring work?"

Coach: "Each basket counts two points, unless the shot is from behind the three-point line. In that case, it's three points. A free throw counts one point. A free throw, by the way, is the penalty a team pays for committing a foul. If a player fouls an opponent, play stops and the opponent gets to shoot at the basket from the free-throw line."

Analyst: "Tell me a little more about what each player does."

Coach: "The guards generally do most of the dribbling and passing. They're typically shorter than the forwards, and the forwards are usually shorter than the center. All the players are supposed to be able to dribble, pass, shoot, and rebound. The forwards do most of the rebounding and intermediate-range shooting, while the center stays near the basket and shoots from close range."

Analyst: "How about the dimensions of the court? And by the way, how long does a game last?"

Coach: "In international play, the court is 28 meters long by 15 meters wide. The basket is 10 feet off the ground. In the pros, a game lasts 48 minutes, divided into four 12-minute quarters. In college and international play, it's 40 minutes divided into two 20-minute halves. A game clock keeps track of the time remaining."

This could go on and on, but let's stop and take stock of where we are. Here are the nouns you've uncovered: ball, basket, team, players, guards, forwards, center, shot, shot clock, three-point line, free throw, foul, free-throw line, court, game clock.

Here are the verbs: shoot, advance, dribble, pass, foul, rebound. You also have some additional information about some of the nouns—like the relative heights of the players at each position, the dimensions of the court, the total amount of time on a shot clock, and the duration of a game.

Finally, your own commonsense knowledge could come into play as you generate a few attributes on your own. You know, for example, that the ball has attributes like volume and diameter.

Using this information, you can create a diagram like the one in Figure 3.15. It shows the classes, and provides some attributes, operations, and constraints. The diagram also shows responsibilities. You could use this diagram as a foundation for further conversations with the coach, to uncover more information.

FIGURE 3.15

An initial class diagram for modeling the game of basketball.

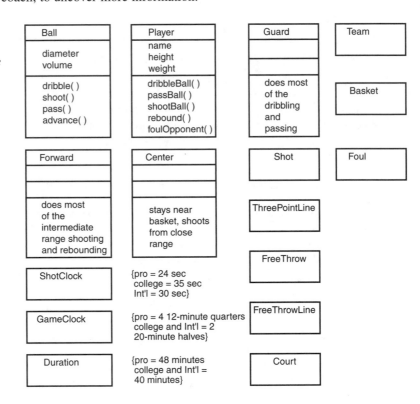

Summary

The rectangle is the UML icon for representing a class. The name, attributes, operations, and responsibilities of the class fit into areas within the rectangle. You can use a stereotype to organize lists of attributes and operations. You elide a class by showing just a subset of its attributes and operations. This makes a class diagram less busy.

You can show an attribute's type and an initial value, and you can show the values an operation works on and their types as well. For an operation, this additional information is called the signature.

To reduce the ambiguity in a class description, you can add constraints. The UML also allows you to say more about a class by attaching notes to the rectangle that represents it.

Classes represent the vocabulary of an area of knowledge. Conversations with a client or an expert in that area reveal nouns that can become classes in a model and verbs that can become operations. You can use a class diagram as a way of stimulating the client to talk more about his or her area and reveal additional knowledge.

Q&A

Q **You mention using "commonsense" knowledge to round out the class diagram for basketball. That's all well and good, but what happens when I have to analyze an area that's new to me—where common sense won't necessarily help?**

A Typically, you'll be thrust into an area that's new for you. Before you meet with a client or with an expert in the field, try to become a "subexpert." Prepare for the meeting by reading as much related documentation as possible. Ask your interviewee for some papers or manuals they might have written. When you've finished reading, you'll know some of the fundamentals and you'll be able to ask pointed questions.

Q **At what point will I want to show an operation's signature?**

A Probably after the analysis phase of a development effort, as you get into design. The signature is a piece of information that programmers will find helpful.

Workshop

To review what you've learned about object-orientation, try your hand at these quiz questions. The answers appear in Appendix A, "Quiz Answers."

Quiz

1. How do you represent a class in the UML?
2. What information can you show on a class icon?
3. What is a constraint?
4. Why would you attach a note to a class icon?

Exercises

1. Here's a brief (and incomplete) description of hockey:

    A hockey team consists of a center, a goalie, two wings, and two defensemen. Each player has a stick, which he uses to advance a puck on the ice. The objective is to use the stick to shoot the puck into a goal. Hockey is played on a rink whose maximum dimensions are 100 feet wide by 200 feet long. The center's job is to pass the puck to the wings, who are typically the better shooters on the team. The defensemen try to stop the opposing players from getting into position to shoot the puck into the goal. The goalie is the last line of defense, blocking opposition shots. Each time he stops the puck from getting into the goal, he's credited with a "save." Each goal is worth one point. A game lasts 60 minutes, divided into three periods of 20 minutes each.

    Use this information to come up with a diagram like the one in Figure 3.15. If you know more about hockey than I've put in the description, add that information to your diagram.

2. If you know more about basketball than I've put in Figure 3.15, add information to that diagram.

3. Go back to the conversation between the analyst and the basketball coach. Take a look at the coach's responses and find at least three areas where you could pursue additional lines of questioning. For example, at one point the coach mentions a "three-point line." Further questioning would reveal the specifics of that term.

HOUR 4

Working with Relationships

In this hour, you'll learn how classes connect with one another. You'll cover

- Associations
- Multiplicity
- Qualified associations
- Reflexive associations
- Inheritance and generalization
- Dependencies

In the model that finished up the last hour, you were left with a set of classes that represent the vocabulary of basketball. Although that provides the basis for further exploration of what basketball is all about, it might be apparent to you that something's missing.

That "something" is a sense of the way the classes relate to one another. If you look at that model (refer to Figure 3.15), you'll see that it doesn't show how a player relates to the ball, how players make up a team, or how a game proceeds. It's as though you've constructed a laundry list of terms, rather than a picture of an area of knowledge.

In this hour, you'll draw the connections among the classes and fill out the picture.

Associations

NEW TERM When classes are connected together conceptually, that connection is called an *association*. The initial basketball model provides some examples. Let's examine one—the association between a player and a team. You can characterize this association with the phrase "a player plays on a team." You visualize the association as a line connecting the two classes, with the name of the association ("plays on") just above the line. It's helpful to indicate the direction of the relationship, and you show that with a filled triangle pointing in the appropriate direction. Figure 4.1 shows how to visualize the Plays On association between the player and the team.

FIGURE 4.1

An association between a player and a team.

When one class associates with another, each one usually plays a role within that association. You can show those roles on the diagram by writing them near the line next to the class that plays the role. In the association between a player and a team, if the team is professional, it's an employer and the player is an employee. Figure 4.2 shows how to represent these roles.

FIGURE 4.2

In an association, each class typically plays a role. You can represent those roles on the diagram.

The association can work in the other direction: A team employs players. You can show both associations in the same diagram, with a filled triangle indicating the direction of each association, as in Figure 4.3.

FIGURE 4.3

*Two associations
between classes can
appear on the same
diagram.*

Associations may be more complex than just one class connected to another. Several
classes can connect to one class. If you consider guards, forwards, and centers, and their
associations with the Team class, you'll have the diagram in Figure 4.4.

FIGURE 4.4

*Several classes can
associate with a par-
ticular class.*

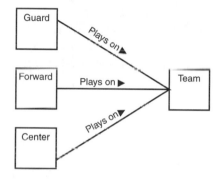

Constraints on Associations

Sometimes an association between two classes has to follow a rule. You indicate that rule
by putting a constraint near the association line. For example, a Bank Teller serves a
Customer, but each Customer is served in the order in which he or she appears in line.
You capture this in the model by putting the word *ordered* inside curly braces (to indicate
the constraint) near the Customer class, as in Figure 4.5.

FIGURE 4.5

*You can place a con-
straint on an associa-
tion. In this example,
the Serves association
is constrained to have
the Bank Teller serve
the Customer in order.*

Another type of constraint is the Or relationship, signified by {or} on a dashed line that
connects two association lines. Figure 4.6 models a high school student choosing either
an academic course of study or a commercial one.

FIGURE 4.6

The Or relationship between two associations is a constraint.

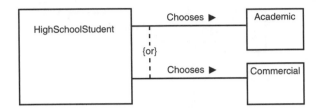

Association Classes

NEW TERM An association can have attributes and operations, just like a class. In fact, when this is the case, you have an *association class*. You visualize an association class the same way you show a regular class, and you use a dashed line to connect it to the association line. An association class can have associations to other classes. Figure 4.7 shows an association class for the Plays On association between a player and a team. The association class, Contract, is associated with the GeneralManager class.

FIGURE 4.7

An association class models an association's attributes and operations. It's connected to an association via a dashed line, and can be associated to another class.

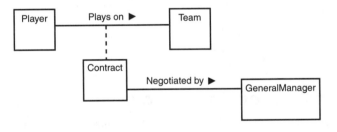

Links

Just as an object is an instance of a class, an association has instances as well. If we imagine a specific player who plays for a specific team, the Plays On relationship is called a *link*, and you represent it as a line connecting two objects. Just as you would underline the name of an object, you underline the name of a link, as in Figure 4.8.

FIGURE 4.8

A link is an instance of an association. It connects objects rather than classes. In a link, you underline the name of the link, just as you underline the name of an object.

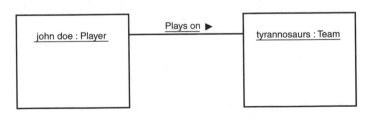

Multiplicity

The association drawn so far between Player and Team suggests that the two classes are in a one-to-one relationship. Common sense tells us that this isn't the case, however. A basketball team has five players (not counting substitutes). The Has association must take this into account. In the other direction, a player can play for just one team, and the Plays On association must account for that.

NEW TERM These specifications are examples of *multiplicity*—the number of objects from one class that relate with a single object in an associated class. To represent these numbers in the diagram, you place them above the association line near the appropriate class, as in Figure 4.9.

FIGURE 4.9

Multiplicity denotes the number of objects of one class that can relate to one object of an associated class.

The multiplicity in this example is not the only type. A variety of multiplicities are possible (a multiplicity of multiplicities, so to speak). One class can relate to another in a one-to-one, one-to-many, one-to-one or more, one-to-zero or one, one-to-a bounded interval (for example, one-to-five through ten), one-to-exactly *n* (as in this example), or one-to-a set of choices (for example, one-to-nine or ten).

The first time you see some of these multiplicities, the phrasing might be a little confusing. So here's a trick to help you through the confusion: Imagine double-quotes around the right-side phrase, so that one-to-one or more becomes one-to-"one or more" and one-to-a bounded interval becomes one-to-"a bounded interval." The double-quotes show the boundaries of that right-side phrase and might make the whole thing easier to understand.

The UML uses an asterisk (*) to represent *more* and to represent *many*. In one context Or is represented by two dots, as in "1..*" ("one or more"). In another context, Or is represented by a comma, as in "5,10" ("5 or 10"). Figure 4.10 shows how to visualize possible multiplicities.

When class A is in a one-to-zero or one multiplicity with class B, class B is said to be *optional* for class A.

FIGURE **4.10**
*Possible multiplicities
and how to represent
them in the UML.*

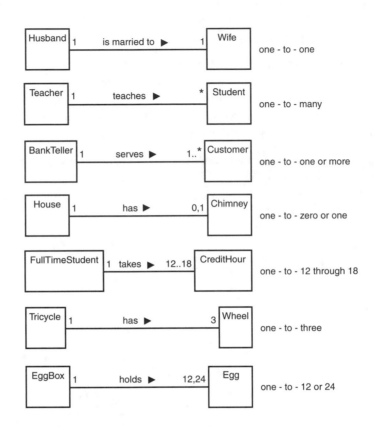

Qualified Associations

When an association's multiplicity is one-to-many, a particular challenge often arises: lookup. When an object from one class has to choose a particular object of another in order to fulfill a role in an association, the first class has to rely on a specific attribute to find the correct object. That attribute is typically an identifier, such as an ID number. When you make a reservation at a hotel, for instance, the hotel assigns you a confirmation number. If you call with questions about the reservation, you have to supply the confirmation number.

NEW TERM   In the UML, the ID information is called a *qualifier*. Its symbol is a small rectangle adjoining the class that does the looking up. Figure 4.11 shows the representation. The idea is to effectively reduce a one-to-many multiplicity to a one-to-one multiplicity.

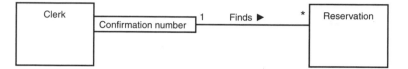

FIGURE 4.11
A qualifier in an association solves the lookup problem.

Reflexive Associations

NEW TERM Sometimes, a class is in an association with itself. Referred to as a *reflexive association*, this can happen when a class has objects that can play a variety of roles. A CarOccupant can be either a driver or a passenger. In the role of the driver, the CarOccupant drives zero or more CarOccupants who play the role of passenger. You represent this by drawing an association line from the class rectangle back to the same class rectangle, and on the association line you indicate the roles, name of the association, direction of the association, and multiplicity as before. Figure 4.12 presents this example.

FIGURE 4.12

In a reflexive association, you draw the line from the class to itself and you can include the roles, association name, direction of the association, and multiplicity.

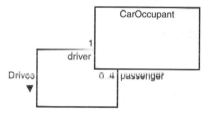

Inheritance and Generalization

One of the hallmarks of object-orientation is that it captures one of the great common-sense aspects of day-to-day life: If you know something about a category of things, you automatically know some things you can transfer to other categories. If you know something is an appliance, you already know it has an on-off switch, a brand name, and a serial number. If you know something is an animal, you take for granted that it eats, sleeps, has a way of being born, has a way of getting from one place to another, and probably a number of other attributes (and operations) you could list if you thought about it for a few minutes.

NEW TERM Object-orientation refers to this as *inheritance*. The UML also refers to this as *generalization*. One class (the child class or subclass) can inherit attributes and operations from another (the parent class or superclass). The parent class is more general than the child class.

 In a generalization, a child is substitutable for a parent. That is, anywhere the parent appears, the child may appear. The reverse isn't true, however.

The inheritance hierarchy doesn't have to end at two levels: A child class can be a parent class for still another child class. Mammal is a child class of Animal, and Horse is a child class of Mammal.

In the UML, you represent inheritance with a line that connects the parent class to the child class. On the part of the line that connects to the parent class, you put an open triangle that points to the parent class. This type of connection stands for the phrase *is a kind of*. A Mammal *is a kind of* Animal, and a Horse *is a kind of* Mammal. Figure 4.13 shows this particular inheritance hierarchy, along with some additional classes. In the figure, note the appearance of the triangle and the lines when more than one child class inherits from a parent class. Setting the diagram up this way results in a less busy diagram than showing all the lines and triangles, but the UML doesn't prohibit putting all of them in the picture. Note also that you don't put the inherited attributes and operations in the subclass rectangles, as you've already represented them in the superclass.

FIGURE 4.13
An inheritance hierarchy in the animal kingdom.

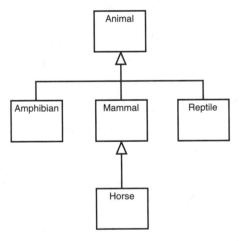

 When modeling inheritance, be sure the child class satisfies the *is a kind of* relationship with the parent class. If the two don't have that kind of relationship, an association of some other kind might be more appropriate.

Child classes often add to the attributes and operations they inherit. For example, a Mammal has hair and gives milk, two attributes not found in the Animal class.

A class may have no parents, in which case it's a *base class* or *root class*. A class may have no children, in which case it's a *leaf class*. If a class has exactly one parent, it has *single inheritance*. If a class has more than one parent, it has *multiple inheritance*.

Discovering Inheritance

In the course of talking to a client, an analyst discovers inheritance in several ways. It's possible that the candidate classes that emerge include both parent classes and child classes. The analyst has to realize that the attributes and operations of one class are general and apply to perhaps several other classes—which may add attributes and operations of their own.

The basketball example from Hour 3, "Working with Object-Orientation," has Player, Guard, Forward, and Center classes. The Player has attributes such as name, height, weight, runningSpeed, and verticalLeap. It has operations such as dribble(), pass(), rebound(), and shoot(). The Guard, Forward, and Center inherit these attributes and operations, and add some of their own. The Guard might have the operations runOffense() and bringBallUpcourt(). The Center might have the operation slamDunk(). Based on the coach's comments about relative heights of the players, the analyst might want to place constraints on the heights of the individuals who play each position.

Another possibility is that the analyst notes that two or more classes have a number of attributes and operations in common. The basketball model has a GameClock (which keeps track of how much time remains in a game period) and a ShotClock (which tracks the time remaining from the instant one team takes possession of the ball until it's supposed to shoot the ball). Realizing that both track time, the analyst could formulate a Clock class with a trackTime() operation that both the GameClock and the ShotClock inherit.

Because the ShotClock tracks 24 seconds (professional) or 35 seconds (college) and the GameClock tracks 12 minutes (professional) or 20 minutes (college), trackTime() is polymorphic.

Abstract Classes

In the basketball model, the two classes I just mentioned—Player and Clock—are useful because they serve as parent classes for important child classes. The child classes are important in the model because you'll ultimately want to have instances of these classes. To develop the model you'll need instances of Guard, Forward, Center, GameClock, and ShotClock.

Player and Clock, however, will not provide any instances for the model. An object from the Player class would serve no purpose, nor would an object from the Clock class.

NEW TERM   Classes like Player and Clock—that provide no objects—are said to be *abstract*. You indicate an abstract class by writing its name in italics. Figure 4.14 shows the two abstract classes and their children.

FIGURE 4.14
Two inheritance hier-
archies with abstract
classes in the basket-
ball model.

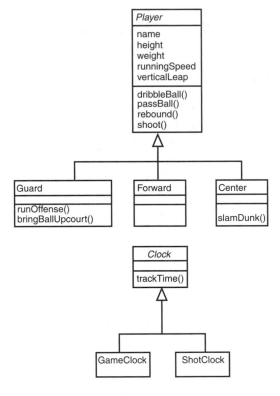

Dependencies

NEW TERM   In another kind of relationship, one class uses another. This is called a *depen-* *dency*. The most common usage of a dependency is to show that the signature of one class's operation uses another class.

Suppose you're designing a system that displays corporate forms onscreen, so employees can fill them out. The employee uses a menu to select the form to fill out. In your design, you have a System class and a Form class. Among its many operations, the System class has displayForm(f:Form). The form the system displays obviously depends on which Form the user selects. The UML notation for this is a dashed line with an arrowhead pointing at the class depended on, as in Figure 4.15.

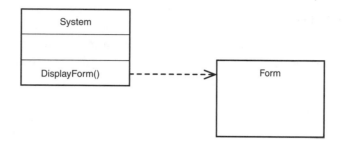

Figure 4.15
A dashed line with an arrowhead represents a dependency.

Summary

Without relationships, a class model would be little more than a laundry list of rectangles that represent a vocabulary. Relationships show how the terms in the vocabulary connect with one another to provide a picture of the slice of the world you're modeling. The association is the fundamental conceptual connection between classes. Each class in an association plays a role, and multiplicity specifies how many objects in one class relate to one object in the associated class. Many types of multiplicities are possible. An association is represented as a line between the class rectangles with the roles and multiplicities at either end. Like a class, an association can have attributes and operations.

A class can inherit attributes and operations from another class. The inheriting class is the child of the parent class it inherits from. You discover inheritance when you find classes in your initial model that have common attributes and operations. Abstract classes are intended only as bases for inheritance and provide no objects of their own. Inheritance is represented as a line between the parent and the child with an open triangle adjoining (and pointing to) the parent.

In a dependency, one class uses another. The most common usage of a dependency is to show that a signature in the operation of one class uses another class. A dependency is depicted as a dashed line joining the two classes in the dependency, with an arrowhead adjoining (and pointing to) the depended-on class.

Q&A

Q **Do you ever provide a name for an inheritance relationship, as you do for an association?**

A The UML doesn't stop you from naming an inheritance relationship, but usually it's not necessary.

Workshop

The quiz and the exercises are designed to firm up your knowledge of the UML in the area of relationships. Each question and exercise requires you to think about the modeling symbology you just learned and apply it to a situation. The answers are in Appendix A, "Quiz Answers."

Quiz

1. How do you represent multiplicity?
2. How do you discover inheritance?
3. What is an abstract class?
4. What's the effect of a qualifier?

Exercises

1. Take the initial basketball model from Hour 3 and add links that express the relationships you covered in this hour. If you know the game of basketball, feel free to add links that represent your knowledge.
2. According to an old adage, "An attorney who defends himself has a fool for a client." Create a model that reflects this piece of wisdom.
3. Draw an inheritance hierarchy of the objects in your residence. Be sure to include any abstract classes as well as all instances.
4. Think back to the subjects you've taken in school. Model this set of subjects as an inheritance hierarchy, again with all abstract classes and instances. In this model include dependencies. (Weren't some courses prerequisites for others?)
5. Imagine an association between the classes "Dog" and "Person." The association is "is a pet of." Now imagine the same association between "Cat" and "Person." Draw each association and attach an association class to each one. Use the association classes to show how these associations, although identically named, differ from one another.

Hour 5

Understanding Aggregations, Composites, Interfaces, and Realizations

In this hour, you'll continue with relationships among classes and learn new concepts about classes and class diagrams. You'll learn about

- Aggregations
- Composites
- Contexts
- Interfaces
- Realizations
- Visibility

You've learned about associations, multiplicities, and inheritance. You're almost ready to create meaningful class diagrams. In this hour, you'll learn the final pieces of the puzzle, as you delve into additional types of relationships and other issues connected with classes. The ultimate goal is to be able to create a static view of a system, complete with all the interconnections among the system's classes.

Aggregations

NEW TERM Sometimes a class consists of a number of component classes. This is a special type of relationship called an *aggregation*. The components and the class they constitute are in a *part-whole* association. In Hour 2, "Understanding Object-Orientation," I mentioned that your home computer system is an aggregation that consists of a CPU box, a keyboard, a mouse, a monitor, a CD-ROM drive, one or more hard drives, a modem, a disk drive, a printer, and possibly some speakers. Along with the drives, the CPU box holds RAM, a graphics card, and a sound card (and probably some other items).

You represent an aggregation as a hierarchy with the "whole" class (for instance, the computer system) at the top, and the components below. A line joins a whole to a component, with an open diamond on the line near the whole. Figure 5.1 shows the computer system as an aggregation.

FIGURE 5.1

An aggregation (part-whole) association is represented by a line between the component and the whole with an open diamond adjoining the whole.

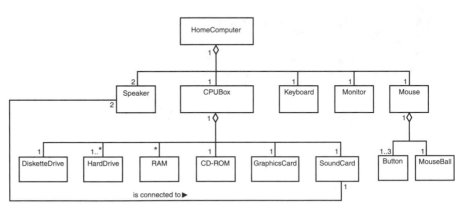

Although this example shows each component belonging to one whole, in an aggregation this isn't necessarily the case. For example, in a home entertainment system, a remote control might be a component of a television, and the same remote control might be a component of a VCR.

Constraints on Aggregations

Sometimes the set of possible components in an aggregation falls into an Or relationship. In some restaurants, a meal consists of soup or salad, main course, and dessert. To model this, you would use a constraint—the word *or* within braces on a dotted line that connects the two part-whole lines, as Figure 5.2 shows.

FIGURE 5.2

You can place a constraint on an aggregation to show that one component or another is part of the whole.

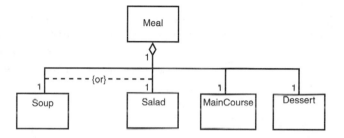

Note the consistency between the use of {or} in Figure 5.2 (which shows a constraint on an aggregation) and the use of {or} previously in Figure 4.6 (which shows a constraint in an association).

Composites

A composite is a strong type of aggregation. Each component in a composite can belong to just one whole. The components of a coffee table—the tabletop and the legs—make up a composite. The symbol for a composite is the same as the symbol for an aggregation except the diamond is filled (See Figure 5.3).

FIGURE 5.3

In a composite, each component belongs to exactly one whole. A closed diamond represents this relationship.

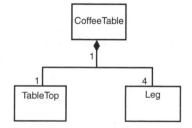

5

Contexts

When you model a system, clusters of classes will emerge, often as aggregations or composites. You'll want to focus attention on one cluster or another, and the UML context diagram provides the modeling feature that does this for you. Composites figure heavily in context diagrams. A context diagram is like a detailed map of a section of a larger map. Several sections might be necessary to capture all the detailed information.

Here's an example. Suppose you're creating a model of a shirt and how it fits into an outfit and a wardrobe. One type of context diagram (see Figure 5.4) shows the shirt as a large class rectangle, with a diagram nested inside. The nested diagram shows how the components of the shirt relate to one another. This is a composite context diagram—*composite* because only the shirt "owns" every component.

FIGURE 5.4

A composite context diagram shows the components of a class as a diagram nested inside a large class rectangle.

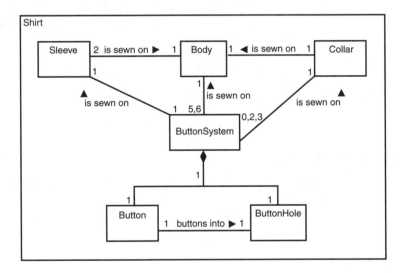

The composite context diagram focuses attention on the shirt and its internal components. To show the shirt in the context of the wardrobe and the outfit, you have to widen your scope. A system context diagram does this for you. You can show how the Shirt class connects with the Wardrobe and Outfit classes, as in Figure 5.5.

You can then zoom in on another class, and present its details in another context diagram.

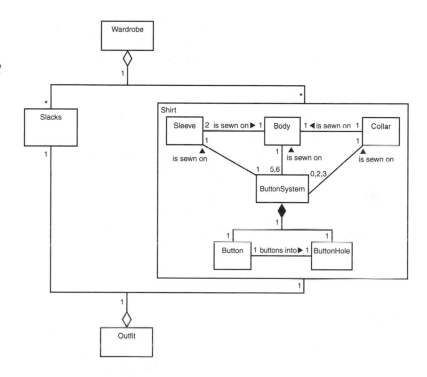

FIGURE 5.5

A system context diagram shows the components of a class and how that class relates to other classes in the system.

Interfaces and Realizations

After you've created a number of classes, you might notice they're not related to a particular parent, but their behaviors might include some of the same operations with the same signatures. You can code the operations for one of the classes and reuse them in the others. Another possibility is that you develop a set of operations for classes in one system, and reuse them for classes in another.

NEW TERM   Either way, you'll want to somehow capture the reusable set of operations. The interface is the UML construct that enables you to do this. An *interface* is a set of operations that specifies some aspect of a class's behavior, and it's a set of operations a class presents to other classes.

An example will help clarify the interface concept. The keyboard that you use to communicate with your computer is a reusable interface. Its keystroke operation has been reused from the typewriter. The placement of keys is the same as on a typewriter, but the main point is that the keystroke operation has been transferred from one system to another. Other operations in the interface—shift, caps lock, and tab—are also reused from the typewriter.

5

Of course, the computer keyboard provides a number of operations that you won't find on a typewriter: control, alt, page up, page down, and more. The interface, then, can specify a subset of a class's operations and not necessarily all of them.

You model an interface the same way you model a class, with a rectangle icon. The difference is that, as a set of operations, an interface has no attributes. You'll recall that you can elide the attributes out of the representation of a class. How then do you distinguish between an interface and a class that just doesn't show its attributes? One way is to use the stereotype construct and put «interface» above the name of the interface in the rectangle. Another is to put the letter "I" at the beginning of the name of any interface.

New Term   In a sense, it's as though the computer keyboard guarantees that part of its behavior will "realize" a typewriter's behavior. Accordingly, the relationship between a class and an interface is called *realization*. This relationship is modeled as a dashed line with a large open triangle adjoining and pointing to the interface. Figure 5.6 shows how it's done.

Figure 5.6

An interface is a collection of operations that a class carries out. A class is related to an interface via realization, indicated by a dashed line with an open triangle that points to the interface.

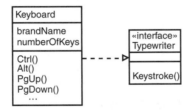

Another (elided) way to represent a class and an interface is with a small circle connected by a line to the class, as in Figure 5.7.

Note the similarity between the symbol for realization and the symbol for inheritance. The only difference between the two is that the line for realization is dashed and the line for inheritance is solid. The notation underscores the similarity—and the difference—between the two relationship types.

Think of inheritance as the relationship between a parent and a child: The parent passes on physical attributes (eye color, hair color, and so on) to the child, and the child also takes on behaviors from the parent. Think of realization as something like the relationship between a teacher and a child: The teacher doesn't pass on any physical attributes to the child, but the child learns behaviors and procedures from the teacher.

FIGURE 5.7

The elided way of representing a class realizing an interface.

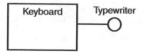

A class can realize more than one interface, and an interface can be realized by more than one class.

Visibility

NEW TERM   Closely related to interfaces and realizations is the concept of visibility. *Visibility* applies to attributes or operations, and specifies the extent to which other classes can use a given class's attributes or operations (or an interface's operations). Three levels of visibility are possible. At the *public* level, usability extends to other classes. At the *protected* level, usability is open only to classes that inherit from the original class. At the *private* level, only the original class can use the attribute or operation. In a television set, changeVolume() and changeChannel() are public operations, paintImageOnScreen() is a private one. In an automobile, accelerate() and brake() are public operations, updateMileageCount() is protected.

Realization, as you might imagine, implies that the public level applies to every operation in an interface. Shielding the operations via either of the other levels would make no sense, as an interface is intended for realization by a multitude of classes.

To denote the public level, precede the attribute or operation with a "+", to denote the protected level, precede it with a "#", and to denote private, precede it with a "-". Figure 5.8 shows the aforementioned public, protected, and private operations in a television and in an automobile.

FIGURE 5.8

Public and private operations in a television, and public and protected operations in an automobile.

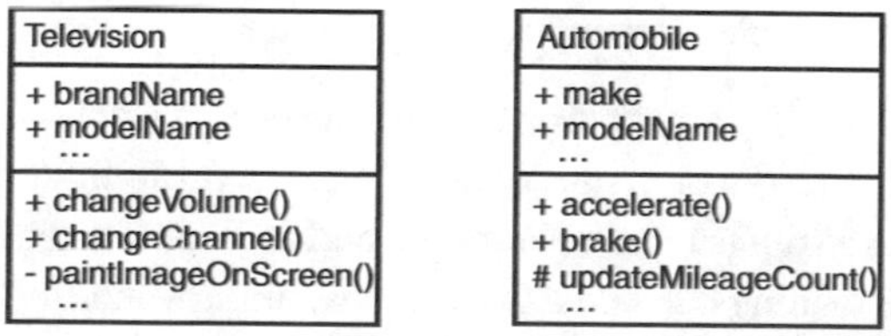

Television
+ brandName
+ modelName
...
+ changeVolume()
+ changeChannel()
- paintImageOnScreen()
...

Automobile
+ make
+ modelName
...
+ accelerate()
+ brake()
# updateMileageCount()
...

Scope

NEW TERM   Scope is another concept relevant to attributes and operations and how they relate across a system. Two kinds of scope are possible. In *instance* scope, each instance of a class has its own value for the attribute or operation. In *classifier* scope, only one value of the attribute or operation exists across all instances of the class.

5

A classifier-scoped attribute or operation appears with its name underlined. This type of scoping is usually used when a specified group of instances (and no others) has to share the exact values of a private attribute. Instance-scoping is by far the more common type of scope.

Summary

To complete your knowledge about classes and how they connect, it's necessary to understand some additional relationships. An aggregation specifies a part-whole association: A "whole" class is made up of component classes. A component in an aggregation may be part of more than one whole. A composite is a strong form of aggregation, in that a component in a composite can be part of only one whole. The UML representation of aggregations is similar to the representation of composites. The association line joining a part to a whole has a diamond adjoining the whole. In an aggregation, the diamond is open; in a composite it's closed.

A context diagram focuses attention on a specific class within a system. A composite context diagram is like a detailed map of a larger map. It shows a class diagram nested inside a large rectangular class icon. A system context diagram shows how the composite class diagram relates to other objects in the system.

A realization is an association between a class and an interface, a collection of operations that a number of classes can use. An interface is represented as a class with no attributes. To distinguish it from a class whose attributes have been elided from the diagram, the stereotype «interface» appears above the interface's name or an uppercase "I" precedes the interface's name. Realization is represented in the UML by a dashed line that connects the class to the interface, with an open triangle adjoining the interface and pointing to it. Another way to represent a realization is with a solid line connecting a class to a small circle, with the circle standing for the interface.

In terms of visibility, all the operations in an interface are *public*, so that any class can use them. Two other levels of visibility are *protected* (usability extends to children of the class that owns the attributes and operations) and *private* (attributes and operations are usable only by the owning class). A "+" denotes public visibility, "#" denotes protected, and "-" denotes private.

Scope is another aspect of attributes and operations. In instance-scoping, each object in a class has its own value of an attribute or operation. In classification-scoping, one value exists for a particular attribute or operation throughout a set of objects in a class. Objects not in that set have no access to the classification-scoped value.

Q&A

Q **Is aggregation considered transitive? In other words, if class 3 is a component of class 2 and class 2 is a component of class 1, is class 3 a component of class 1?**

A Yes, aggregation is transitive. In our example, the mouse buttons and mouse ball are part of the mouse and also part of the computer system.

Q **Does "interface" imply "user interface" or GUI?**

A No. It's more generic than that. An interface is just a set of operations that one class presents to other classes, one of which may (but not necessarily) be the user.

Workshop

The quiz and exercises will test and strengthen your knowledge about aggregations, composites, contexts, and interfaces. The answers appear in Appendix A, "Quiz Answers."

Quiz

1. What is the difference between an aggregation and a composite?

2. What is realization? How is realization similar to inheritance? How does realization differ from inheritance?

3. Name the three levels of visibility and describe what each one means.

Exercises

1. Create a composite context diagram of a magazine. Consider the Table of Contents, Editorial, Articles, and Columns. Then create a system context diagram that shows the Magazine along with Subscriber and NewsstandBuyer.

2. Today's most popular type of GUI is the WIMP (Windows, Icons, Menus, Pointer) interface. Using all the appropriate UML knowledge you've acquired thus far, draw a class diagram of the WIMP interface. In addition to the classes named in the acronym, include related items such as the scrollbar and cursor, and any other necessary classes.

3. Construct a model of an electric pencil sharpener showing all relevant attributes and operations. In your model, show how it inherits from the Appliance class and how it realizes the operations of the class ManualPencilSharpener.

5

HOUR 6

Introducing Use Cases

Now that you've learned about classes and their relationships, it's time to turn our attention to another major area of the UML—use cases. In this hour, you'll cover these topics:

- What use cases are
- Creating use cases
- Including use cases
- Extending use cases
- Starting a use case analysis

In the past three hours, we've dealt with diagrams that provide a static view of the classes in a system. We're going to ultimately move into diagrams that provide a dynamic view and show how the system and its classes change over time. The static view helps an analyst communicate with a client. The dynamic view, as you'll see, helps an analyst communicate with a team of developers, and helps the developers create programs.

The client and the development team make up an important set of stakeholders in a system. One equally important part of the picture is missing, however—the user.

Neither the static view nor the dynamic view shows the system's behavior from the user's point of view. Understanding that point of view is key to building systems that are both useful and usable—that is, that meet requirements and are easy (and even fun) to work with.

Modeling a system from a user's point of view is the job of the use case. In this hour, you'll learn all about what use cases are and what they do. In the next hour, you'll learn how to use the UML's use case diagram to visualize a use case.

Use Cases: What They Are

A few years ago, I bought a fax machine. When I was shopping for it in an office supply store, I encountered a wide array of choices. How did I decide on the ultimate winner? I asked myself exactly what I wanted to do with a fax machine. What features did I want? What functions did I absolutely have to have? Did I want to make copies? Connect with my computer? Use the fax machine as a scanner? Did I have to send faxes so quickly that I'd need a speed dial function? Did I want to use the fax machine to sense the difference between an incoming phone call and an incoming fax?

We all go through a process like this when we make a non-impulse purchase. What we're doing is a form of *use case analysis*: We're asking ourselves how we're going to use the product or system we're about to shell out good money for, so we can settle on something that meets our requirements. The important thing is to know what those requirements are.

This kind of process is particularly crucial for the analysis phase of system development. How users will use a system drives the way you're going to design and build it.

The use case is a construct that helps analysts work with users to determine system usage. A collection of use cases depicts a system in terms of what users intend to do with it.

NEW TERM   Think of a use case as a collection of scenarios about system use. Each scenario describes a sequence of events. Each sequence is initiated by a person, another system, a piece of hardware, or by the passage of time. Entities that initiate sequences are called *actors*. The result of the sequence has to be something of use either to the actor who initiated it or to another actor.

Use Cases: Why They're Important

Just as the class diagram is a great way to stimulate a client to talk about a system from his or her viewpoint, the use case is an excellent tool for stimulating potential users to talk about a system from their own viewpoints. It's not always easy for users to articulate how they intend to use a system. Because traditional system development was often a haphazard process that was short on upfront analysis, users are sometimes stunned when anyone asks for their input.

The idea is to get system users involved in the early stages of system analysis and design. This increases the likelihood that the system ultimately becomes a boon to the people it's supposed to help—instead of a monument to clever cutting-edge computing concepts that business users find incomprehensible and impossible to work with.

An Example: The Soda Machine

Suppose you're starting out to design a soda machine. In order to get the user's point of view, you interview a number of potential users as to how they'll interact with the machine.

Because the main function of a soda machine is to allow a customer to buy a can of soda, it's likely the users will quickly tell you that you're concerned with a set of scenarios—a use case, in other words—that you could label "Buy soda." Let's examine each possible scenario in this use case. In normal system development, remember, these scenarios would emerge through conversations with users.

FIGURE 6.1

A use case specifies a set of scenarios for accomplishing some thing useful for an actor. In this example, one use case is "Buy soda."

The "Buy Soda" Use Case

The actor in this use case is a customer who wants to purchase a can of soda. The customer initiates the scenario by inserting money into the machine. He or she then makes a selection. If everything goes smoothly, the machine has at least one can of the selected soda in stock, and presents a cold can of the soda to the customer.

In addition to the sequence of steps, other aspects of the scenario deserve consideration. What preconditions motivate the customer to initiate this scenario in the "Buy soda" use case? Thirst is the most obvious one. What postconditions result as a consequence of the scenario's steps? Again, the obvious one is that the customer has a soda.

Is the scenario I described the only possible one for "Buy soda"? Others immediately come to mind. It's possible that the machine is out of the soda the customer wants.

6

It's possible that the customer doesn't have the exact amount of money the soda costs. How should you design the soda machine to handle these scenarios?

Let's turn to the out-of-soda scenario, another sequence of steps in the "Buy soda" use case. Think of it as an alternative path through the use case. The customer initiates the use case by inserting money into the machine. He or she then makes a selection. The machine does not have at least one can of the selected soda, so it presents a message to the customer, saying it's out of that brand. Ideally, the message should prompt the customer to make another selection. The machine should also offer the customer the option of getting his or her money back. At this point, the customer selects another brand and the machine delivers (if it's not sold out of the new selection), or takes the option of receiving the money. The precondition is a thirsty customer. The postcondition is either a can of soda or the returned money.

> Of course, another out-of-soda scenario is possible: The "out of brand" message could display as soon as the machine's stock disappears and remain on until the machine is resupplied. In that case, the user might not insert money in the first place. The client for whom you're designing the machine might prefer the first scenario: If the customer has already inserted money, the tendency might be to make another selection rather than to ask the machine to return the money.

Now let's look at the incorrect-amount-of-money scenario. Once again, the customer initiates the use case in the usual way, and then makes a selection. Let's assume the machine has the selection in stock. If the machine has a reserve of appropriate change on hand, it returns the difference and delivers the soda. If the machine doesn't have a reserve of change, it returns the money and presents a message that prompts the user for correct change. The precondition is the usual one. The postcondition is either a can of soda along with change, or the returned money originally deposited.

Another possibility is that as soon as the machine's change reserve is depleted, a message appears informing potential customers that correct change is required. The message would remain visible until the machine's reserve is resupplied.

Additional Use Cases

You've examined the soda machine from the viewpoint of one user: the customer. Other users enter the picture as well. A supplier has to restock the machine, and a collector (possibly the same person as the supplier) has to collect the accumulated money from the machine. This tells us we should create at least two more use cases, "Restock" and "Collect money," whose details emerge through interviews with suppliers and collectors.

Consider the "Restock" use case. The supplier initiates this use case because some interval (say, two weeks) has passed. The supplier's representative unsecures the machine (probably by unlocking a lock, but that gets into implementation), pulls open the front of the machine, and fills each brand's compartment to capacity. The representative also refills the change reserve. The representative then closes the front of the machine and secures it. The precondition is the passage of the interval, the postcondition is that the supplier has a new set of potential sales.

For the "Collect Money" use case, the collector also initiates because an interval has passed. He or she would follow the same sequence of steps as in "Restock" to unsecure the machine and pull open the front. The collector then removes the money from the machine, and follows the "Restock" steps of closing and securing the machine. The precondition is the passage of the interval, and the postcondition is the money in the hands of the collector.

Notice that when we derive a use case, we don't worry about how to implement it. In our example, we're not concerned with the insides of the soda machine. We don't care about how the refrigeration mechanism works, or how the machine keeps track of its money. We're just trying to see how the soda machine will look to someone who has to use it.

The objective is to derive a collection of use cases that we ultimately show the people who will design the soda machine and the people who will build it. To the extent our use cases reflect what customers, collectors, and suppliers want, the result will be a machine that all these groups can easily use.

Including a Use Case

In the "Restock" use case and the "Collect" use case, you'll note some common steps. Both begin with unsecuring the machine and pulling it open, both end with closing the machine and securing it. Can we eliminate the duplication of steps from use case to use case?

We can. The way to do it is to take each sequence of common steps and form an additional use case from each one. Let's combine the "unsecure" and "pull open" steps into a use case called "Expose the inside" and the "close machine" and "secure" steps into a use case called "Unexpose the inside."

With these new use cases in hand, the "Restock" use case starts off with the "Expose the inside" use case. The supplier's representative then goes through the steps as before, and concludes with the "Unexpose the inside" use case. Similarly, the "Collect" use case starts off with the "Expose the inside" use case, proceeds as before, and finishes with the "Unexpose the inside" use case.

6

As you can see, Restock and Collect include the new use cases. Accordingly, this technique of reusing a use case is referred to as *including a use case*.

 Early versions of the UML referred to *including a use case* as *using a use case*. You might still see the old way in print. The term *including* has two advantages. First, it's clearer: The steps in one use case "include" the steps of another. Second, it avoids the potential confusion of putting "using" near the "use" in "use case." That way, we won't have to say we "promote reuse by using a use case."

Extending a Use Case

It's possible to reuse a use case in a way other than inclusion. Sometimes we create a new use case by adding some steps to an existing use case.

Let's go back to the "Restock" use case. Before putting new cans of soda into the machine, suppose the supplier's representative notes the brands that sold well and the brands that did not. Instead of simply restocking all the brands, the rep might pull out the brands that haven't sold well and replace them with cans of the brands that have proven to be more popular. He or she would then also have to indicate on the front of the machine the new assortment of available brands.

If we add these steps to "Restock" we'll have a new use case that we can call "Restock according to sales." This new use case is an extension of the original, and this technique is called *extending a use case*.

Starting a Use Case Analysis

In our example, we jumped right into use cases and focused on a few of them. In the real world, you usually follow a set of procedures when you start a use case analysis.

You begin with the client interviews (and interviews with experts) that lead to the initial class diagrams we discussed in Hour 3. This gives you some idea of the area you're working in and a familiarity with the terms you'll be using. You then have a basis for talking with users.

You interview users (preferably in a group) and ask them to tell you everything they would do with the system you're getting ready to design. Their answers form a set of candidate use cases. Next, it's important to briefly describe each use case. You also have to derive a list of all the actors who will initiate and benefit from the use cases. As you get more into this phase, you'll increase your ability to speak to the users in their language.

Use cases will crop up in several phases of the development process. They help with the design of a system's user interface, they help developers make programming choices, and they provide the basis for testing the newly constructed system.

To go any further with use case analysis you're going to have to apply the UML, and that's the subject for the next hour.

Summary

The use case is a construct for describing how a system will look to potential users. It's a collection of scenarios initiated by an entity called an *actor* (a person, a piece of hardware, a passage of time, or another system). A use case should result in something of value for either the actor who initiated it or for another actor.

It's possible to reuse use cases. One way ("inclusion") is to use the steps from one use case as part of the sequence of steps in another use case. Another way ("extension") is to create a new use case by adding steps to an existing use case.

Interviewing users is the best technique for deriving use cases. When deriving a use case, it's important to note the preconditions for initiating the use case, and the postconditions that result as a consequence of the use case.

You do the user interviews after you interview clients and generate a list of candidate classes. This will give you a foundation in the terminology that you'll use to talk with the users. It's a good idea to interview a group of users. The objective is to derive a list of candidate use cases and all possible actors.

Q&A

Q Why do we really need the use case concept? Can't we just ask users what they want to see in a system and leave it at that?

A Not really. We have to add structure to what the users tell us, and use cases provide the structure. The structure comes in handy when you have to take the results of your interviews with users and communicate those results to clients and developers.

Q How difficult is it to derive use cases?

A In my experience, listing the use cases—at least the high-level ones—isn't all that difficult. Some difficulty arises when you're delving into each one and trying to get the users to list the steps in each scenario. When you're building a system that replaces an existing way of doing things, users typically know these steps so well and have used them so often they find it difficult to articulate them. It's a good idea to have a panel of users, as the discussion in the group typically brings out ideas that an individual user might have trouble expressing.

6

Workshop

This hour was theory rather than UML. For this workshop, the objective is to understand the theoretical concepts and apply them in several contexts. The practice will firm up the concepts for you in advance of the next hour when you'll learn how to visualize them in the UML. The answers appear in Appendix A, "Quiz Answers."

Quiz

1. What do you call the entity that initiates a use case?

2. What is meant by "including a use case"?

3. What is meant by "extending a use case"?

4. Is a use case the same as a scenario?

Exercises

1. For our soda machine example, create another use case that includes the "Expose the inside" and the "Unexpose the inside" use cases.

2. Use cases can help you analyze a business as well as a system. Consider a computer superstore that sells hardware, peripherals, and software. Who are the actors? What are some of the major use cases? What are some scenarios within each use case?

HOUR 7

Working with Use Case Diagrams

The use case is a powerful concept for helping an analyst understand how a system should behave. It helps you gather requirements from the users' point of view. In this hour, you'll learn to visualize the use case concepts you learned in the last hour. Specifically, you'll

- Represent a use case model
- Visualize relationships among use cases
- Understand the role of use case diagrams in the development process
- Create and apply use case models
- Look at the big picture of the UML

As powerful as the use case concept is, use cases become even more powerful when you use the UML to visualize them. Visualization allows you to show use cases to users so they can give you additional information. It's a fact of life that users often know more than they can articulate: The use case helps break the ice. Also, a visual representation allows you to combine use case diagrams with other kinds of diagrams.

One of the objectives of the system analysis process is to generate a collection of use cases. The idea is to be able to catalog and reference this collection, which serves as the users' view of the system. When it's time to upgrade the system, the use case catalog serves as a basis for gathering the requirements of the upgrade.

Representing a Use Case Model

An actor initiates a use case, and an actor (possibly the initiator, but not necessarily) receives something of value from the use case. The graphic representation is straightforward. An ellipse represents a use case, a stick figure represents an actor. The initiating actor is on the left of the use case, and the receiving actor is on the right. The actor's name appears just below the actor. The name of the use case appears either inside the ellipse or just below it. An association line connects an actor to the use case, and represents communication between the actor and the use case. The association line is solid, like the line that connects associated classes.

One of the benefits of use case analysis is that it shows the boundary between the system and the outside world. Actors are typically outside the system, whereas use cases are inside. You use a rectangle (with the name of the system somewhere inside) to represent the system boundary. The rectangle encloses the system's use cases.

NEW TERM   The actors, use cases, and interconnecting lines make up a *use case model.* Figure 7.1 shows the symbols.

FIGURE 7.1

In a use case model, a stick figure represents an actor, an ellipse represents a use case, and an association line represents communication between the actor and the use case.

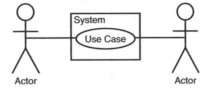

The Soda Machine Revisited

Let's apply the symbols to the example from the previous hour. As you'll recall, you developed use cases for a soda machine. The "Buy soda" use case sits inside the system along with "Restock" and "Collect." The actors are Customer, Supplier's Representative, and Collector. Figure 7.2 shows a UML use case model for the soda machine.

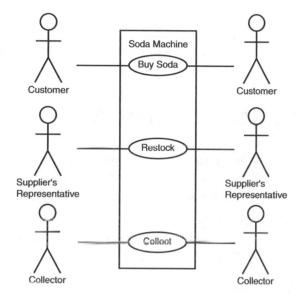

FIGURE 7.2

A use case model of the soda machine from Hour 6.

Tracking the Steps in the Scenarios

Each use case is a collection of scenarios, and each scenario is a sequence of steps. As you can see, those steps do not appear on the diagram. They're not in notes attached to the use cases. Although the UML doesn't prohibit this, clarity is key in creating any diagram and attaching notes to every use case would make the diagram too busy. How and where do you keep track of the steps?

Your use case diagrams will usually be part of a design document that the client and the development team refer to. Each diagram will have its own page. Each scenario of each use case will also have its own page, listing in text form the

- Actor who initiates the use case
- Preconditions for the use case
- Steps in the scenario
- Postconditions when the scenario is complete
- Actor who benefits from the use case

You can also list assumptions for the scenario (for example, one customer will use the soda machine at a time), and a brief one-sentence description of the scenario.

Hour 6, "Introducing Use Cases," presented some alternative scenarios for the "Buy soda" use case. In your description, you can either list these scenarios separately ("Out-of-brand" and "Incorrect change"), or you can consider them exceptions to the first scenario in the use case. Exactly how you do all this is up to you, your client, and the users.

7

To show the steps in a scenario, another possibility is to use a UML activity diagram (discussed in Hour 11, "Working with Activity Diagrams").

Visualizing Relationships Among Use Cases

NEW TERM   The example in Hour 6 also showed two ways that use cases can relate to one another. One way, *inclusion*, enables you to reuse one use case's steps inside another use case. The other way, *extension*, allows you to create a new use case by adding steps to an existing use case.

NEW TERM   Two other kinds of relationships are generalization and grouping. As is the case for classes, *generalization* has one use case inheriting from another. *Grouping* is a simple way of organizing a set of use cases.

Inclusion

Let's examine the "Restock" and "Collect" use cases from the Hour 6 example. Both begin with unsecuring the machine and pulling it open, and both end with closing the machine and securing it. The "Expose the inside" use case was created to capture the first pair of steps, and the "Unexpose the inside" use case to capture the second. Both "Restock" and "Collect" include these two use cases.

To represent inclusion, you use the symbol you used for dependency between classes—a dashed line connecting the classes with an arrowhead pointing to the depended-on class. Just above the line, you add a stereotype—the word "include" enclosed in guillemets. Figure 7.3 shows the inclusion relationship in the use case model of the soda machine.

Bear in mind that an included use case never stands on its own. It only works as part of a use case that includes it.

In the text notation that tracks the steps in the sequence, you indicate the included use cases. The first step in the "Restock" use case would be include (Expose the inside).

FIGURE 7.3

The soda machine use case model with inclusion.

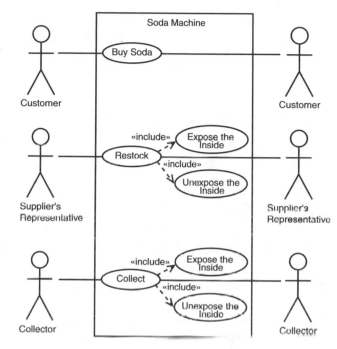

Extension

NEW TERM   Hour 6 showed that the "Restock" use case could be the basis of another use case: "Restock according to sales." Instead of just restocking the soda machine so that all brands end up with the same number of cans, the supplier's representative could take note of the brands that sold well and the brands that did not, and restock accordingly. The new use case is said to *extend* the original one because it adds new steps to the sequence in the original use case, also called the *base* use case.

NEW TERM   Extension can only take place at specific designated points within the base use case's sequence. These points are called, appropriately, *extension points*. In the Restock use case, the new steps (noting the sales and refilling accordingly) would occur after the supplier's representative opened the machine and was ready to fill the compartments of the soda brands. For this example, the extension point is "fill the compartments."

Like inclusion, you visualize extension with a dependency line (dashed line and arrowhead), along with a stereotype that shows "extends" in guillemets. Within the base use case, the extension point appears below the name of the use case. Figure 7.4 shows the extension relationship for "Restock" and "Restock according to sales" along with the inclusion relationships for "Restock" and "Collect."

7

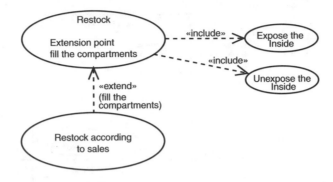

Generalization

Classes can inherit from one another and so can use cases. In use case inheritance, the
child use case inherits behavior and meaning from the parent, and adds its own behavior.
You can apply the child wherever you apply the parent.

In the example, you might imagine a "Buy a cup of soda" use case that inherits from the
"Buy soda" use case. The child adds behaviors such as "add ice" and "mix soda brands."
You model generalization of use cases the same way you model generalization of classes—
with a solid line that has an open triangle pointing at the parent, as in Figure 7.5.

FIGURE 7.5
*One use case can
inherit the meaning
and behavior of
another.*

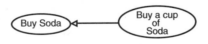

The generalization relationship can exist between actors as well as use cases. You might
have represented both the supplier's representative and the collector as agents of the supplier. If you rename the representative as the Restocker, the Restocker and Collector are
both children of the Supplier Agent, as Figure 7.6 shows.

FIGURE 7.6
*Like classes and use
cases, actors can be in
a generalization rela-
tionship.*

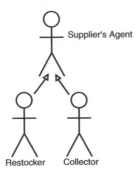

Grouping

In some use case diagrams, you might have a multitude of use cases and you'll want to organize them. This could happen when a system consists of a number of subsystems. Another possibility is when you're interviewing users in order to gather requirements for a system. Each requirement would be represented as a separate use case. You'll need some way of categorizing the requirements.

The most straightforward way to organize is to group related use cases into a package. A package, remember, appears as a tabbed folder. The grouped use cases appear inside the folder.

Use Case Diagrams in the Analysis Process

Given the example you worked with, you dived right in and applied the use case symbols. Now it's time to step back and put use cases in the context of an analysis effort.

Client interviews should start the process. These interviews will yield class diagrams that serve as the foundation for your knowledge of the system's domain (the area in which it will solve problems). After you know the general terminology of the client's area, you're ready to start talking to users.

Interviews with users begin in the terminology of the domain, but should then shift into the terminology of the users. The initial results of the interviews should reveal actors and high-level use cases that describe functional requirements in general terms. This information provides the boundaries and scope of the system.

Later interviews with users delve into these requirements more closely, resulting in use case models that show the scenarios and sequences in detail. This might result in additional use cases that satisfy inclusion and extension relationships. In this phase, it's important to rely on your understanding of the domain (from the class diagrams derived from client interviews). If you don't understand the domain well, you might create too many use cases and too much detail—a situation that could greatly impede design and development.

Applying Use Case Models: An Example

To further your understanding of use case models and how to apply them, let's take a look at a more complex example than a soda machine. Suppose you have to design a local area network (LAN) for a consulting firm, and you have to figure out the functionality to build into the LAN. How do you start?

7

A LAN is a communication network that an organization uses over a limited distance. It allows users to share resources and information.

Understanding the Domain

Begin with client interviews to create a class diagram that reflects what life is like in the world of consulting. The class diagram might include these classes: Consultant, Client, Project, Proposal, Data, and Report. Figure 7.7 shows what the diagram might look like.

FIGURE 7.7

A class diagram for the consulting world.

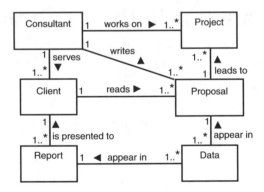

Understanding the Users

Now that the domain is in hand, turn your attention to the users because the objective is to figure out the kinds of functionality to build into the system.

In the real world, you would interview users. For this example, you'll base your ideas on some general knowledge about LANs and about the domain. Bear in mind, however, that in real-world systems analysis, nothing can substitute for interviews with real people.

One group of users will be consultants. Another will be clerical staff. Other potential users include corporate officers, marketers, network administrators, office managers, and project managers. (Can you think of any others?)

At this point, it's helpful to show the users in a generalization hierarchy, as in Figure 7.8.

FIGURE 7.8

The hierarchy of users who will interact with the LAN.

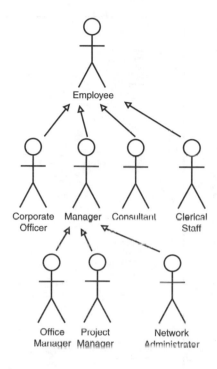

Understanding the Use Cases

What about the use cases? Here are some possibilities: "Provide security levels," "Create a proposal," Store a proposal," "Use e-mail," "Share database information," "Perform accounting," "Connect to the LAN from outside the LAN," "Connect to the Internet," "Share database information," "Catalog proposals," "Use prior proposals," and "Share printers." Based on this information, Figure 7.9 shows the high-level use case diagram that we build.

This set of use cases constitutes the functional requirements for the LAN.

Drilling Down

Let's elaborate on one of the high-level use cases and build a use case model. One extremely important activity in a consulting firm is writing proposals, so let's examine the "Create a proposal" use case.

7

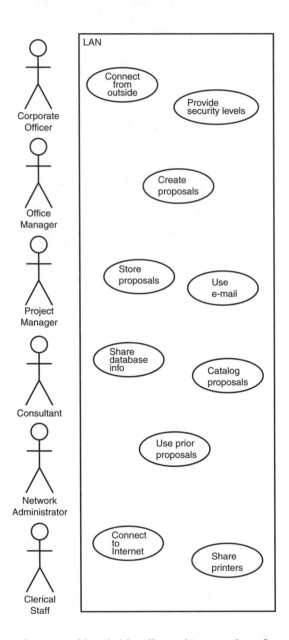

FIGURE 7.9

A high-level use case diagram of a LAN for a consulting firm.

Interviews with consultants would probably tell you that a number of steps are involved in this use case. First of all, the initiating actor is a consultant. The consultant has to log on the LAN and be verified as a valid user. Then he or she has to use office suite software (word processing, spreadsheet, and graphics) to write the proposal. In the process, the consultant might reuse portions of prior proposals. The consulting firm might have a policy that one corporate officer and two other consultants review a proposal before it goes to a client. To satisfy this policy, the consultant stores the proposal in a central repository accessible to the LAN and e-mails the three reviewers with a message telling them that the proposal is ready and informing them of its location. After receiving feedback and making necessary modifications (again, using the office suite software), the consultant prints out the proposal and mails it to the client. When everything's finished, the consultant logs off the network. The consultant has completed a proposal, and is the actor who benefits from the use case.

> When an interview reveals something like that "three reviewers" policy I just mentioned, take careful note. It means that you're starting to hear about a company's *business logic*—its set of rules for how it conducts itself. The more business logic you can find out, the better off you'll be as an analyst. You'll understand your client's corporate culture and you'll be better able to understand organizational needs.

From the preceding sequence, it's clear some of the steps will be repeated from one use case to another, and thus lead to other (possibly included) use cases you might not have thought of before. Logging on and getting verified are two steps that numerous use cases can include. For this reason, you'd create a "Verify user" use case that "Create a proposal" includes. Two other included use cases are "Use office suite software" and "Log off the network."

Additional thought about the proposal process might make you realize that the proposals written for new clients differ from the proposals written for existing clients. In fact, new-client proposals probably provide promotional information about the firm. With existing clients, it's not necessary to send that kind of information. Thus, another new use case, "Create a proposal for a new client" extends "Create a proposal."

Figure 7.10 shows the use case diagram that results from this analysis of the "Create a proposal" use case.

FIGURE 7.10

The "Create a proposal" use case in the LAN for a consulting firm.

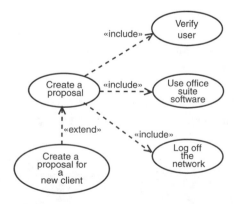

7

This example brings home an important point—a point I stressed before: The use case analysis describes the behavior of a system. It doesn't touch the implementation. This is particularly important here because the design of a LAN is far beyond the scope of this book!

Taking Stock of Where We Are

This is a good time to look at the overall structure of the UML because you've gone through two of its major aspects—object-orientation and use case analysis. You've seen their foundations and symbols, and explored some applications.

In Hours 2–7, you worked with

Classes
Objects
Interfaces
Use cases
Actors
Associations
Generalizations
Dependencies
Realizations
Aggregations
Composites
Stereotypes
Constraints
Notes
Packages
Extensions
Inclusions

Let's try to partition this set of items into categories.

Structural Elements

Classes, objects, actors, interfaces, and use cases are five of the structural elements in the UML. Although they have a number of differences (which, as an exercise, you ought to enumerate), they are similar in that they represent either physical or conceptual parts of a model. As you proceed through Part I, you'll encounter additional structural elements.

Relationships

Associations, generalizations, dependencies, aggregations, composites, and realizations are the relationships in the UML. (Inclusion and extension are two kinds of dependencies.) Without relationships, UML models would just be lists of structural elements. The relationships connect those elements and thereby connect the models to reality.

Grouping

The package is the only grouping element in the UML. It allows you to organize the structural elements in a model. A package can hold any kind of structural element, and can hold many different kinds at once.

Annotation

The note is the UML's annotation element. Notes enable you to attach constraints, comments, requirements, and explanatory graphics to your models.

Extension

Stereotypes and constraints are two constructs the UML provides for extending the language. They allow you to create new elements out of existing ones, so that you can adequately model the slice of reality your system will play in.

...And More

In addition to structural elements, relationships, grouping, annotation, and extension, the UML has another category—behavioral elements. These elements show how parts of a model (such as objects) change over time. You haven't dealt with these yet, but you will learn about one in the next hour.

The Big Picture

Now you have an idea of how the UML is organized. Figure 7.11 visualizes this organization for you. As you go through the remaining hours in Part I, keep this organization in mind. You'll keep adding to it as you go along, and this "big picture" will show you where to add the new knowledge you acquire.

7

FIGURE **7.11**

The organization of the UML, in terms of the elements you've dealt with thus far.

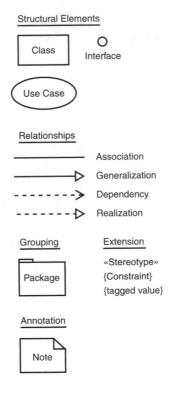

Structural Elements

Class	○ Interface
Use Case	

Relationships

———————— Association

————————▷ Generalization

- - - - - - - → Dependency

- - - - - - - ▷ Realization

Grouping   Extension

Package   «Stereotype»
                            {Constraint}
                            {tagged value}

Annotation

Note

Summary

The use case is a powerful tool for gathering functional requirements. Use case diagrams add still more power: Because they visualize use cases, they facilitate communication between analysts and users, and between analysts and clients. In a use case diagram, the symbol for a use case is an ellipse. The symbol for an actor is a stick figure. An association line joins an actor to a use case. The use cases are usually inside a rectangle that represents the system boundary.

Inclusion is represented by a dependency line with an «includes» stereotype. Extension is represented by a dependency line with an «extends» stereotype. Two other relationships between use cases are generalization, in which one use case inherits the meaning and behaviors of another, and grouping, which organizes a set of use cases. Generalization is represented by the same generalization line that shows inheritance among classes. Grouping is represented by the package icon.

Use case diagrams figure heavily into the analysis process. Begin with client interviews that yield class diagrams. The class diagrams provide a foundation for interviewing users. User interviews result in a high-level use case diagram that shows the functional requirements of the system. To create use case models, drill down into each high-level use case. The resulting use case diagrams provide the foundation for design and development.

Object-orientation and use cases are the two heavyweight concepts behind the UML. Now that you've seen them, you're ready for the big picture of the UML. The elements you've learned about in Hours 2–7 fall into these categories: structural elements, relationships, organization, annotation, and extension. In the next hour, you'll learn about an element in the remaining category: behavioral elements. Keeping this big picture in mind will help you as you learn more about the UML.

Q&A

Q I noticed that in the high-level use case diagram, you don't show associations between the actors and the use cases. Why is that?

A The high-level use case diagram emerges at the early stages of interviews with users. It's still more or less a brainstorming exercise at that point, and the objective is to find the overall requirements, scope, and boundaries of the system. The associations make more sense when subsequent client interviews get you deeper into each requirement and use case models take shape.

Q Why is it important to have that "big picture" of the UML? Can't I just know when to use each type of diagram?

A If you understand the organization of the UML, you'll be able to handle situations that you haven't encountered before. You'll be able to recognize when an existing UML element won't do the job, and you'll know how to construct a new one. You'll also know how to create a hybrid diagram (a diagram that encompasses a diverse set of UML elements) if it turns out to be the only way to clearly present a model.

Workshop

In this workshop, you'll continue with the knowledge you gained in Hour 6, using it as a foundation for the knowledge from Hour 7. The objective is to use your new knowledge to visualize use cases and their relationships. The answers appear in Appendix A, "Quiz Answers."

7

Quiz

1. Name two advantages to visualizing a use case.

2. Describe generalization and grouping, the relationships among use cases that you learned about in this hour. Name two situations in which you would group use cases.

3. What are the similarities between classes and use cases? What are the differences?

Exercises

1. Sketch the diagram of a use case model for a TV remote control. Be sure to include all the functions of the remote as use cases for your model.

2. In the second exercise in Hour 6, you listed the actors and use cases for a computer superstore. This time, draw a high-level use case diagram based on the work you did for that exercise. Then create a use case model for at least one of the high-level use cases. In your work, try to incorporate the "includes" or "extends" relationships.

3. Consider what happens when you go shopping for groceries and other necessities in a supermarket. Create the concept for a device that eliminates some of the annoyances associated with this experience and model the use cases for that device. In your set of use cases, use inclusion, extension, and generalization wherever they're appropriate.

Hour 8

Working with State Diagrams

So far, you've learned about the important structural elements of the UML. Now you'll learn about an element that shows how change proceeds over time. Here are the topics you'll cover in this hour:

- What a state diagram is
- Events, actions, and guard conditions
- Substates: sequential and concurrent
- History states
- Why state diagrams are important
- Adding the state diagram to the big picture of the UML

NEW TERM At the end of the last hour, I said this hour would cover a category you haven't worked with before. This new category, the *behavioral element*, shows how parts of a UML model change over time. You'll learn about a particular member of this category, the state diagram.

Each year brings new styles in clothes and cars, seasons change the color of leaves on trees, and passing years see children grow and mature. Without becoming any more like a greeting card, the point is that as time passes and events occur, changes take place in the objects around us.

This also holds true in any system. As the system interacts with users and (possibly) with other systems, the objects that make up the system go through necessary changes to accommodate the interactions. If you're going to model systems, you must have a mechanism to model change.

What Is a State Diagram?

One way to characterize change in a system is to say that its objects change their *state* in response to events and to time. Here are some quick examples:

When you throw a switch, a light changes its state from Off to On.

When you click a remote control, a television changes its state from showing you one channel to showing you another.

After an appropriate amount of time, a washing machine changes its state from Washing to Rinsing.

 The UML *state diagram* captures these kinds of changes. It presents the states an object can be in along with the transitions between the states, and shows the starting point and endpoint of a sequence of state changes.

  A state diagram is also referred to as a *state machine*.

Bear in mind that a state diagram is intrinsically different from a class diagram, an object diagram, or a use case diagram in a very important way. The diagrams you've already studied model the behavior of a system, or at least a group of classes, objects, or use cases. A state diagram shows the states of a single object.

It's customary to capitalize the initial letter of a state's name. Also, it's a good idea to give a state a name that ends in "ing" whenever possible (for example, "Dialing," "Faxing"). Sometimes it's not possible ("Idle" is an example, as you'll see in a moment).

The Symbol Set

Figure 8.1 shows the rounded rectangle that represents a state, along with the solid line and arrowhead that represents a transition. The arrowhead points to the state being transitioned into. The figure also shows the solid circle that symbolizes a starting point and the bull's-eye that symbolizes an endpoint.

FIGURE 8.1

The UML symbols in a state diagram. The icon for a state is a rounded rectangle, and the symbol for a transition is a solid line with an arrowhead. A solid circle stands for the starting point of a sequence of states, and a bull's-eye represents the endpoint.

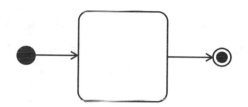

Adding Details to the State Icon

The UML gives you the option of adding detail to these symbols. Just as you have the option of dividing a class icon into three areas (for name, attributes, and operations), you can divide the state icon into three areas. The top area holds the name of the state (which you have to supply whether you subdivide the icon or not), the middle area holds state variables, and the bottom area holds activities. Figure 8.2 shows these details.

FIGURE 8.2

You can subdivide a state icon into areas that show the state's name, state variables, and activities.

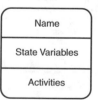

State variables, like timers or counters, are sometimes helpful. Activities consist of events and actions: Three frequently used ones are *entry* (what happens when the system enters the state), *exit* (what happens when the system leaves the state), and *do* (what happens while the system is in the state). You can add others as necessary.

The fax machine provides an example of an object with a state that has state variables and activities. When it's sending a fax—that is, when it's in the Faxing state—the fax machine notes the date and time it started sending the fax (the values of the state variables "date" and "time"), and notes its phone number as well as the name of the owner (the values of the state variables "phone number" and "owner"). While in this state, the fax machine engages in the activities of adding a datestamp and timestamp to the fax, and adding its phone number and the name of its owner. In other activities in this state, the machine pulls the pages through, paginates the fax, and completes the transmission.

While it's in the Idle state, the fax machine presents the date and time on a display. Figure 8.3 shows a state diagram.

FIGURE 8.3

The fax machine provides an example of an object with a state that has state variables and activities.

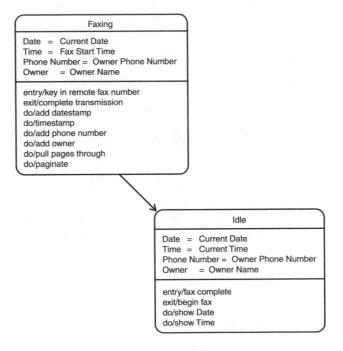

Adding Details to the Transitions: Events and Actions

NEW TERM You can also add some details to the transition lines. You can indicate an event that causes a transition to occur (a *trigger event*), and the computation (the *action*) that executes and makes the state change happen. To add events and actions you write them near the transition line, using a slash to separate a triggering event from an action. Sometimes an event causes a transition without an associated action, and sometimes a transition occurs because a state completes an activity (rather than because of an event). This type of transition is called a *triggerless transition*.

The graphical user interface (GUI) you interact with gives examples of transition details. For the moment, let's assume the GUI can be in one of three states:

Initializing

Working

Shutting Down

When you turn your PC on, bootup takes place. Turning the PC on, then, is a triggering event that causes the GUI to transition to the Initializing state, and booting up is an action that takes place during the transition.

As a result of activities in the Initializing state, the GUI transitions into the Working state. When you choose to shut down the PC, you generate a trigger event that causes the transition to the Shutting Down state, and eventually the PC turns off. Figure 8.4 shows the state diagram that captures these states and transitions in the GUI.

FIGURE 8.4

The states and transitions of a graphical user interface include trigger events, actions, and triggerless transitions.

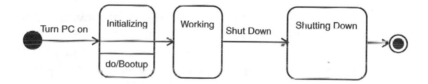

Adding Details to the Transitions: Guard Conditions

The preceding account of GUIs leaves a lot to be desired. First of all, if you leave your computer unattended or if you just sit idly by and don't type or use the mouse, a screen-saver appears and rescues your pixels from potential burnout. To say this in state-change terms, if enough time passes without a user input the GUI transitions from the Working state into a state I didn't show in Figure 8.4—the Screensaving state.

The time interval is specified in your Windows Control Panel. It's usually 15 minutes. Any keystroke or mouse movement transitions the monitor from the Screensaving state back to the Working state.

NEW TERM   That 15-minute interval is a *guard condition*—when it's met, the transition takes place. Figure 8.5 shows the state diagram for the GUI with the Screensaving state and the guard condition added. Notice that the guard condition, [is Timeout], is written as a Boolean expression.

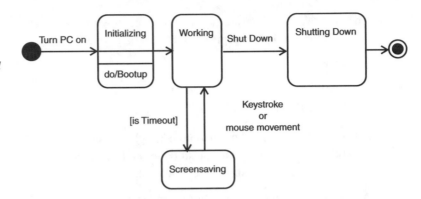

FIGURE 8.5
*The state diagram for
the GUI, with the
Screensaving state and
a guard condition.*

Substates

Our model of the GUI is still somewhat empty. The Working state, in particular, is a lot richer than I've indicated in Figures 8.4 and 8.5.

When the GUI is in the Working state, a lot is happening behind the scenes, although it might not be particularly evident onscreen. The GUI is constantly waiting for you to do something—to type a keystroke, move the mouse, or press a mouse button. Then it must register those inputs and change the display to visualize those actions for you onscreen— for example, by moving the cursor when you move the mouse, or displaying an "a" when you press the "a" key.

NEW TERM   Thus the GUI goes through changes while it's within the Working state. Those changes are changes of state. Because these states reside within a state, they're called *substates*. Substates come in two varieties: *sequential* and *concurrent*.

Sequential Substates

As the name implies, sequential substates occur one after the other. Recapping the afore-mentioned substates within the GUI's Working state, you have this sequence:

Awaiting User Input

Registering User Input

Visualizing User Input

User input triggers the transition from Awaiting to Registering. Activities within Registering transition the GUI into Visualizing. After the third state, the GUI goes back to Awaiting User Input. Figure 8.6 shows how to represent these sequential substates within the Working state.

FIGURE 8.6

Sequential substates within the GUI's working state.

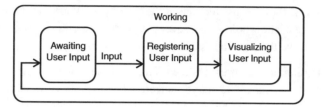

Concurrent Substates

Within the Working state, the GUI isn't just waiting for you. It's also watching the system clock and (possibly) updating an application's display after a specific interval. For example, an application might include an onscreen clock that the GUI has to update.

All this is going on at the same time as the sequence I just discussed. Although each sequence is, of course, a set of sequential substates, the two sequences are concurrent with one another. You represent concurrency with a dotted line between the concurrent states, as in Figure 8.7.

FIGURE 8.7

Concurrent substates proceed at the same time. A dotted line separates concurrent substates.

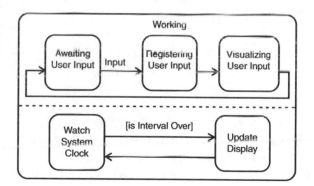

NEW TERM   Separating the Working state into two components might remind you of something. Remember when I discussed aggregations and composites? When each component is part of just one "whole," you are dealing with a composite. The concurrent parts of the Working state have that same kind of relationship to the Working state. For this reason, the Working state is a *composite state*. A state that consists of just sequential substates is also a composite state.

History States

When your screensaver is on and you move your mouse to get back to the Working state, what happens? Does your display go back to looking as it did right after the GUI was initialized? Or does it look exactly the way you left it before the screensaver came on?

Obviously, if the screensaver caused the display to revert back to the beginning of the Working state, the whole screensaver idea would be counterproductive. Users would lose work and have to restart a session from square one.

The state diagram captures this idea. The UML supplies a symbol that shows that a composite state remembers its active substate when the object transitions out of the composite state. The symbol is the letter "H" enclosed in a small circle connected by a solid line to the remembered substate, with an arrowhead that points to that substate. Figure 8.8 shows this symbol in the Working state.

FIGURE 8.8

The history state, symbolized by the "H" in the small circle, shows that a composite state remembers its active substate when the object transitions out of that composite state.

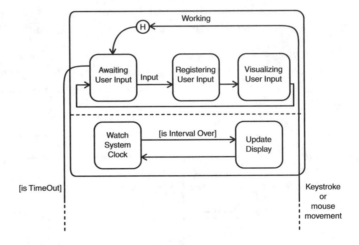

NEW TERM   In the state diagram, I haven't dealt with windows that are opened by other windows—in other words, with substates nested within other substates. When a history state remembers substates at all levels of nesting (as the Windows Working state does), the history state is *deep*. If it only remembers the highest nested substate, the history state is *shallow*. You represent a deep history by putting "H*" in the circle.

NEW TERM   The history state, the initial state (represented by the solid black circle), and the final state (represented by the bull's-eye) are termed *pseudostates*. They have no state variables and no activities, and therefore aren't "full" states.

Messages and Signals

In the example, the trigger event that causes the transition from Screensaving to Working is a keystroke, a mouse movement, or a mouse click. Any of these events is, in effect, a message from the user to the GUI. This is an important concept because objects communicate by sending messages to each other. In this case, the trigger event is a message from one object (the user) to another (the GUI).

NEW TERM   A message that triggers a transition in the receiving object's state diagram is called a *signal*. In the object-oriented world, sending a signal is the same as creating an instance of a signal class and transmitting it to the receiving object. The signal has properties that are represented as attributes. If you think of a signal as a class you can create class diagrams that show inheritance hierarchies of signals.

The remote control that you use to operate your TV set is a good example of a signal-sender and gives us an opportunity to model signal hierarchies. This example also gives us an opportunity to talk about stereotypes. Stereotypes, remember, are the UML's way of extending itself. The UML provides no special icon for signals as classes, so we extend the class diagram by including «Signal» in each class icon that represents a signal. Figure 8.9 shows the hierarchy of signals for one brand of remote control. The one you use might differ slightly. If it does, model its signals.

FIGURE 8.9

A hierarchy of signals for a TV's remote control.

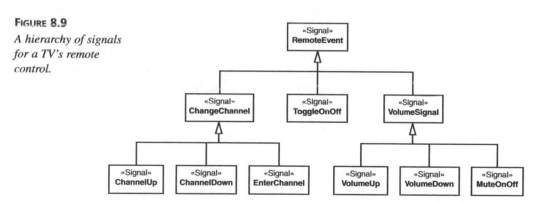

Incidentally, you can use the «Signal» class icon as a way of elaborating on the event that takes an object from one state to another, as Figure 8.10 shows.

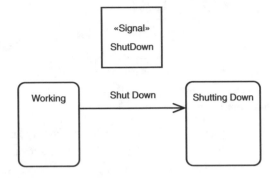

FIGURE 8.10
Using a «Signal» class icon to elaborate on an event that causes a state transition.

Why Are State Diagrams Important?

The UML state diagram provides a variety of symbols and encompasses a number of ideas—all to model the changes that just one object goes through. This type of diagram has the potential to get very complex very quickly. Is it really necessary?

In fact, it is. It's necessary to have state diagrams because they help analysts, designers, and developers understand the behavior of the objects in a system. A class diagram and the corresponding object diagram show only the static aspects of a system. They show hierarchies and associations, and tell you what the behaviors are. They don't show you the dynamic details of the behaviors.

Developers, in particular, have to know how objects are supposed to behave because they have to implement these behaviors in software. It's not enough to implement an object: Developers have to make that object *do* something. State diagrams ensure that they won't have to guess about what the object is supposed to do. With a clear picture of object behavior, the likelihood increases that the development team will produce a system that meets requirements.

Building the Big Picture

Now you can add "behavioral elements" to your big picture of the UML. Figure 8.11 presents the picture with the state diagram included.

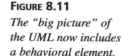

FIGURE 8.11

The "big picture" of the UML now includes a behavioral element, the state diagram.

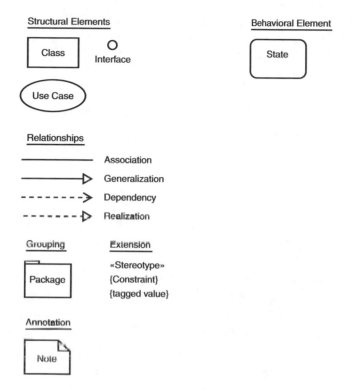

Structural Elements

Class
Interface
Use Case

Relationships

Association
Generalization
Dependency
Realization

Grouping
Package

Extension
«Stereotype»
{Constraint}
{tagged value}

Annotation
Note

Behavioral Element

State

8

Summary

Objects in a system change their states in response to events and to time. The UML state diagram captures these state changes. A state diagram focuses on the state changes in just one object. A rounded rectangle represents a state, and a line with an arrowhead represents a transition from one state to another.

The state icon has the name of the state, and can hold state variables and activities as well. A transition can occur in response to a trigger event and can entail an action. A transition can also occur because of an activity in a state: A transition that takes place in this fashion is termed a *triggerless transition*. Finally, a transition can occur because a particular condition—a *guard condition*—holds true.

Sometimes, a state consists of substates. Substates may either be sequential (occurring one after the other) or concurrent (occurring at the same time). A state that consists of substates is called a composite state. A history state indicates that a composite state remembers its substate when the object transitions out of that composite state. A history state may be either shallow or deep. These terms pertain to nested substates. A *shallow* history remembers only the top-level substate. A *deep* history remembers all levels of substates.

When an object sends a message that triggers a transition in another object's state diagram, that message is a *signal*. By using class diagrams extended with a «Signal» stereotype, you can build an inheritance hierarchy of signals.

It's necessary to have state diagrams because they help analysts, designers, and developers understand the behavior of the objects in a system. Developers, in particular, have to know how objects are supposed to behave because they have to implement these behaviors in software. It's not enough to implement an object: Developers have to make that object *do* something.

Q&A

Q What's the best way to start creating a state diagram?

A It's much like creating a class diagram or a use case model. In the class diagram, you list all the classes and then wrestle with the interclass associations. In the state diagram, first list the states of the object, and then focus on the transitions. As you work through each transition, figure out whether a trigger event sets it off and if any action takes place.

Q Must every state diagram have a final state (the one represented by the bull's-eye)?

A No. An object that never turns off won't have this state.

Q Any hints on laying out a state diagram?

A Try to arrange the states and transitions so that you minimize crossing lines. One objective of this diagram (and any other) is clarity. If people can't understand the models you build, no one will use them and your efforts—no matter how thorough and insightful—will be wasted.

Workshop

The quiz and exercises will transition you into the "Learned state diagrams" state. As always, you'll find the answers in Appendix A, "Quiz Answers."

Quiz

1. In what important way does a state diagram differ from a class diagram, an object diagram, or a use case diagram?

2. Define these terms: *transition, event,* and *action.*

3. What is a *triggerless transition*?

4. What is the difference between sequential substates and concurrent substates?

5. What is a *pseudostate*? Give examples.

Exercises

1. Suppose you're designing a toaster. Create a state diagram that tracks the states of bread in the toaster. Include necessary triggering events, actions, and guard conditions.

2. In Windows, users can send a number of signals to the GUI. Create a class diagram of the possible signals, showing all inheritance relationships. Remember to include «Signal» in your diagram.

3. Figure 8.7 shows the concurrent substates within the GUI's Working state. Draw a diagram of the Screensaving state that includes concurrent substates.

8

HOUR 9

Working with Sequence Diagrams

State diagrams focus on the states of an object. That's only a small part of the picture. The UML sequence diagram takes the next step and shows how objects communicate with one another over time. In this hour, you'll cover

- What a sequence diagram is
- Applying sequence diagrams
- Instance diagrams and generic diagrams
- Using "if" and "while"
- Creating an object in the sequence
- Representing recursion
- Sequence diagrams in the big picture of the UML

The state diagrams you learned about in the last hour zoom in on a single object. They show the changes an object goes through.

The UML enables you to expand your field of view and show how an object interacts with other objects. In this expanded field of view, you'll include an important dimension: time. The key idea here is that interactions among objects take place in a specified sequence, and the sequence takes time to go from beginning to end. When you create a system, you specify the sequence, and you use the UML sequence diagram to do it.

What Is a Sequence Diagram?

NEW TERM   The *sequence diagram* consists of objects represented in the usual way—as named rectangles (with the name underlined), messages represented as solid-line arrows, and time represented as a vertical progression.

Objects

The objects are laid out near the top of the diagram from left to right. They're arranged in any order that simplifies the diagram.

NEW TERM   Extending downward from each object is a dashed line called the object's *lifeline*. Along the lifeline is a narrow rectangle called an *activation*. The activation represents an execution of an operation the object carries out. The length of the rectangle signifies the activation's duration. Figure 9.1 shows an object, lifeline, and activation.

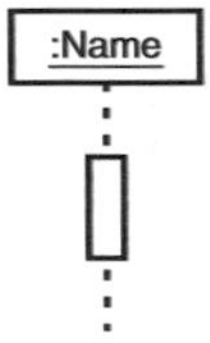

FIGURE 9.1

Representing an object in a sequence diagram.

:Name

Messages

A message that goes from one object to another goes from one object's lifeline to the other object's lifeline. An object can send a message to itself—that is, from its lifeline back to its own lifeline.

NEW TERM   A message can be *simple, synchronous,* or *asynchronous.* A simple message is a transfer of control from one object to another. If an object sends a synchronous message, it waits for an answer to that message before it proceeds with its business. If an object sends an asynchronous message, it doesn't wait for an answer before it proceeds.

In the sequence diagram, a simple message has a two-line arrowhead, a synchronous message has a full arrowhead, and an asynchronous message has a half-arrowhead, as shown in Figure 9.2.

FIGURE 9.2

Symbols for messages in the sequence diagram.

9

Time

The diagram represents time in the vertical direction. Time starts at the top and progresses toward the bottom. A message that's closer to the top occurs earlier in time than a message that's closer to the bottom.

Thus, the sequence diagram is two-dimensional. The left-to-right dimension is the layout of the objects, and the top-to-bottom dimension shows the passage of time. Figure 9.3 shows the essential symbol set of the sequence diagram, with the symbols working together. The objects are laid out across the top. Each object's lifeline is a dashed line extending downward from the object. A solid line with an arrowhead connects one lifeline to another, and represents a message from one object to another. The figure shows an actor initiating the sequence, although strictly speaking, the stick figure isn't part of the sequence diagram's symbol set.

FIGURE 9.3

The symbols in a sequence diagram. (Although an actor typically initiates the sequence, the actor symbol isn't part of the sequence diagram's symbol set.)

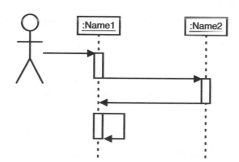

In order to bring this important UML tool to life, let's apply it to examples you've covered in previous hours. Each application will show you some important concepts that relate to sequence diagrams.

The GUI

In the last hour, you developed state diagrams that show the changes a GUI goes through. Now you'll draw a sequence diagram that represents the GUI's interactions with other objects.

The Sequence

Suppose the user of a GUI presses an alphanumeric key on the keyboard. Assuming he or she is using an application such as a word processor, the corresponding alphanumeric character appears immediately onscreen. What goes on behind the scenes to make this happen?

1. The GUI notifies the operating system about the keystroke.
2. The operating system notifies the CPU.
3. The operating system updates the GUI.
4. The CPU notifies the video card.
5. The video card sends a message to the monitor.
6. The monitor presents the alphanumeric character onscreen, providing visual feed-back to the user.

All this happens so quickly that we forget these steps take place. (If, in fact, we ever even knew about them!)

The Sequence Diagram

Figure 9.4 presents the sequence diagram for the GUI. As you can see, the messages are asynchronous: None of the components waits for anything before moving on. In your dealings with some Windows applications, you might have experienced some of the effects of asynchronous communication, particularly on a slower machine. When you type in a word processor, sometimes you don't see the result of a keystroke before you perform subsequent ones, and then two or more characters appear on the screen.

Sometimes it's instructive to show the states of one or more of the objects on the sequence diagram. Because you've already analyzed the states of the GUI (in the last hour), this is easy to do. Figure 9.5 shows a hybrid—the GUI sequence diagram with the GUI's states. Note that the sequence originates and ends in the GUI's Working state, as you would expect.

In a sequence diagram, another way to show an object's change of state is to include the object more than once in the diagram.

FIGURE 9.4

A sequence diagram that shows how a GUI interacts with other objects.

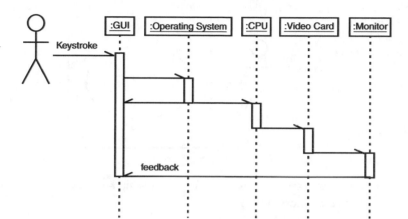

FIGURE 9.5

A sequence diagram can show an object's states.

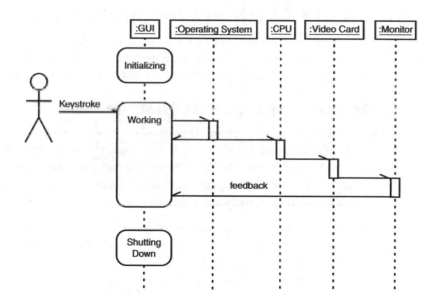

The Use Case

What exactly is a sequence diagram a diagram of? In this example, the sequence diagram shows the object interactions that take place during a simple scenario—the user presses a key. This scenario might be part of a use case called "Perform a keystroke" (see Figure 9.6). By diagramming the system interactions in the use case, the sequence diagram has, in effect, "mapped" the use case onto the system.

FIGURE 9.6
*The use case dia-
grammed by the
sequence diagram in
Figure 9.4.*

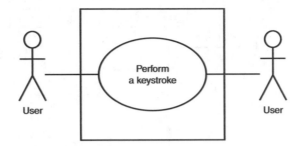

In the next example, I examine the relationship between use cases and sequence diagrams a bit more closely.

The Soda Machine: Instance and Generic

The preceding example began with a state diagram. This one begins with a use case.
"Buy soda" was one of the use cases in the Soda Machine example in Hours 6,
"Introducing Use Cases," and 7, "Working with Use Case Diagrams."

An Instance Sequence Diagram

In the best-case scenario of the "Buy soda" use case, remember that the actor is a customer who wants to purchase a can of soda. The customer initiates the scenario by inserting money into the machine. He or she then makes a selection. Because we're talking
about the best-case scenario, the machine holds least one can of the selected soda, and
presents a cold can of that soda to the customer.

Let's assume that in the soda machine, three objects do the work we're concerned with:
the front (the interface the soda machine presents to the customer), the money register
(which collects the money), and the dispenser (which holds the soda and delivers it
through the front). We'll also assume that the money register controls the dispenser. The
sequence goes like this:

1. The customer inserts the money into the money slot in the front of the machine.

2. The customer makes a selection.

3. The money travels to the register.

4. Because this is the best-case scenario, assume the soda is in stock, and the register
   has the dispenser deliver the soda to the front of the machine.

NEW TERM   As the corresponding sequence diagram covers only one scenario (that is, one
instance) in the "Buy soda" use case, it's called an *instance sequence diagram*.
Figure 9.7 shows this diagram. Note that the diagram shows simple messages. Each message moves the flow of control from one object to another.

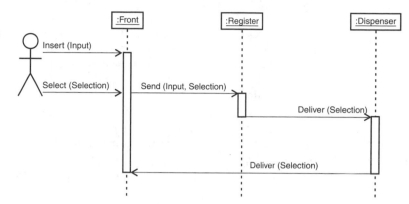

FIGURE 9.7
This sequence diagram models just the best-case scenario in the "Buy soda" use case. Hence, it's an instance sequence diagram.

A Generic Sequence Diagram

As you'll recall, the "Buy soda" use case consisted of two additional scenarios. One dealt with the machine being out of the selected soda. The other dealt with the customer having an incorrect amount of money. If you consider all of a use case's scenarios when you draw a sequence diagram, you create a *generic sequence diagram*.

In this case, you can build the generic sequence diagram out of the instance sequence diagram. In order to do this, you have to account for flow of control. That is, you have to represent the conditions and consequences for incorrect-amount-of-money and out-of-selected-soda.

For the incorrect-amount-of-money scenario

1. The register checks to see whether the customer's input amount matches the price of the soda.

2. If the amount is greater than the price, the register calculates the difference and checks its cash reserve.

3. If the difference is present in the cash reserve, the register returns the change to the customer and everything proceeds as before.

4. If the difference is not in the cash reserve, the register returns the input amount and displays a message that prompts the customer for the correct amount.

5. If the amount is less than the price, the register does nothing and the machine waits for more money.

If you were designing a soda machine for a client, you might have to make a design decision regarding step 5. You can choose to have the machine wait a certain interval, calculate the difference between the price and the input amount, and display a message that prompts the customer to insert the difference.

As part of the decision, you would have to answer these questions: How much is that capability worth to the client? How much would it cost to implement the technology that makes it work?

This is a good example of how a sequence diagram can catalyze the analysis process.

To represent each "if" in the sequence, you put the condition of the "if" in square brackets. Above the appropriate message-arrows, add [input > price], [input – price not present], and [input – price present].

Each condition causes a "fork" of control in the message, separating the message into separate paths. Different message-paths can ultimately arrive at the same object. To accommodate this, the receiving object's lifeline branches into separate paths. At some point in the sequence, the branches in the message merge, as do the paths in the lifeline.

Figure 9.8 shows the diagram after adding the incorrect-amount-of-money scenario.

FIGURE 9.8
The sequence diagram after adding the incorrect-amount-of-money scenario to the "Buy soda" use case.

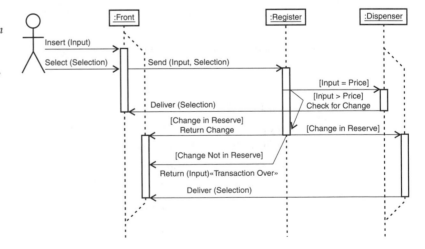

Now let's add the out-of-selection scenario.

1. After the customer selects a sold-out brand, the machine flashes a "sold out" message.

2. The machine displays a message that prompts the customer to make another selection.

3. The customer has the option of pushing a button that returns his or her money.

4. If the customer selects an in-stock brand, everything proceeds as in the best-case scenario if the input amount is correct. If not, the machine follows the incorrect-amount-of-money scenario.

5. If the customer selects another sold-out brand, the process repeats until the customer selects an in-stock brand or pushes a button that returns his or her money.

Figure 9.9 shows the soda machine's generic sequence diagram with the incorrect-amount-of-money and out-of-selection scenarios.

FIGURE 9.9

The soda machine's generic sequence diagram after adding the out-of-selection scenario to Figure 9.8.

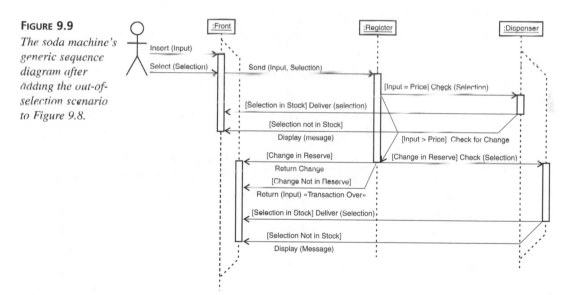

If you're starting to think that a sequence diagram lurks behind every use case, you're getting the idea.

Creating an Object in the Sequence

In the examples so far, you've learned about different types of messages, instance and generic sequence diagrams, and control structures. Another important sequence diagram-related concept, particularly when you're designing software, is object creation.

It's often the case that an object-oriented program has to create a new object. Recall that in the software realm, a class is a template for creating an object (like a cookie-cutter is a template for creating a cookie). How do you represent object creation when you diagram a sequence of object interactions?

The "Create a proposal" use case from the consulting-firm LAN example provides an instance of object creation. For this example, you'll abstract out the LAN, with the understanding that everything takes place via the network. Assuming, then, that the consultant is already logged on to the LAN, the sequence you'll model is as follows:

1. The consultant wants to reuse parts of an existing proposal, and searches the networked central repository for an appropriate proposal.

2. If the consultant finds an appropriate proposal, he or she opens the file and in the process opens the office software suite. The consultant saves the file under a new name, thus creating a new file for the new proposal.

3. If the consultant does not find a proposal, he or she opens the office software suite and creates a new file for the proposal.

4. While working on the proposal, the consultant uses applications from the office software suite.

5. When the consultant finishes the proposal, he or she stores it in the central repository.

In addition to object creation (in this case, file creation), this sequence involves the use of "if" as well as a "while" loop.

NEW TERM   First, let's attack object creation. When a sequence results in the creation of an object, you represent the created object in the usual way—as a named rectangle. The difference is that you don't position it at the top of the sequence diagram as you do with the other objects. Instead, you position it along the vertical dimension so that its location corresponds to the time when it's created. The message that creates the object is labeled "Create()". The parentheses imply an operation: In an object-oriented language, a *constructor* operation creates an object.

> Instead of using "Create()" to label the object creation message-arrow, another option is to use a «Create» stereotype.

As for the "while" statement, you represent this flow of control by putting the while condition ("while working on proposal") in square brackets and preceding the left bracket with an asterisk.

Figure 9.10 shows a sequence diagram of the "Create a proposal" use case.

FIGURE 9.10

The sequence diagram for the "Create a proposal" use case.

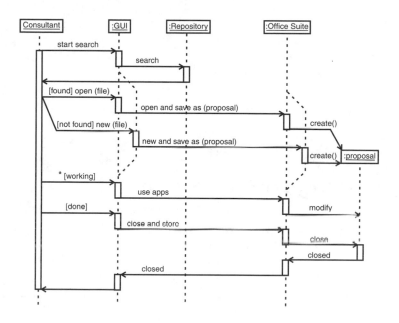

This example presents a look at abstraction in that I've omitted details that don't particularly concern us. I've done this in two ways. First, I left out details about the LAN, as I mentioned earlier. Also, notice that the GUI is an object in the sequence diagram, and I haven't included all the intricacies of the "Perform a keystroke" use case from the earlier GUI example. The details of the GUI's interactions with the operating system, the CPU, and the monitor aren't important for our purposes here.

Representing Recursion

NEW TERM   Sometimes an object has an operation that invokes itself. This is called *recursion*, and it's a mainstay of many programming languages.

Here's an example. Suppose one of the objects in your system is a calculator, and suppose one of its operations computes interest. In order to compute compound interest for a time-frame that encompasses several compounding periods, the object's interest-computation operation has to invoke itself a number of times.

To represent this in the UML, you draw a message-arrow out of the activation that signifies the operation, and draw a small rectangle overlaid on top of the activation. Draw the arrow so that it points back to the small rectangle, and draw a return arrow to the object that initiated the recursion. Figure 9.11 is a snippet of a sequence diagram that shows recursion.

FIGURE 9.11

Representing recursion in a sequence diagram.

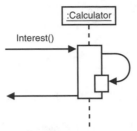

Building the Big Picture

You can now add one more diagram to your big picture of the UML. As it deals with the behaviors of objects, the sequence diagram goes under the "Behavioral Elements" category. Figure 9.12 updates your growing picture.

FIGURE 9.12

The "big picture" of the UML with the addition of the sequence diagram.

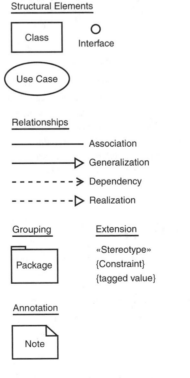

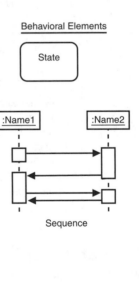

Summary

The UML sequence diagram adds the dimension of time to object interactions. In the diagram, objects are laid out across the top, and time proceeds from top to bottom. An object lifeline descends from each object. A narrow rectangle on an object's lifeline represents an *activation*—an execution of one of that object's operations. You can incorporate an object's states by placing them along its lifeline.

Messages (simple, synchronous, or asynchronous) are arrows that connect one lifeline to another. A message's location in the vertical dimension represents the time of its occurrence within the sequence. Messages that occur early are close to the top of the diagram, and messages that occur late are close to the bottom.

A use case diagram can show either an instance (one scenario) of a use case, or it can be generic and incorporate all of a use case's scenarios. Generic sequence diagrams often provide opportunities to represent "if" statements and "while" loops. Enclose each condition for an "if" statement in square brackets. Do the same for the condition that satisfies a "while" loop, and prefix the left bracket with an asterisk.

When a sequence includes the creation of an object, you represent the newly created object as a rectangle in the usual way. Its position in the vertical dimension represents the time it's created.

In some systems, an operation can invoke itself. This is called *recursion*. Represent it with an arrow that goes from an activation back to itself, and a small rectangle overlaid on top of the activation.

Q&A

Q **The sequence diagram looks like it might be useful for more than just system analysis. Can I use it to show interactions in an organization?**

A Yes, you can. The objects can be principal players, and the messages can be simple transfers of control.

Q **You show how newly created objects are represented in the sequence diagram. Do objects ever die, and if so, how do I represent that?**

A Objects do die. You represent an object's death by putting an "X" at the bottom of that object's lifeline.

Workshop

Now that you've stepped back and taken a long view of object interactions, step up to the plate, answer a few questions, and do a couple of exercises to firm up your knowledge of sequence diagrams. You'll find the answers in Appendix A, "Quiz Answers."

Quiz

1. Define *synchronous message* and *asynchronous message*.

2. In a generic sequence diagram, how do you represent the flow of control implied by an "if" statement?

3. How do you represent the flow of control implied by a "while" statement?

4. In a sequence diagram, how do you represent a newly created object?

Exercises

1. Create an instance sequence diagram that shows what happens when you successfully send a fax. That is, model the object interactions in the best-case scenario of the "send fax" use case of a fax machine. Include objects for the sending machine, the receiving machine, the fax, and a central "exchange" that routes faxes and phone calls.

2. Create a generic sequence diagram that includes unsuccessful scenarios (line busy, error on sending machine) as well as the best-case scenario from Exercise 1.

3. Create a sequence diagram for an electric pencil sharpener. Include as objects the actor, the pencil, the insertion point (that is, the place where you put the pencil into the sharpener), the motor, and the sharpening element. What messages should you include? What are the activations? Should your diagram incorporate recursion?

HOUR 10

Working with Collaboration Diagrams

In this hour, you'll learn about a diagram that's similar to the one you covered in the last hour. This one also shows the interaction among objects, but in a way that's slightly different from the sequence diagram. Sharpen your pencil and get ready to discover

- What a collaboration diagram is
- How to apply a collaboration diagram
- Working with "if" and "while"
- Nesting
- Active objects and concurrency
- Synchronization
- Where collaboration diagrams fit into the UML

Like the sequence diagram, the collaboration diagram shows how objects interact. It shows the objects along with the messages that travel from one to another. So now you may be asking yourself, "If the sequence diagram does that, why does the UML need another diagram? Don't they do the same thing? Is this just overkill?"

The two types of diagrams *are* similar. In fact, they're *semantically equivalent*. That is, they present the same information, and you can turn a sequence diagram into an equivalent collaboration diagram and vice versa.

As it turns out, it's helpful to have both forms. The sequence diagram emphasizes the time-ordering of interactions. The collaboration diagram emphasizes the context and overall organization of the objects that interact. Here's another way to look at the distinction: The sequence diagram is arranged according to time, the collaboration diagram according to space.

What Is a Collaboration Diagram?

An object diagram shows the objects and their relationships with one another. A collaboration diagram is an extension of the object diagram. In addition to the associations among objects, the collaboration diagram shows the messages the objects send each other. You usually omit the multiplicities because they would add clutter.

To represent a message, you draw an arrow near the association line between two objects. The arrow points to the receiving object. A label near the arrow shows what the message is. The message typically tells the receiving object to execute one of its operations. A pair of parentheses ends the message. Inside the parentheses, you put the parameters (if any) the operation works on.

I mentioned that you can turn any sequence diagram into a collaboration diagram, and vice versa. Thus, you have to be able to represent sequence information in a collaboration diagram. To do this, you add a number to the label of a message, with the number corresponding to the message's order in the sequence. A colon separates the number from the message.

Figure 10.1 shows the symbol set for the collaboration diagram.

FIGURE 10.1

The symbol set for the collaboration diagram.

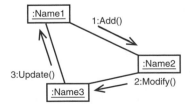

Let's take advantage of the equivalence of the two types of diagrams. In order to develop the collaboration diagram's concepts, you'll revisit the examples you worked with in the previous hour. As you do this, additional concepts will emerge.

The GUI

This example is the most straightforward case. An actor initiates the interaction sequence by performing a keystroke, and messages occur in sequence. That sequence (from the last hour) is

1. The GUI notifies the operating system about the keystroke.
2. The operating system notifies the CPU.
3. The operating system updates the GUI.
4. The CPU notifies the video card.
5. The video card sends a message to the monitor.
6. The monitor presents the alphanumeric character onscreen, providing visual feedback to the user.

Figure 10.2 shows how to represent this sequence of interactions in a collaboration diagram. The diagram includes the stick figure representing the user who initiates the sequence, although this figure isn't part of this diagram's symbol set.

FIGURE 10.2

A collaboration diagram for the GUI example.

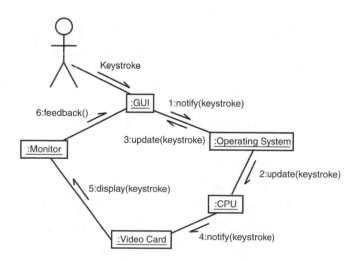

State Changes

You can show an object's changes of state in a collaboration diagram. In the object rectangle, indicate the state of the object. To the diagram, add another rectangle that stands for the object and indicate the changed state. Connect the two with a dashed line and label the line with a «become» stereotype.

Figure 10.3 illustrates a state change for the GUI, showing that the Initializing state becomes the Working state.

FIGURE 10.3

A collaboration diagram can incorporate changes of state.

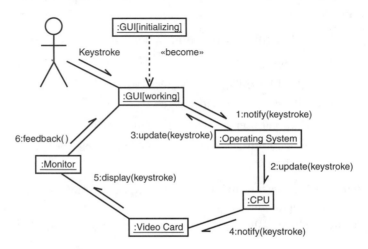

The Soda Machine

Things get a little more interesting when you bring conditions into the picture, as you did in the last hour in the soda machine example. Let's start with the best-case scenario of the "Buy soda" use case, where the sequence is

1. The customer inserts the money into the money slot in the front of the machine.
2. The customer makes a selection.
3. The money travels to the register.
4. Because this is the best-case scenario, assume the soda is in stock, and the register has the dispenser deliver the soda to the front of the machine.

The collaboration diagram is straightforward, as Figure 10.4 shows.

Now let's add the incorrect-amount-of-money scenario. The diagram has to account for a number of conditions:

1. The user has input more money than the purchase price.
2. The machine has the correct amount of change.
3. The machine does not have the correct amount of change.

FIGURE 10.4

The collaboration diagram for the best-case scenario of "Buy soda."

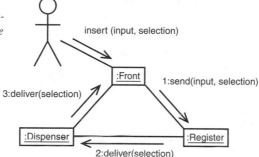

You represent conditions the same way you represented them the sequence diagram. You put the condition inside a pair of square brackets, and the condition precedes the message-label. The important thing is to coordinate the conditions with the numbering.

This can get a bit complicated, so let's build up this diagram in stages. You start with the condition where the user has input more money than the purchase price and the register has the correct change on hand. You add the step of the machine returning the change to the customer, and you add the bracketed conditions. The step that returns the change is an outgrowth of the step that checks to see whether the correct change is present. To indicate this in the return-change step, you use the same number as the message that checks for change, and you add a decimal point and a 1. This is called *nesting*. Figure 10.5 shows the details.

FIGURE 10.5

The collaboration diagram with part of the incorrect-amount of-money scenario.

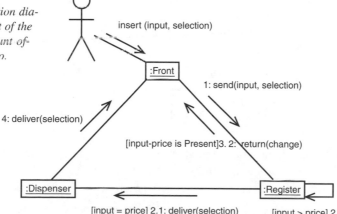

What happens when the machine doesn't have the correct change? The machine has to display an out of change message, return the money, and prompt the customer for the correct change. In effect, the transaction is over.

When you add this condition, you add a branch to the flow of control. You number this branch as a nested message. Because it's the second nested message, 2 goes after the decimal point. Finally, because the transaction is over, you clarify by adding a «transaction over» stereotype to this message, and another one to the message that delivers the soda. Figure 10.6 presents the scenario.

FIGURE **10.6**

The "Buy soda"
collaboration dia-
gram with the
whole incorrect-
amount-of-money
scenario.

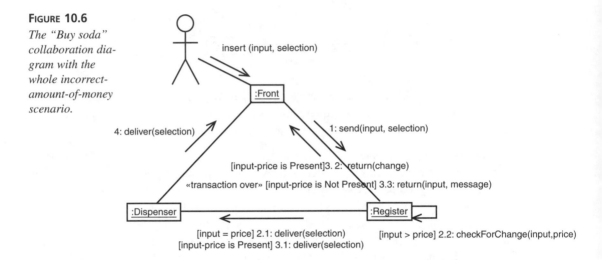

In the Workshop at the end of this hour, an exercise asks you to complete the collaboration diagram by adding the out-of-soda scenario.

Creating an Object

To show object creation, I return to the "Create a proposal" use case from the consulting firm. Once again, the sequence you'll model is

1. The consultant searches the networked central repository for an appropriate proposal to reuse.

2. If the consultant finds an appropriate proposal, he or she opens the file and in the process opens the office software suite. The consultant saves the file under a new name, thus creating a new file for the new proposal.

3. If the consultant does not find a proposal, he or she opens the office software suite and creates a new file for the proposal.

4. While working on the proposal, the consultant uses applications from the office software suite.

5. When the consultant finishes the proposal, he or she stores it in the central repository.

To show object creation, you add a «create» stereotype to the message that creates the object.

Once again, you deal with "if" statements and nested messages. You also work with a "while" loop. As in the sequence diagram, to represent the "while," you put its condition in square brackets and precede the left bracket with an asterisk.

Figure 10.7 shows this collaboration diagram, complete with object creation and "while."

FIGURE **10.7**
The "Create a pro-
posal" collaboration
diagram.

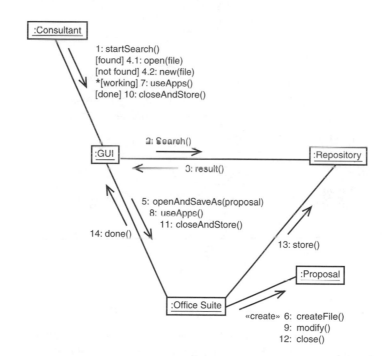

A Few More Concepts

Although you've covered a lot of ground, you haven't exhausted all the concepts related to collaboration diagrams. The concepts in this section are a little esoteric, but they might come in handy in your system analysis efforts.

Multiple Receiving Objects in a Class

Sometimes an object sends a message to multiple objects in the same class. A professor, for example, asks a group of students to hand in an assignment. In the collaboration diagram, the representation of the multiple objects is a stack of rectangles extending "backward." You add a bracketed condition preceded by an asterisk to indicate that the message goes to all objects. Figure 10.8 shows the details.

FIGURE 10.8

An object sending a message to multiple objects in a class.

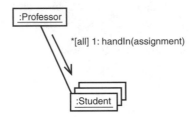

In some cases, the order of message sending is important: A bank clerk serves each customer in the order that he or she appears in line. Represent this with a "while" whose condition implies order (such as "line position = 1...n") along with the message and the stacked rectangles (see Figure 10.9).

FIGURE 10.9

An object sending a message to multiple objects in a class, in a specified order.

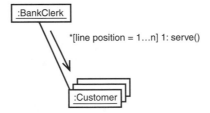

Representing Returned Results

A message can be a request for an object to perform a calculation and return a value. A customer object might request a calculator object to compute a total price that's the sum of an item's price and sales tax.

The UML provides a syntax for representing this situation. You write an expression that has the name of the returned value on the left, followed by ":=", followed by the name of the operation and the quantities it operates on to produce the result. For this example, that expression would be totalPrice := compute(itemPrice,salesTax). Figure 10.10 shows the syntax on a collaboration diagram.

FIGURE 10.10

A collaboration diagram that includes the syntax for a returned result.

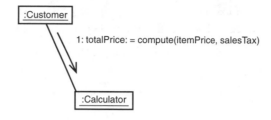

NEW TERM   The right side of the expression is called a *message-signature.*

Active Objects

NEW TERM   In some interactions, a specific object controls the flow. This *active object* can send messages to passive objects and interact with other active objects. In a library, a librarian takes reference requests from a patron, looks up reference information in a database, gives an answer back to the requester, assigns workers to restock books, and more. A librarian also interacts with other librarians who are carrying out the same operations. When two or more active objects do their work at the same time, that's called *concurrency.*

The collaboration diagram represents an active object the same as any other, except that its border is thick and bold. (See Figure 10.11.)

FIGURE 10.11

An active object controls the flow in a sequence. It's represented as a rectangle with a thick, bold border.

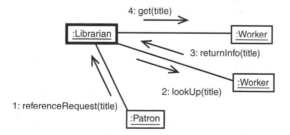

Synchronization

Another case you might run into is an object sending a message only after several other (possibly nonconsecutive) messages have been sent. That is, the object must "synchronize" its message with a set of other messages.

An example will clarify this for you. Suppose your objects are people in a corporation, and they're concerned with a new product campaign. Here is a sequence of interactions:

1. The Senior VP of Marketing asks the VP of Sales to create a campaign for a particular product.

2. The VP of Sales creates the campaign and assigns it to a Sales Manager.

3. The Sales Manager directs a Salesperson to sell the product according to the campaign.

4. The Salesperson makes sales calls on potential customers.

5. After the VP of Sales has made the assignment and the Sales Manager has issued the directive, (that is, when steps 2 and 3 are complete) a corporate Public Relations Specialist calls the local newspaper and places an ad about the campaign.

How do you represent step 5's position in the sequence? Again, the UML provides a syntax. Instead of preceding this message with a numerical label, you precede it with a list of the messages that have to be completed prior to step 5 taking place. A comma separates one list-item from another, and the list ends with a slash. Figure 10.12 shows the collaboration diagram for this example.

FIGURE 10.12
Message synchronization in a collaboration diagram.

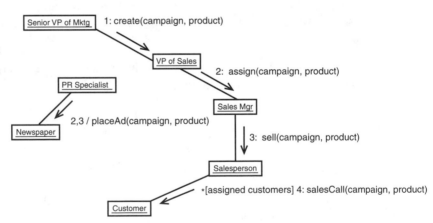

Building the Big Picture

Now you can add the collaboration diagram to your picture of the UML. It's another behavioral element, as Figure 10.13 shows.

FIGURE 10.13

The big picture of the UML, including the collaboration diagram.

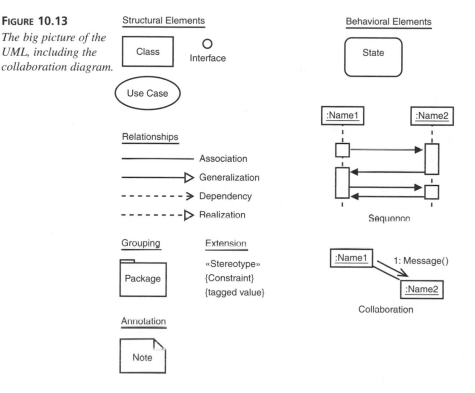

Summary

A collaboration diagram is another way of presenting the information in a sequence diagram. The two types of diagrams are semantically equivalent, but it's a good idea to use both when you construct a model of a system. The sequence diagram is organized according to time, and the collaboration diagram is organized according to space.

The collaboration diagram shows the associations among objects, as well as the messages that pass from one object to another. An arrow near an association line represents a message, and a numbered label shows the content of the message. The number represents the message's place in the sequence of messages.

Conditionals are represented as before—by putting the conditional statement in square brackets. To represent a "while" loop, precede the left bracket with an asterisk.

Some messages are subsidiaries of others. The label numbering scheme represents this in much the same way that some technical manuals show headings and subheadings—with a numbering system that uses decimal points to show levels of nesting.

Collaboration diagrams allow you to model multiple receiving objects in a class whether or not the objects receive the message in a specified order. You can also represent active objects that control the flow of messages, as well as messages that synchronize with other messages.

Q&A

Q Will I really have to include both a collaboration diagram and a sequence diagram in most UML models I build?

A It's a good idea to include both. The two types of diagrams are likely to stimulate different thought processes during the analysis segment of the development effort. The collaboration diagram clarifies the relationships among the objects because it includes the interobject links. The sequence diagram focuses attention on the sequence of interactions. Also, your client organization might include people whose thought processes differ from one another. When you have to present your model, one type of diagram might be better suited than the other for a particular individual.

Workshop

Now that you've learned about sequence diagrams and their siblings, collaboration diagrams, test and strengthen your knowledge with the quiz and the exercises. As always, you'll find the answers in Appendix A, "Quiz Answers."

Quiz

1. How do you represent a message in a collaboration diagram?

2. How do you show sequential information in a collaboration diagram?

3. How do you show changes of state?

4. What is meant by the "semantic equivalence" of two diagram types?

Exercises

1. In the soda machine example, I only showed a collaboration diagram equivalent to an instance sequence diagram for the incorrect-amount-of-money scenario. Create a collaboration diagram that corresponds to Hour 9's generic sequence diagram for the "Buy soda" use case. That is, add the out-of-selected-soda scenario to the collaboration diagram of Figure 10.5.

2. In the collaboration diagram for the "Create a proposal" use case, the consultant searches the central repository for an appropriate proposal to reuse. Think of "search" as a message sent in order to a sequence of files, and use modeling techniques from the "A Few More Concepts" section to change the collaboration diagram in Figure 10.6.

3. Create a collaboration diagram that's equivalent to the sequence diagram you created to model the electric pencil sharpener in Hour 9.

HOUR 11

Working with Activity Diagrams

In this hour, you'll get into a type of diagram that might seem familiar to you. This diagram shows the steps in an operation or process. Specifically, you learn

- What an activity diagram is
- How to apply an activity diagram
- How to work with swimlanes
- Where activity diagrams fit into the big picture of the UML

If you've ever taken an introductory course in programming, you've probably encountered the flowchart. One of the first visual models ever applied to computing, the flowchart shows a sequence of steps, processes, decision points, and branches. Novice programmers are encouraged to use flowcharts to conceptualize problems and derive solutions. The idea is to make the flowchart the foundation of the code. With its multiple features and diagram types, the UML is in some ways a flowchart on steroids.

The UML activity diagram, the subject of this hour, is much like the flowcharts of old. It shows steps (called, appropriately enough, *activities*) as well as decision points and branches. It's useful for showing what happens in a business process or an operation. You'll find it an integral part of system analysis.

What Is an Activity Diagram?

First and foremost, an activity diagram is designed to be a simplified look at what happens during an operation or a process. It's an extension of the state diagram you learned about in Hour 8, "Working with State Diagrams." The state diagram shows the states of an object and represents activities as arrows connecting the states. The activity diagram highlights the activities.

Each activity is represented by a rounded rectangle—narrower and more oval-shaped than the state icon. The processing within an activity goes to completion and then an automatic transmission to the next activity occurs. An arrow represents the transition from one activity to the next. Like the state diagram, the activity diagram has a starting point represented by a filled-in circle, and an endpoint represented by a bull's-eye.

Figure 11.1 shows the startpoint, endpoint, two activities, and a transition.

FIGURE 11.1

Transitioning from one activity to another.

Decisions, Decisions, Decisions

A sequence of activities almost always comes to a point where a decision has to take place. One set of conditions leads to one path, another set of conditions to another path, and the two paths are mutually exclusive.

You can represent a decision point in either of two ways. (Hmmm…sounds like a decision.) One way is to show the possible paths coming directly out of an activity. The other is to have the activity transition to a small diamond—reminiscent of the decision symbol in a flowchart—and have the possible paths flow out of the diamond. (As an old flowcharter, I prefer the second way.) Either way, you indicate the condition with a bracketed condition statement near the appropriate path. Figure 11.2 shows you the possibilities.

FIGURE 11.2

*The two ways of show-
ing a decision.*

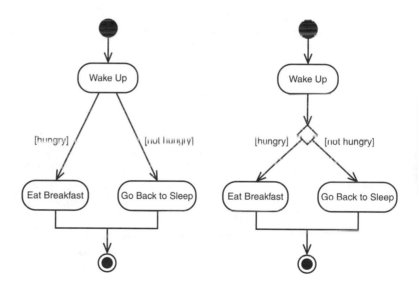

Concurrent Paths

As you model activities, you'll have occasion to separate a transition into two separate paths that run at the same time (that is, concurrently), and then come together. To represent the split, you use a solid bold line perpendicular to the transition and show the paths coming out of the line. To represent the merge, show the paths pointing at another solid bold line (see Figure 11.3).

FIGURE 11.3
*Representing a transi-
tion split into two
paths that run concur-
rently and then come
together.*

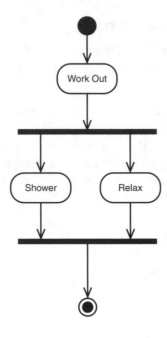

Signals

During a sequence of activities, it's possible to send a signal. When received, the signal causes an activity to take place. The symbol for sending a signal is a convex pentagon, and the symbol for receiving a signal is a concave polygon. Figure 11.4 will clarify this.

> In UML terms, the convex polygon symbolizes an *output event*; the concave polygon symbolizes an *input event*.

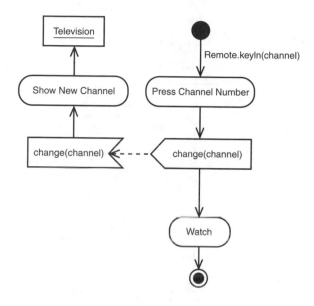

FIGURE 11.4
Sending and receiving a signal.

Applying Activity Diagrams

Let's look at some examples. First, you'll diagram an operation and then you'll diagram a process.

An Operation: Fibs

Have you ever seen this series of numbers? 1,1,2,3,5,8,13,.... It's called the "Fibonacci series," after the medieval mathematician who wrote about it 800 years ago. Each number is a "fib," so the first fib—or fib(1)—is 1, fib(2) is 1, fib(3) is 2, and so on. The rule is that each fib, except for the first two, is the sum of the preceding two fibs. (Fib(8), then, is 21.)

Suppose one of your classes is a calculator, and one of its operations is to compute the *n*th fib and print it. You might call the operation *computeFib(n)*. Let's create an activity diagram that models this operation.

You'll require a few variables. You'll need a counter to keep track of whether or not the operation has reached the *n*th fib, a variable to keep track of your computations, and two more to store two fibs that you'll have to add to each other. Figure 11.5 shows the activity diagram that makes it all happen.

FIGURE 11.5
An activity diagram for computeFib(n), an operation that calculates the nth Fibonacci number.

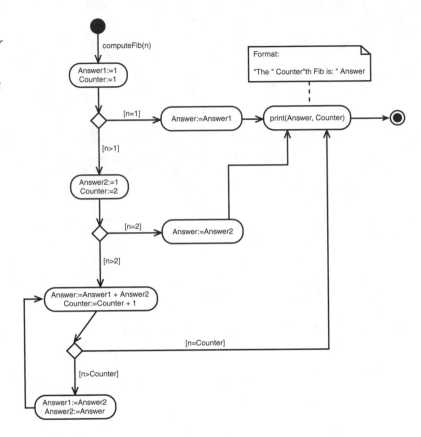

A Process: Creating a Document

Let's turn our attention from an operation to a process. Think of the activities that go into using an office software suite to create a document. One possible sequence of activities is

1. Open the word processing package.

2. Create a file.

3. Save the file under a unique name within its directory.

4. Type the document.

5. If graphics are necessary, open the graphics package, create the graphics, and paste the graphics into the document.

6. If a spreadsheet is necessary, open the spreadsheet package, create the spreadsheet, and paste the spreadsheet into the document.

7. Save the file.

8. Print a hard copy of the document.

9. Exit the office suite.

The activity diagram for this sequence is in Figure 11.6.

FIGURE 11.6

An activity diagram for the process of creating a document.

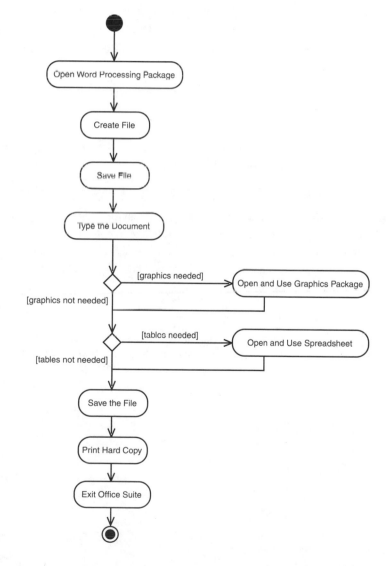

11

Swimlanes

One of the handier aspects of the activity diagram is its ability to expand and show who has the responsibility for each activity in a process.

Consider a consulting firm and the business process involved in meeting a new client. The activities would occur like this:

1. A salesperson calls the client and sets up an appointment.

2. If the appointment is onsite (in the consulting firm's office), corporate technicians prepare a conference room for a presentation.

3. If the appointment is offsite (at the client's office), a consultant prepares a presentation on a laptop.

4. The consultant and the salesperson meet with the client at the agreed-upon location and time.

5. The salesperson follows up with a letter.

6. If the meeting has resulted in a statement of a problem, the consultant creates a proposal and sends it to the client.

A standard activity diagram would look like Figure 11.7.

NEW TERM   The activity diagram adds the dimension of visualizing roles. To do that, you separate the diagram into parallel segments called *swimlanes*. Each swimlane shows the name of a role at the top, and presents the activities of each role. Transitions can take place from one swimlane to another. Figure 11.8 shows the swimlane version of the activity diagram in Figure 11.7.

> Both activity diagrams for "Meeting a new client" show creating a proposal as an activity. In each case, that activity could attach to a note that cites the activity diagram for creating a document.

FIGURE 11.7

An activity diagram for the business process of meeting a new client.

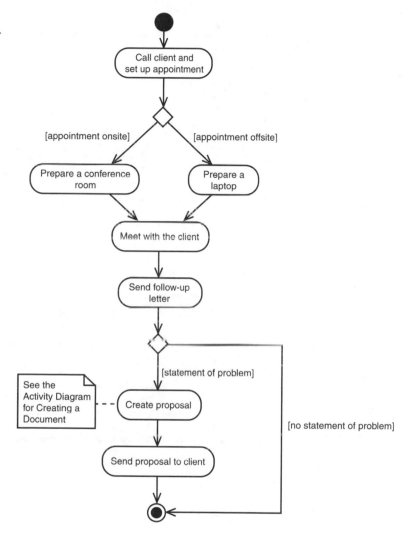

11

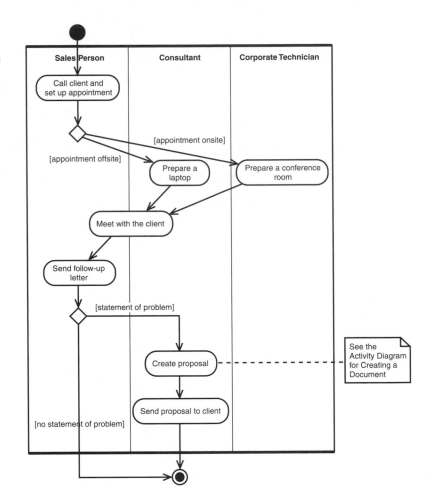

FIGURE **11.8**

*The swimlane version
of the activity diagram
in Figure 11.7 shows
the activities that each
role performs.*

Hybrid Diagrams

Let's revisit the activity diagram for creating a document. You can refine the activity for
printing a hard copy of the document. Instead of just showing a "Print Hard Copy" activity, you can be a little more specific. Printing takes place because a signal containing the
document's file transmits from the word processing package to the printer, which
receives the signal and prints the copy.

Figure 11.9 shows that you can represent this with the symbols for signal transmission
and signal reception, along with a printer object that receives the symbol and performs
its print operation. This is an example of a hybrid diagram because it has symbols you
normally associate with different types of diagrams.

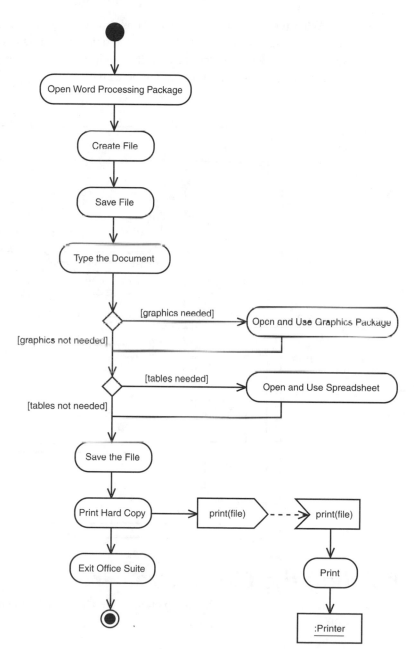

FIGURE 11.9
Refining the "Print Hard Copy" activity results in a hybrid diagram.

11

Here's another possibility for a hybrid diagram: You can show an activity diagram for an operation inside an object symbol, and show the object receiving a request to perform the operation. Suppose you modeled the calculator object that computes Fibonacci numbers. Developers might find it helpful if you presented them with a hybrid diagram like Figure 11.10.

FIGURE 11.10

A hybrid diagram can show an activity diagram inside an object.

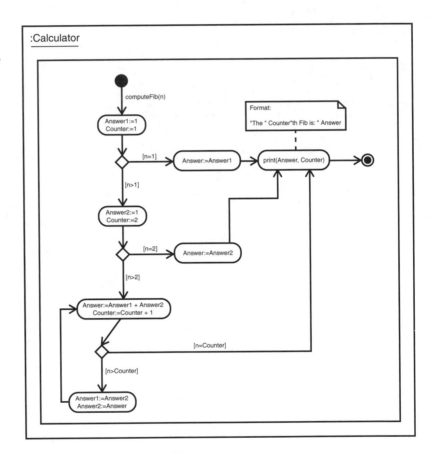

Building the Big Picture

Figure 11.11 shows the growing big picture of the UML, including the activity diagram. This diagram is a behavioral element.

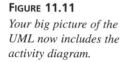

Figure 11.11

Your big picture of the UML now includes the activity diagram.

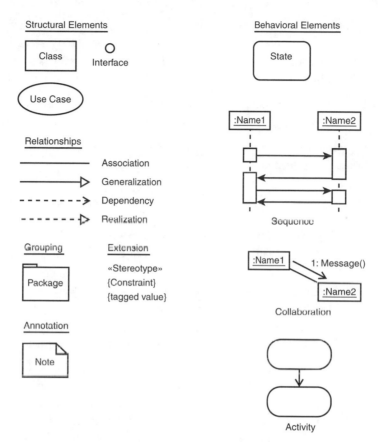

Structural Elements

Class   ○ Interface

Use Case

Relationships

———————— Association

————————▷ Generalization

- - - - - - -> Dependency

- - - - - -▷ Realization

Grouping   Extension

Package   «Stereotype»
                 {Constraint}
                 {tagged value}

Annotation

Note

Behavioral Elements

State

:Name1   :Name2

Sequence

:Name1   1: Message()

:Name2

Collaboration

Activity

11

Summary

The UML activity diagram is much like a flowchart. It shows steps, decision points, and branches. This type of diagram is useful for representing an object's operations and a business's processes.

The activity diagram is an extension of the state diagram. State diagrams highlight states and represent activities as arrows between states. Activity diagrams put the spotlight on the activities. Each activity is represented as a rounded rectangle, more oval in appearance than the state icon. The activity diagram uses the same symbols as the state diagram for the startpoint and the endpoint.

When a path diverges into two or more paths, you represent the divergence with a solid bold line perpendicular to the paths, and you represent the paths coming together with the same type of line. Within a sequence diagram you can show a signal: Represent a signal transmission with a convex pentagon and a signal reception with a concave pentagon.

In an activity diagram, you can represent the activities each role performs. You do this by dividing the diagram into swimlanes—parallel segments that correspond to the roles.

It's possible to combine the activity diagram with symbols from other diagrams and thus produce a hybrid diagram.

Q&A

Q **This is another one of those "Do I really need it?" questions. With everything that a state diagram shows, do I really need activity diagrams?**

A My recommendation is that you include activity diagrams in your analyses. They'll clarify some processes and operations in your own mind, and in your clients'. They're also very useful for developers. It's likely that a good activity diagram will go a long way toward helping a developer code an operation.

Q **You've shown two types of hybrid diagram here. Does the UML limit the kinds of hybrids you can create?**

A It does not limit you. The UML is not meant to be restrictive. Although it does have syntactical rules, the idea is for analysts to build a model that conveys a consistent vision to clients, designers, and developers—not to satisfy narrow linguistic rules. If you can build a hybrid diagram that helps all stakeholders understand a system, by all means do it.

Workshop

The quiz questions and exercises will get you thinking about activity diagrams and how to use them. Answers are in Appendix A, "Quiz Answers."

Quiz

1. What are the two ways of representing a decision point?
2. What is a swimlane?
3. How do you represent signal transmission and reception?

Exercises

1. Create an activity diagram that shows the process you go through when you start your car. Begin with putting the key in the ignition, end with the engine running, and consider the activities you perform if the engine doesn't start immediately.

2. What can you add to the activity diagram for the business process of meeting a new client?

3. If you lay out three stones so that one stone is in one row and two are in the next row, they form a triangle. If you lay out six stones so that one is in one row, two are in the next, and three are in the next, they form a triangle, too. For this reason, 3 and 6 are called *triangle numbers*. The next triangle number is 10, the one after that 15, and so on. The first triangle number is 1. Create two different activity diagrams for a process that computes the *n*th triangle number. For one, start with *n* and work backward. For the other, start with 1 and move forward. (You may have noticed that the *n*th triangle number is equal to $[(n)(n + 1)]/2$. In order to get the full benefit of this exercise, however, avoid this solution.)

4. Here's an exercise for the mathematically inclined. If you were comfortable with Exercise 3, you might like this one. If not, just move on to the next hour. (You might try diagramming what I said in these last two sentences!) In coordinate geometry, you represent a point in space by showing its x-position and its y-position. Thus, you can say that point 1's location is X1,Y1. Point 2's location is X2,Y2. To find the distance between these two points, you square X2-X1 and then you square Y2-Y1. Add these two squared quantities together, and take the square root of the sum. Create an activity diagram for an operation *distance (X1,Y1,X2,Y2)* that finds the distance between two points.

11

HOUR 12

Working with Component Diagrams

In this hour, you'll learn to use a diagram that's somewhat different from the ones you learned about before. Here are the topics you'll cover:

- What a component is
- Components and interfaces
- What a component diagram is
- Applying component diagrams
- Component diagrams in the big picture of the UML

In previous hours, you learned about diagrams that deal with conceptual entities. A class diagram represents a concept—an abstraction of items that fit into a category. A state diagram also represents a concept—changes in the state of an object.

In this hour, you're going to learn about a UML diagram that represents a real-world entity: a software component.

What Is a Component?

A software component is a physical part of a system. It resides in a computer, not in the mind of an analyst. What qualifies as a component? A table, data file, executable, dynamic link library, document, and more.

What's the relationship between a component and a class? Think of a component as the software implementation of a class. The class represents an abstraction of a set of attributes and operations. An important point to remember about components and classes: One component can be the implementation of more than one class.

You may be wondering, if the component lives in a computer and it's a working part of the system, why bother to model it? You model components and their relationships so that

1. Clients can see the structure in the finished system
2. Developers have a structure to work toward
3. Technical writers who have to provide documentation and help files can understand what they're writing about
4. You're ready for reuse

Let's explore that last one. One of the most important aspects of components is the potential they provide for reusability. In today's rapid-fire business arena, the quicker you bring a system to fruition, the greater your competitive edge. If you can build a component for one system and reuse it for another, you contribute to that edge. Taking the time and the effort to model a component helps reuse occur.

We'll revisit reuse at the end of the next section.

Components and Interfaces

When you deal with components, you have to deal with their interfaces. Early in my discussion of classes and objects, I talked about interfaces. As you might recall from Hour 2, "Understanding Object-Orientation," an object hides what it does from other objects and from the outside world. (I referred to that as *encapsulation* or *information-hiding*.) The object has to present a "face" to the outside world so that other objects (including, potentially, humans) can ask the object to execute its operations. This "face" is the object's *interface*.

NEW TERM   I elaborated on this idea in Hour 5, "Understanding Aggregations, Composites, Interfaces, and Realizations." As I mentioned then, a number of classes might not be related to one parent (as in inheritance), but their behaviors might include some of the same operations with the same signatures. You can reuse this set of operations from class to class. The *interface* is the UML construct that allows you to do this. An interface is a set of operations that specifies something about a class's behavior. Think of an interface as a class that only has operations—no attributes. Bottom line: The interface is a set of operations that a class presents to other classes.

In my discussion of interfaces in Hour 5, I also mentioned that the relationship between a class and its interface is called *realization*.

Wait a second. It sounds like modeling an interface is an exercise in modeling a concept. At the top of this hour, I said that when you model a component you model something that's not conceptual, but lives in a computer. What's the connection?

In fact, an interface can be either conceptual or physical. The interface a class uses is the same as the interface its software implementation (a component) uses. For you as a modeler, this means that the way you represent an interface for a class is the same as the way you represent an interface for a component. Although the UML symbology distinguishes between a class and a component, it makes no distinction between a conceptual interface and a physical one.

NEW TERM Here's an important point to remember about components and interfaces: You can only reach a component's operations through its interface. As is the case with a class and its interface, the relation between a component and its interface is called *realization*.

NEW TERM Here's another important point: A component can make its interface available so that other components can utilize the interface's operations. In other words, a component can access the services of another component. The component that provides the services is said to provide an *export interface*. The component that accesses the services is said to use an *import interface*.

Replacement and Reuse

Interfaces figure heavily into the important concepts of component replacement and component reuse. You can replace one component with another if the new component conforms to the same interfaces as the old one. You can reuse a component in another system if the new system can access the reused component through that component's interfaces. You can engineer a component for reuse in development projects across your whole enterprise if you can refine its interfaces so that a wide array of components can access them.

This is where modeling interfaces comes in handy. Life is easier for a developer trying to replace or reuse a component if the component's interface information is readily available

12

in the form of a model. If not, the developer has to go through the time-consuming process of stepping through code.

Types of Components

As you progress in your modeling career, you'll deal with three kinds of components:

1. *Deployment components*, which form the basis of executable systems (for example, Dynamic Link Libraries [DLLs], executables, ActiveX controls, and Java Beans)

2. *Work product components*, from which deployment components are created (for example, data files and source code files)

3. *Execution components*, created as a result of a running system

If you're a Windows user, you encounter examples of all three when you use Help—although you might not know it. The deployment component is the .HLP file: When you click on a Help file's icon (a book with a question-mark on its cover), you typically open the Help Topics dialog box and start searching for the topic of your choice. The first time you click on the Help Topics Find tab, you'll notice a little page-flipping animation of a book as the system creates a contents/index page for you. A .CNT (Contents Topic) file describes the layout of the contents. Because this file helps create a deployment component (you can use the index page forever after), it's a work product component. Also, the created index resides in a newly created .FTS (Full Text Search) file. Finally, the first time you open Help, it creates a .GID (General Index) file, the result of an analysis by the Windows Help system that speeds up access to help file topics. Thus, the .FTS and .GID files are execution components.

What Is a Component Diagram?

A component diagram contains—appropriately enough—components, interfaces, and relationships. Other types of symbols that you've already learned can also appear in a component diagram.

Representing a Component

The component diagram's main icon is a rectangle that has two rectangles overlaid on its left side. Shown in Figure 12.1, this icon represents a component. You put the name of the component inside the icon. The name is a string.

FIGURE 12.1
*The icon that repre-
sents a component.*

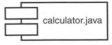

Figure 12.2 shows that if the component is a member of a package, you can prefix the component's name with the name of the package. You can also add information that shows some detail about the component.

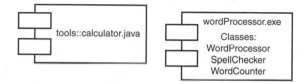

The icon on the right in Figure 12.2 shows the classes that one particular component implements. Figure 12.3 shows another way to do this, although this technique usually adds too much clutter to a diagram. Note the dependency relationships between the component and the classes.

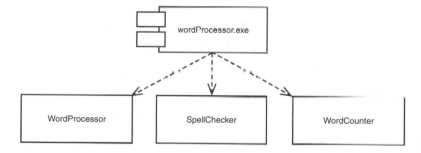

Representing Interfaces

A component and the interfaces it realizes can be represented in two ways. One shows the interface as a rectangle that contains interface-related information. It's connected to the component by the dashed line and large open triangle that indicate realization. (See Figure 12.4.)

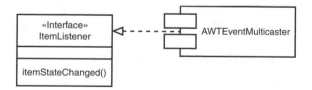

Figure 12.5 shows the other way. It's iconic: You represent the interface as a small circle connected to the component by a solid line. In this context, the solid line represents a realization relationship. (Compare Figures 12.4 and 12.5 with Figures 5.6 and 5.7.)

FIGURE 12.5

You can represent an interface as a small circle connected to the component by a solid line that in this context stands for realization.

In addition to realization, you can represent dependency—the relationship between a component and an import interface. As you'll recall, dependency is visualized as a dashed line with an arrowhead. You can show realization and dependency on the same diagram, as in Figure 12.6.

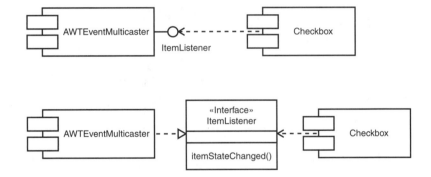

FIGURE 12.6

An interface that one component realizes and another depends on.

Applying Component Diagrams

A few examples will get you started with component diagrams. The first is a model of a Web page that presents a Java applet. The next is a model of a Web page that uses ActiveX controls. You finish with a model of a Microsoft package called PowerToys. Downloadable from Microsoft, this package enables you to modify aspects of Windows 95.

A Web Page with a Java Applet

This example models a program taken from Rogers Cadenhead's excellent and entertaining *Teach Yourself Java 1.1 Programming in 24 Hours* (Sams.net Publishing, 1997). It appears in Hour 22, "Writing a Game for the Web." Rogers shows how to build an applet that plays the dice game "Craps" on a Web page, and uses a class called "Die" (to create the dice) from Hour 21, "Playing Games with Java." For the details of the programming, you'll just have to read the book. (Be sure to also check his latest edition, which covers the most recent version of Java.) Here, we're only concerned with the components.

 An *applet* is a Java program designed to work inside a Web page.

The Web page is the file Craps.html. The applet's source code is the file Craps.java, and the object code is the file Craps.class. The source code for the Die class is in Die.java and the object code is in Die.class. All five files live in the same directory—let's call it Crapshoot (that's not Rogers's name for it).

Craps.html obviously depends on Craps.class and Die.class. Each .class file is a component and each one is the implementation of a class. What's not so immediately obvious (you would have to read the source code to see it) is that both Craps.java and Die.java import (use the classes of) java.awt, a group of classes that display and control a GUI. (The "awt" stands for "Abstract Windowing Toolkit.")

In the context of Java, *importing* enables a developer to use just the name of an operation when writing that operation in a program instead of having to use the operation's full pathname (which could be very long). Importing doesn't "read a class into" another class. It just allows the shorthand.

Craps.java is an applet, and thus inherits from java.applet.Applet class. Finally, Craps.java imports java.awt.event and implements an ActionListener interface (in order to respond to user-initiated events like mouse clicks).

Within the code, the ActionListener interface supplies a button for the to user click in order to "roll the dice." Consulting a Java reference would tell you the java.awt.AWTEventMulticaster class implements this interface.

You know what? This will all be a lot easier to understand if you look at a UML model! Figure 12.7 shows the component diagram. One package corresponds to the directory the files live in, the other to the JDK (Java Development Kit).

FIGURE **12.7**

*The diagram for
Rogers Cadenhead's
Web-based craps
game.*

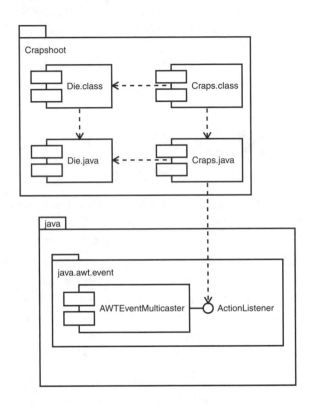

 NEW TERM   The exercise we've just gone through—building a model from
an existing piece of code—is called *reverse engineering*.

A Web Page with ActiveX Controls

ActiveX is Microsoft's way of adding components to applications. With so many different kinds of ActiveX components (controls) available, you can find one that does almost
anything an application requires. One property of an ActiveX component is its unique
32-digit hexadecimal ID number, called a CLASS ID (abbreviated CLSID).

If your needs are special, you can build your own ActiveX component in Visual Basic or
Visual C++. You can then reuse it from application to application.

On Web pages, ActiveX components live and work with code written in a scripting language like VBScript. In this example, the Web page has an ActiveX timer control, two
ActiveX combo boxes, and three ActiveX buttons. The Web page allows a user to set the

parameters for animating the movement of a sphere (a .gif image) across the screen. From one combo box, the user selects the number of pixels per move. From the other, he or she selects the number of milliseconds between movements. One button starts the movement, another stops the movement, and the third resets the sphere to its starting position. The timer moves the sphere after the user-selected number of milliseconds elapses.

The ActiveX controls reside in a separate component called a *layout*. The HTML page and the layout are in the same directory.

Figure 12.8 shows the component diagram for this page. Note the use of the note symbol to represent the VBScript. Although this isn't absolutely necessary, it highlights a difference between the scripting language and the compiled ActiveX components.

FIGURE 12.8

The component diagram for a Web page with ActiveX components.

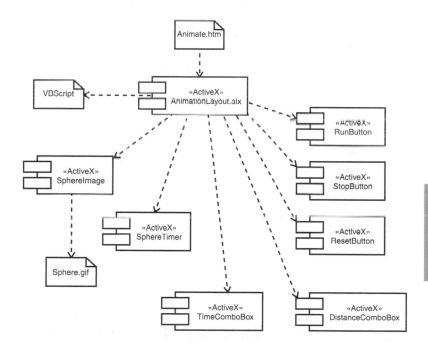

PowerToys

If you use Windows 95, you're familiar with the unsightly little arrows at the lower-left corner of each desktop shortcut icon. Microsoft has a package called PowerToys that lets you eliminate those arrows and do all kinds of other things to your GUI, via an application called TweakUI that's part of the package. (PowerToys won't work with later versions of Windows.)

You can download PowerToys from the Microsoft Web site. It's free. When you download it into its own directory and open that directory, you'll see a number of files with .dll extensions. You'll also see a Help file and a .CNT file. Click on the Help file, and it manufactures a .GID file. Use the Help file's Find feature and it creates a .FTS file.

Although the "classic" PowerToys isn't designed for versions of Windows later than 95, if you're really, *really* interested in tweaking your operating system, visit www.createwindow.com/wininfo/powertoys.htm to find out how.

Figure 12.9 shows a component diagram that models TweakUI in the PowerToys package, showing the dependencies among the different types of components.

FIGURE 12.9

Modeling TweakUI in the PowerToys package.

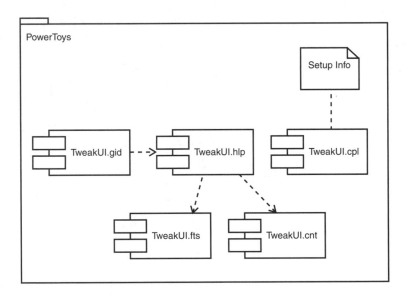

Component Diagrams in the Big Picture

You're almost done with the big picture. Figure 12.10 includes the component diagram, which focuses on a system's software architecture. In the next hour, you'll learn how to model the hardware architecture.

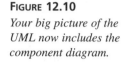

FIGURE 12.10
Your big picture of the UML now includes the component diagram.

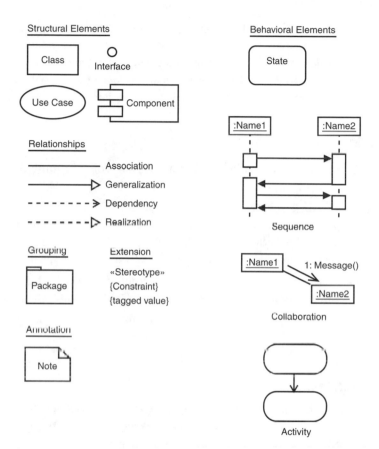

Summary

The UML component diagram is a departure of sorts from the diagrams you learned before. Instead of representing a conceptual entity such as a class or a state, a component diagram represents a real-world item—a software component. Software components reside in computers, not in the minds of analysts.

A component is accessible through its interface, a collection of operations. The relationship between a component and its interface is called *realization*. One component can access the services of another. When it does, it uses an *import interface*. The component that realizes the interface with those services provides an *export interface*.

12

The component icon is a rectangle with two small rectangles overlaid on its left side. You can represent an interface in either of two ways. One representation is a rectangle containing information about the interface and connected to the component with a dashed line and an empty triangle. The other is a small circle connected to the component with a solid line. Both connection types are intended to show a realization relationship.

Q&A

Q In a component diagram, what's a good rule of thumb for using symbols that aren't component icons?

A You do this when you want to indicate something that's a bit different from a compiled component. It's not necessary, but it might help get the point across. You might use the note symbol to signify header files, DLLs, or script files. Another possibility is to use the regular component symbol with a stereotype that indicates the file type.

Q You've shown VBScript as one component of the Web page. VBScript code consists of a number of subroutines. Can't I model each one as a component?

A Yes, you can. It might clutter up your model to refine the VBScript (or JavaScript) to that level, however, so you can attach a note that elaborates on the subroutines.

Workshop

In this workshop, you get to solidify your knowledge about components and how to model them. One of the exercises covers Web page concepts, the other covers DLLs. You can find answers to the Quiz questions in Appendix A.

Quiz

1. What are the three types of components?
2. What do you call the relationship between a component and its interface?
3. What are the two ways of representing this relationship?
4. What is an *export interface*? What is an *import interface*?

Exercises

1. Take a shot at reverse engineering a model for a Web page. Visit `http://www.samspublishing.com`, the home page of Sams Publishing . Use your browser's View menu to make the selection that reveals the page's source code. You won't find any ActiveX components or Java applets, but you'll see a number of .gif files and some JavaScript. Don't include all the gifs in your model—just do a few to get the hang of it. Toward the top of the code, you'll see a reference to a style sheet.

The reference is inside an HTML LINK element. This is a separate file that holds styling information for the Web page. Be sure to include it in your model.

2. If you have Office 97, explore the directory that contains Excel. It's probably in something like C:\Program Files\Microsoft Office\Office. (Your disk drive letter might be different.) Note the DLLs Excel uses. They begin with "Xl" and end with .dll. Model these dependencies with a component diagram. Excel depends on more DLLs than those, but this will be good practice for you.

12

Hour **13**

Working with Deployment Diagrams

In this hour, I focus on a system's hardware architecture. You'll learn

- What a deployment diagram is
- Applying deployment diagrams
- Deployment diagrams in the big picture of the UML

So far, I've stayed mainly in the conceptual realm, turning in the last hour to models of software architecture. Now I look at the hardware. As you can see, I've moved from items (like classes) that live in analyses, to components that live in computers, to hardware that lives in the real world.

Hardware, of course, is a prime topic in a multicomponent system. In today's world of computing, a system is likely to encompass numerous types of platforms in far-flung locations. A solid blueprint for hardware deployment is essential to system design. The UML provides you with symbols for creating a clear picture of how the final hardware setup should look.

What Is a Deployment Diagram?

NEW TERM   The main hardware item is a *node*, a generic name for any kind of computing
            resource. Two types of nodes are possible. A *processor* is a node that can execute
a component. A *device* is a node that can't. A device (such as a printer or a monitor) typically interfaces in some way with the outside world.

In the UML, a cube represents a node. You supply a name for the node, and you can use
a stereotype to indicate the type of resource it is. Figure 13.1 shows a node.

FIGURE **13.1**

*Representing a node in
the UML.*

The name is a text string. If the node is part of a package, its name can contain the name
of the package as well. You can divide the cube into compartments that add information
(such as components deployed on the node), as in Figure 13.2.

FIGURE **13.2**

*Adding information to
a node.*

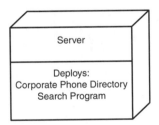

Another way to indicate the deployed components is to show them in dependency relationships with a node (see Figure 13.3).

FIGURE **13.3**

*You can show compo-
nents in dependency
relationships with a
node.*

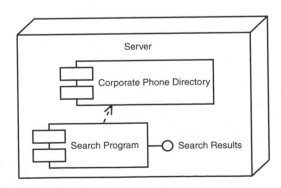

A line joining two cubes represents a connection between two nodes. You can use a stereotype to provide information about the connection. Figure 13.4 provides examples of internode connections.

> Bear in mind that a connection isn't necessarily a piece of wire or cable. You can also visualize wireless connections such as infrared and satellite.

FIGURE 13.4

Representing internode connections.

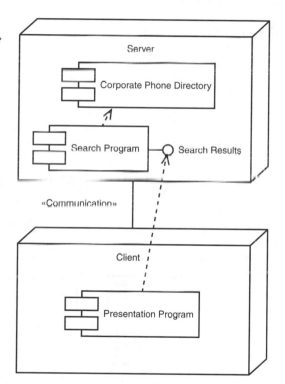

Although the connection is the most common type of association between two nodes, other types of association (such as aggregation and dependency) are possible. You represent them in the usual ways.

Applying Deployment Diagrams

A good place to start is with a home computer system, so the first example is a deployment diagram of the system I used to write this book.

13

As I said earlier, however, today's multiprocessor systems connect nodes that might live far away from each other. To round out the picture, then, you'll also look at examples of deployment diagrams applied to networks. I'll include examples that you might find useful and adaptable to your own work. Each example includes constraints that reflect the rules of the particular network.

A Home System

In modeling my home system, I've included the processor and devices of course, and I also modeled the dialup connection with my Internet service provider and its connection to the Internet. The cloud that represents the Internet is not a part of the UML symbol set, but it's useful for clarifying the model. Figure 13.5 presents the deployment diagram.

FIGURE 13.5

*Deployment diagram
of my home system.*

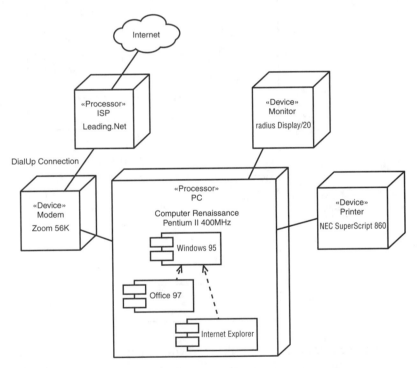

A Token-Ring Network

In a token-ring network, computers equipped with network interface cards (NICs) connect to a central multistation access unit (MSAU). Multiple MSAUs are connected together in a series that looks like a ring (hence the "ring" part of the name). The ring of MSAUs combines to act as a traffic cop, using a signal called a *token* to let each computer know when it can transmit information (hence, the "token" part of the name).

In effect, the token moves from computer to computer until one computer has information to send. In reality, the token moves around the ring of MSAUs.

When it gets the token, only that computer's information can go to the network. After it is sent, the information travels to its destination. When the information reaches its destination, an acknowledgement can go back to the computer that sent it.

In this example, shown in Figure 13.6, I've modeled a network that consists of three MSAUs and their respective computers.

FIGURE 13.6

Deployment diagram for a token-ring network that consists of three MSAUs.

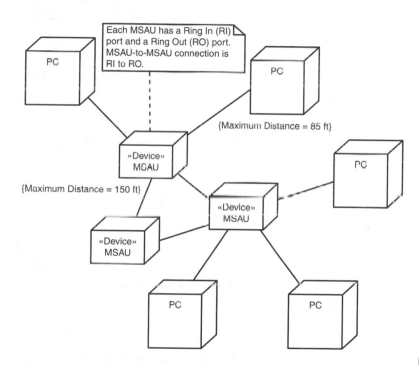

ARCnet

Like a token-ring network, an ARCnet (Attached Resources Computing network) involves passing a token from computer to computer. The difference is that in an ARCnet each computer has an assigned number. The numerical order determines which computer gets the token. Each computer connects to a hub which is either active (amplifies incoming information before passing it on) or passive (passes information without amplifying it).

Unlike the MSAUs in a token-ring network, the ARCnet hubs don't move the token around in a ring. The computers pass the token to one another.

13

Figure 13.7 models an ARCnet with a passive hub, an active hub, and several computers.

FIGURE 13.7

Deployment diagram
of an ARCnet.

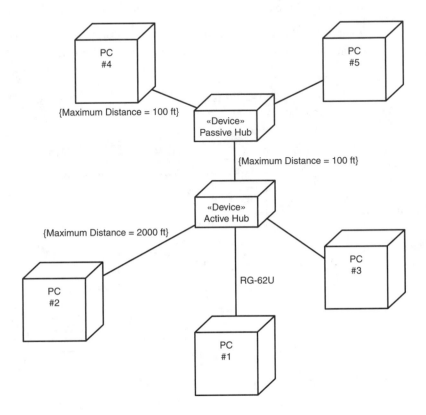

Thin Ethernet

NEW TERM The thin ethernet is a popular type of network. Computers connect to a network cable via connection devices called T-connectors. One network segment may join another via a *repeater*, a device that amplifies a signal before passing it on.

Figure 13.8 models a thin ethernet network.

Metricom's Ricochet Wireless Network

Los Gatos, CA–based Metricom, Inc. provides a wireless modem solution for mobile Internet access. Its wireless modem plugs into a computer's serial port and broadcasts to its Ricochet network.

The Ricochet network consists of radio transmitter-receivers, each about the size of a shoebox. These microcell radios are mounted on top of streetlights a quarter- to a half-mile apart, arranged in a checkerboard pattern. Equipped with a special adapter, each microcell radio draws a small amount of power from its streetlight.

FIGURE **13.8**

Deployment diagram of a thin ethernet network.

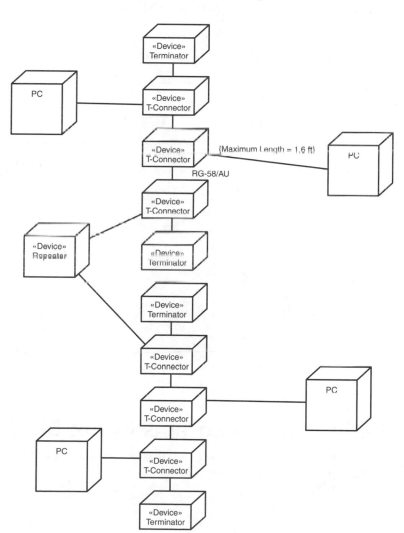

13

The microcell radios broadcast signals to Wired Access Points that move the information to a Network Interconnection Facility (NIF). The NIF consists of a name server (a database that validates connections), a router (a device for linking networks together), and a gateway (a device for translating information from one communications protocol to another). Information moves from the NIF to the Internet.

Figure 13.9 shows the deployment diagram for this network.

FIGURE 13.9
Metricom's Ricochet Wireless Network.

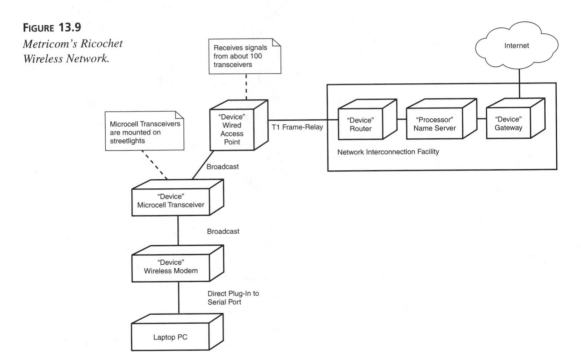

Deployment Diagrams in the Big Picture

You've come to the end of the UML diagram set. The big picture (Figure 13.10) includes the deployment diagram, and is complete.

FIGURE 13.10

Your big picture of the UML includes the deployment diagram, and is complete.

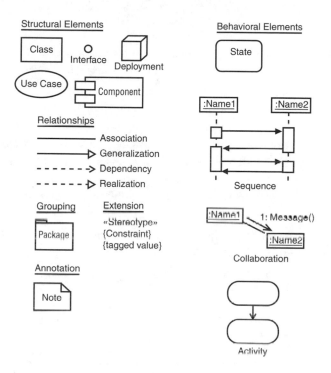

Summary

The UML deployment diagram provides a picture of how the physical system will look when it's all put together. A system consists of nodes, with each node represented by a cube. A line joining two cubes symbolizes a connection between two nodes. The two types of nodes are a processor (which can execute a component) and a device (which can't). Devices typically interface with the real world.

As you might imagine, deployment diagrams are useful for modeling networks. Models presented in this hour include token-ring networks, ARCnet, thin ethernet, and the Ricochet Wireless Network.

13

Q&A

Q **You used a cloud to represent the Internet, and said it wasn't part of the UML symbol set. Can a modeler use other symbols that aren't in the symbol set?**

A Yes. If you do, the UML Police will not hunt you down. The idea is to use the UML to express a vision. Nowhere is this more useful than with deployment diagrams. If you have clip art that clearly shows desktops, laptops, servers, and other processors (and devices), you can use them in your diagrams. In effect, you're creating a graphic stereotype. I'll show an example of this in the next hour. (The cloud symbol, by the way, is an interesting footnote in UML lore. One of the UML creators, Grady Booch, used to represent objects as clouds in the symbol set of his modeling scheme before he became part of the UML team.)

Q **Suppose you have clip art available for some objects but not others. Can you mix them in with the UML symbols?**

A Yes, you can. The object is to draw diagrams that clarify a vision, not (pardon the pun) cloud it.

Workshop

Now that you've finished the set of UML diagrams, test your knowledge about how to represent hardware. The answers are deployed in Appendix A, "Quiz Answers."

Quiz

1. How do you represent a node in a deployment diagram?
2. What kinds of information can appear on a node?
3. What are the two kinds of nodes?
4. How does a token-ring network work?

Exercises

1. Consider your home computer system to be a set of nodes. Draw a deployment diagram that includes your CPU box, monitor, printer, and any other peripherals. Include any necessary stereotypes and compartments to clarify the information. (It will probably look a bit different from the model of my system.)
2. It's possible to connect one network to another. One way to do this is to connect each network to a router, and each router to a (possibly very long) LAN-to-LAN circuit. Draw a deployment diagram of a small token-ring network connected to a small thin ethernet network.

Hour **14**

Understanding the Foundations of the UML

Now that you've seen the diagrams in the UML, you're ready for some of the foundational concepts. In this hour, you'll learn about

- The structure of the UML
- The metamodel layer
- Extending the UML
- Stereotypes, constraints, and tagged values

If this were an academically oriented text instead of a *Teach Yourself* book, this hour would have appeared at the beginning of Part I, rather than toward the end. I've done it this way to give you a chance to get into the trenches with the UML—to understand what the UML is and what it does. That way, you'll be ready to understand the foundations and work with them.

Now that you've seen the diagrams and know how to use them, why bother with this type of hour at all? If you understand what the UML is based on, you'll be able to extend it and adapt it when you start using it in the real world. As any systems analyst can tell you, every project is different. No reference book, text, or tutorial can prepare you for every situation you'll encounter. A good grounding in the foundational concepts, however, will get you ready for most of the systems you'll have to model.

It's much the same as learning a foreign language. The best way to do it is to immerse yourself, as you've done in Hours 1–13 (and will do in Part II, "A Case Study"). Then you can start to pick up the rules of grammar and syntax because you'll be prepared to understand them. (Unfortunately, many academic-world foreign language courses proceed in the opposite order!)

The Structure of the UML

Your big picture of the UML shows the categories of the diagrams and the diagrams in each category. As I mentioned in Hour 1, "Introducing the UML," you need all these diagrams because they enable you to look at a system from a number of different viewpoints. Because different stakeholders care about a system for different reasons, you have to be able to communicate a consistent vision of the system in many different ways.

Although your big picture is helpful as a way of keeping the UML's elements in mind, it won't do as a definition of the UML. The Three Amigos structured the UML in a formal way to ensure that the elements they created would show a clear vision of a proposed system, or a reengineered one.

The UML has a four-layer architecture. The layers are distinguished by the generality in the elements that inhabit them.

> Nowadays, the word *architecture* pops up a lot in the world of system development. Think of an architecture as a kind of summary shorthand for a set of decisions about the way a system is organized. Those decisions focus strongly on the system's elements—what they are, what they do, how they behave, how they interface, and how they combine.

In the preceding hours, you've usually operated at the two most specific layers. When you followed an example or did an exercise that involved specific instances from a particular domain (such as the component diagram of my home computer system), you were in the most specific layer. This layer is called the *user objects layer*, where "user" refers to a user of the UML (not to the user of a system).

NEW TERM You were in the next layer when you worked with classes—as in the example when the analyst spoke to the basketball coach to discern classes in the domain of basketball. The early stages of analysis deal with this layer—you work with an expert or a client to get a handle on a domain, and with potential system users to understand the use cases that will go into making the system. This layer is called the *model layer*.

NEW TERM When were you in a still less-specific layer? At the beginning of each hour when you learned a concept such as a class or a node, you were in the third of the four layers. This layer defines the language for specifying a model. After a little experience, you'll be familiar enough with the UML that this third layer will be second nature to you. Because this layer defines what goes into a model, it's called the *metamodel layer*.

Because your big picture shows the symbols for classes, nodes, components, use cases, and so on, it pertains to the metamodel layer.

NEW TERM And the fourth layer? During your career as an analyst, you'll probably never have to deal with that one. Think of it as a way of defining a language that specifies classes, use cases, components, and all the other UML elements you'll work with. It's more the province of theoreticians who design and compare languages than analysts who have to use them. Because this layer defines what goes into a metamodel, it's called the *metametamodel layer*.

Figure 14.1 shows the four layers.

FIGURE 14.1
The four layers of the UML.

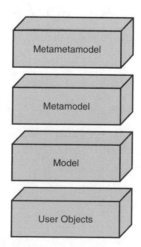

14

The Metamodel Layer: Up Close and Personal

Because the metamodel layer is the basis for your big picture, let's examine it a bit more deeply.

Think of this layer as consisting of three packages: *Foundation*, *Behavioral Elements*, and *Model Management*. Figure 14.2 shows what I mean.

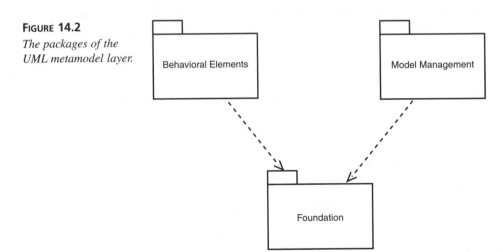

FIGURE **14.2**

The packages of the UML metamodel layer.

As is the case with any package, each one of these groups related items together. (Are we using the UML to model the UML here? Absolutely!)

What are those items? The Foundation package holds the

- Core
- Auxiliary Elements
- Data Types
- Extension Mechanisms

The Behavioral Elements package holds

- Common Behavior
- Collaborations
- Use Cases
- State Machines

The Model Management package is itself a model. It's a class diagram that shows how UML elements, such as packages and subsystems, are related to one another.

The Foundation Package

Let's double back and drill down another level. I'll start with the Foundation package, whose constituents appear in Figure 14.3.

FIGURE 14.3

The packages in the Foundation package.

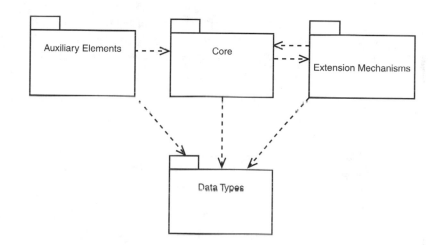

The Core defines what you need in order to build a UML model. Each of the defined items is either *abstract*—meaning you can't make instances of it—or *concrete*, meaning you can. Abstract items include *ModelElement*, *GeneralizableElement*, and *Classifier*. Concrete items include *Class*, *Interface*, *Association*, and *Data Type*.

You'll notice throughout this section I say a package "defines," "specifies," or "gives the formal details for" an item (or a concept). That means three things: (1) The package shows the item within a class diagram (another example of using the UML to model the UML), (2) The package contains rules for using the item, and (3) The package provides information about the meaning of the item.

The class diagram is called the *abstract syntax*, the rules are called *well-formedness rules*, and the meaning is called the *semantics*.

14

Here's another way to look at the abstract-concrete distinction. You would never have anything in your model that you would explicitly call a ModelElement or a Classifier—although you of course use *kinds* of ModelElements and Classifiers all the time. A Classifier, for instance, is any element that describes structure and behavior. Think of a Classifier as a shorthand way of talking about a *class, component, node, actor, interface, signal, subsystem, use case,* or *data type*. To say that something applies to a classifier is to say that it applies to any of these others.

Well, then, are the concrete items children of the abstract items? Indeed they are. Does that mean we're talking about classes and inheritance? We are, but because we're in the metamodel layer, we're talking about *metaclasses*. Thus, a "classifier" is a "metaclass." (How much sense would that sentence have made in Hour 1?)

Let's move on to the other packages within the Foundation. Auxiliary Elements, a package that rounds out the Core, defines Dependency, Component, and Node, among others. The Data Types package specifies the data types the UML uses including primitive types (integer, string, and time) and enumerations. An enumeration, such as a Boolean for example, lists possible values. The Extension Mechanisms package specifies how you can extend the UML, and includes some ready-made extensions. We'll get into this package in much greater detail later in this hour in the section "Extending the UML."

The Behavioral Elements Package

The Behavioral Elements package is the part of the UML that deals with modeling the behavior of a system. The packages it consists of appear in Figure 14.4.

FIGURE **14.4**

The packages that make up the Behavioral Elements package.

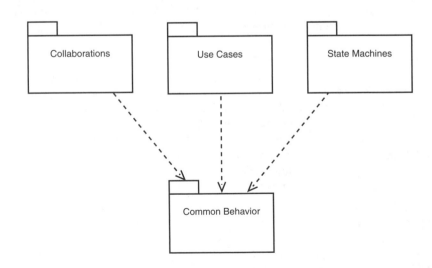

The Common Behavior package provides the concepts for the dynamic elements, and supports the other packages—Use Cases, State Machines, and Collaborations. These "concepts" include *Signal*, *Link*, and *Association End*.

The Collaborations package encompasses a broader scope than just the collaboration diagrams you worked with in Hour 10, "Working with Collaboration Diagrams." In this context, a "collaboration" describes how classifiers and their associations work together to accomplish a particular task. Collaboration diagrams and use case diagrams are part of the picture. The idea is that the classifiers form the *context* of the collaboration; the associations form the *interaction*.

The Use Cases package, unsurprisingly, details the concepts—such as *Actor* and *UseCase*—behind use cases. (Both concepts are classifiers, as I said in a previous section.) The overall objective is to be able to describe a system's behavior without getting into the system's internals.

Also unsurprisingly, the State Machines package gives the formal details for the concepts behind the state diagrams and activity diagrams you've worked with.

Model Management

The Model Management package defines *Model*, *Subsystem*, and *Package*. These items' main purpose in life is to group *ModelElements* of all kinds.

Extending the UML

As you've already seen in previous hours, you can refine your UML diagrams by adding details that further explain their meaning. Stereotypes, constraints, and tagged values are useful devices within the UML.

You can create an extension on-the-fly to add important facts and ideas from your domain to your model. This was evident in the last hour: Constraints on some of the internode communications reveal rules of the different network types.

The UML comes with ready-made stereotypes, constraints, and tagged values. As I mentioned earlier, they're part of the Extensions package which, in turn, is in the metamodel layer's Foundation package. Each of these built-in extensions is appropriate for one (sometimes two) of the UML's elements. The sections that follow cover these extensions.

14

Stereotypes

Appearing inside guillemets, a stereotype is intended to extend a UML element so that it's an instance of a new metaclass. This adds great flexibility. It means you can use an existing UML element as the basis for a type of element you create—an element that captures some aspect of your own system or domain in ways that standard UML elements can't.

The intent of the stereotype is to allow the newly created entity to play well with others inside a modeling tool. Modeling tools (such as Rational Rose or Visual UML) have to store and manipulate classes for code generation and report writing. The stereotyping mechanism allows them to do that with your creations.

The UML comes with an extensive set of ready-made stereotypes. You can add each one to one or two elements. The subsections that follow organize the stereotypes in terms of the elements they match up with.

Dependency

The dependency relationship can take the largest number of ready-made stereotypes. Each one extends a dependency relationship between a source (the element the dashed arrow starts from) and a target (the element the arrow points to). Let's look quickly at each stereotyped dependency.

A «becomes» dependency shows that the source and the target are the same object at different times. The source becomes the target with (possibly) different roles and values. «call» has an operation as its source and an operation as its target. In this stereotyped dependency, the source operation invokes the target operation. A «copy» dependency indicates that the target is an exact copy of the source. In a «derived» dependency, the source is derived from the target.

Remember the visibility concept from Hour 5, "Understanding Aggregations, Composites, Interfaces, and Realizations"? If you have an operation that's private within a particular class, you can still make it accessible to another class. Put the other class (source) and the operation (target) in a «friend» dependency. The source will have access to the target regardless of the visibility.

A dependency between two use cases can also have a stereotype. You've already used two of them, «extends» and «uses», although you substituted «includes» for «uses». «extends» tells you the behaviors of the source use case are added to the target use case. «uses» indicates that a number of use cases have some common behavior, and this stereotype enables you to use that behavior without having to repeat it again and again.

An «import» dependency sits between two packages. This stereotype adds the contents of the target to the source's namespace (the aspect of the package that groups its constituents' names).

The «instance» stereotype indicates that the source is an instance of its target, which is always a classifier. In a «metatarget» dependency, both target and source are classifiers, and the target is the metaclass of the source.

In a «send» stereotype, the source is an operation and the target is a signal. The stereotype shows that the source sends the signal.

Classifier

Stereotypes extend classifiers in a variety of ways. The «metaclass» stereotype shows that the classifier it's attached to is a metaclass of another class. The «powertype» indicates that a classifier has objects that are the children of a particular parent. You can also use «powertype» on a dependency to show that the target is a powertype of the source. (You normally use this one when you model databases.)

The «process» and «thread» stereotypes deal with the flow of control. Both indicate that their classifier is an active class—that is, its objects can initiate control activity. A process can consist of many threads (flows of control), and can execute at the same time as other processes. A thread can execute along with other threads in the same process.

A «utility» stereotyped classifier is a named collection of attributes and operations that aren't members of that classifier—a classifier that has no instances.

Finally, a classifier can have the granddaddy (almost literally!) of all stereotypes—«stereotype». This one indicates that the classifier serves as a stereotype, and enables you to model hierarchies of stereotypes.

Class

You can get more specific than classifiers: It's possible to extend a class as well. A «type» is a class that specifies a domain of objects along with attributes, operations, and associations. The «type» contains no methods (executable algorithms for its operations).

An «implementationClass» is the opposite of a «type». It represents the implementation of a class in a programming language.

Generalization

Generalization, a relationship between classifiers, has its own small set of stereotypes. «inherits» means that instances of the subtype are not substitutable for instances of the supertype. «subclass» does the same thing for classes—it means that instances of the subclass are not substitutable for instances of the superclass. «private» denotes private inheritance: It hides the inherited attributes and operations of a class from its ancestors.

Package

The stereotypes for packages are straightforward. A «facade» is a package that contains references to elements in another package, and no elements of its own. A «system» is a collection of models of a system. A «stub» is a package that provides just the public parts of another package.

14

NEW TERM   In addition to elements I've discussed, a package can contain patterns. A *pattern* is a type of interelement collaboration that's proven effective in numerous situations. A «framework» is a stereotyped package that only contains patterns.

Because packages can reside inside packages, it's helpful to have a stereotype that denotes which package is at the top level. That stereotype is «topLevelPackage». (I told you the package stereotypes were straightforward!)

Component

The stereotypes for components are even more straightforward. You can show that a component is a document, an executable, a file, a data table, or a library. The respective stereotypes are «document», «executable», «file», «table», and «library».

A Few More Stereotypes

In this subsection, I've lumped together some stereotypes used with other UML elements.

A comment that appears on an attached note can take a «requirement» stereotype, denoting that the comment indicates a requirement for the element attached to the note.

Within a class, an operation or a method can create an instance or destroy an instance. (Perhaps you've seen *constructor* and *destructor* methods in Java.) You indicate these features by «create» and «destroy», respectively.

Constraints, the extension mechanism I take up next, can work with stereotypes, too. Sometimes you use a constraint to show an operation's preconditions; sometimes you show its postconditions. You stereotype those constraints with «precondition» and «postcondition». Sometimes you attach a constraint to a set of classifiers or relationships, and you want to indicate that the conditions of the constraint must hold for all the classifiers, relationships, and instances. To do this, you stereotype the constraint as «invariant».

Graphic Stereotypes

Sometimes in your domain, you might have to bring in a new symbol or two to convey a meaning to a client. As I mentioned in the last hour, deployment diagrams typically provide the greatest potential for this. Clip art of processors and devices is usually available, and can replace the plain-vanilla cubes you learned about in Hour 13, "Working with Deployment Diagrams." Figure 14.5 shows an example. It's a stylized version of Figure 13.7, a model of an ARCnet.

FIGURE 14.5

A stylized model of an ARCnet.

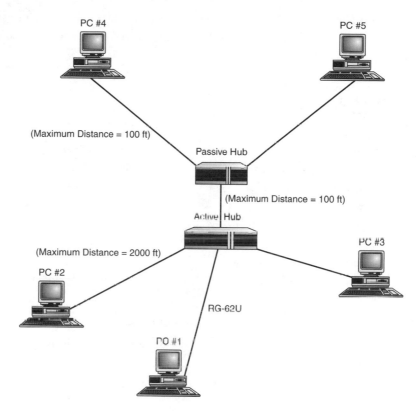

PC #4

PC #5

(Maximum Distance = 100 ft)

Passive Hub

(Maximum Distance = 100 ft)

Active Hub

(Maximum Distance = 2000 ft)

PC #3

PC #2

RG-62U

PC #1

Constraints

Constraints appear in braces. They supply conditions for associations, link-ends, generalizations, and requests (transmissions of signals or calls for operations).

The {or} constraint is applied to a set of associations, and shows that only one association is in play for that set. Another association-based constraint, {implicit}, indicates that an association is conceptual.

Link-ends, the endpoints of links between objects, can hold any of a number of constraints. Each constraint tells why the object at the link-end is visible. {parameter} shows that the object is a parameter relative to the link. {self} tells you the object is the dispatcher of a request. {global} and {local} indicate the object's scope with respect to the link. {association} denotes that the object is visible because of an association.

A set of generalizations can be {complete} (all its subtypes have been specified) or {incomplete} (additional subtypes are possible). A set of generalizations can be {overlapping} (more than one subtype can serve as an instance-type) or {disjoint} (only one subtype can be a type for an instance—this is the default for generalization).

14

If a request is sent to multiple target instances in an unspecified order, it's a {broadcast}. If the multiple instances all return values, and the majority of these values determine a single value, the constraint is a {vote}.

Tagged Values

A tagged value is written inside braces. It consists of a *tag*, an equal sign (=), and a *value*.

Ready-made tag values are appropriate for classifiers, components, attributes, instances, and operations. One tag, {documentation = }, is applicable to any element. On the right of the equal sign, you put a description, explanation, or a comment about the element you attach this tagged value to.

You can attach {location = } to a classifier or a component. When you attach it to a classifier, you supply the component that the classifier is part of. When you attach it to a component, you supply the node where the component resides.

The {persistence = } tagged value can go on an attribute, classifier, or an instance. It denotes the permanence of the state of the element you've attached it to. Possible values are *permanent* (the state remains when the instance is destroyed) and *transitory* (when the instance dies, the state dies).

{semantics = } specifies the meaning of a classifier or an operation. {responsibility} is an obligation of a classifier.

Summary

This hour dealt with the concepts at the base of the UML. The objective was to give you an in-depth understanding that will enable you to apply the UML in real-world situations that don't always mirror textbook exercises. We covered these concepts after all the diagrams so that you would understand the elements of the language before delving into the foundations.

The UML consists of four layers: user objects, model, metamodel, and metametamodel (moving from specific to general). When you analyze a system, you typically work in the first and second layers. When you learn UML concepts, you're usually in the third. The fourth layer is more for language designers and theoreticians, rather than for language users and systems analysts.

The UML comes with a set of built-in extensions. Each of these ready-made stereotypes, constraints, and tagged values is intended for use with one or two of the UML symbols.

Now if I had told you all these foundational concepts at the beginning of Hour 1, would they have been comprehensible?

Q&A

Q I can see that the UML has a number of rules. Who enforces these rules?

A As I mentioned before, the UML Police don't come around and check your model for correctness. A modeling tool, however, gently helps you stick to the rules. Visual UML, for example, has a file of stereotypes that you use in a context-sensitive fashion: When you try to put a stereotype on a particular element, it only allows you to select from stereotypes appropriate for that element. It also allows you to add stereotypes to its stereotype file.

Q Tagged values seem esoteric. Will I ever use them?

A Yes, and frequently. The built-in tagged values, although useful, pale in comparison to tagged values you'll define for yourself. You can use a tagged value to keep important project management–related information in your model—like version numbers and authors of classes. In other words, "status," "version," or "author" would be your tags, and you supply the appropriate values.

Workshop

This workshop firms up your knowledge of the UML's foundations. Use your thought processes on the quiz questions and find the answers in Appendix A, "Quiz Answers." This is a theoretical hour, so I haven't included any exercises. As a general exercise, however, you might try to find some clip art pictures of components and devices and use them to refine the deployment diagrams you saw in Hour 13.

Quiz

1. What are the four layers of the UML?
2. What is a classifier?
3. Why is it important to be able to extend the UML?
4. What are the UML's extension mechanisms?

14

Hour 15

Fitting the UML into a Development Process

Now that you've learned about the UML's diagrams and its structure, it's almost time for the rubber to meet the road. The UML is a wonderful tool, but you don't use it in isolation. It's intended to fuel software development. In this hour, you're going to learn about development processes/methodologies as a vehicle for understanding the use of the UML in a context. Specifically, you'll learn

- Why a development process is important
- Why older development methodologies are inappropriate for today's systems
- The GRAPPLE development process
- How to incorporate the UML into the process

Your organization needs a new computer-based system. New hardware and software will result in a competitive advantage, and you want that advantage. Development has to start, and soon.

You're the one who made the decision to build the new system. You've put a development team in place, complete with a project manager, modelers, analysts, programmers, and system engineers. They're champing at the bit, anxious to get started.

You are, in other words, a client. What work-products will you expect to see from the team? How do you want the project manager to report to you? At the end, of course, you'll want the system up and running. Before that, you'll want indications that the team understands the problem you're trying to solve and clearly comprehends your vision of how to solve it. You'll want a look at their solution-in-progress, and you'll want an idea of how far along the team is at any point.

These are common concerns for any client, and for any system development project that involves an appreciable amount of time, money, and personpower.

Methodologies: Old and New

You won't want the development team to rush off and start coding. After all, what will they code? The development team has to proceed in a structured, methodical way. The structure and nature of steps in a development effort are what I mean by a *methodology*.

Before they begin programming, the developers have to fully understand the problem. This requires that someone analyze your needs and requirements. After that analysis is done, can coding start? No. Someone has to turn the analysis into a design. Coders then work from the design to produce code, which, after testing and deployment, becomes a system.

The Old Way

This oversimplified look at a sequence of segments of effort might give you the idea that the segments should neatly occur in clearly defined chunks of time, one right after the other. In fact, early development methodologies were structured in that way. Figure 15.1 shows one way of thinking that was highly influential for a number of years. Dubbed the "waterfall" method, it specifies that analysis, design, coding, and deployment follow one another like activities in an activity diagram: Only when one is complete can the next one begin.

This way of doing things has some ominous overtones. For one thing, it encourages compartmentalization of effort. If an analyst hands off an analysis to a designer, who hands off a design to a developer, chances are that the three team members will rarely work together and share important insights.

FIGURE 15.1

The waterfall method of software develop-ment.

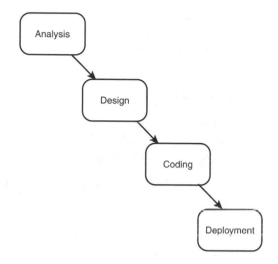

Another problem with this method is that it minimizes the impact of understanding gained over the course of a project. (Make no mistake, understanding evolves during the life of a project—even after an analysis has turned into a design.) If the process can't go back and revisit earlier stages, it's possible that evolving ideas will not be utilized. Trying to shoehorn new insights into a project during development is difficult at best. Revisiting an analysis and a design—and then incorporating an evolved understanding—provides a much better chance of success.

A New Way

In contrast to the waterfall method, contemporary software engineering stresses continuing interplay among the stages of development. Analysts and designers, for example, go back and forth to evolve a solid foundation for the programmers. Programmers, in turn, interact with analysts and designers to share their insights, modify designs, and strengthen their code.

The advantage is that as understanding grows, the team incorporates new ideas and builds a stronger system. The downside (if there is one) is that some people like closure and want to see intermediate stages come to a discrete end. Sometimes, project managers like to be able to say something to clients like, "Analysis is complete, and we're going into design. Two or three days of design, and we'll begin coding."

That mentality is fraught with danger. Setting up artificial barriers between stages will ultimately result in a system that doesn't do exactly what a client wants.

The old way fosters another problem: It's usually the case that adherents of the waterfall method allot the lion's share of project time to coding. The net effect of this is to take valuable time away from analysis and design.

What a Development Process Must Do

In the early years of computer programming, one person could analyze a problem, come up with a solution, and write a program. In the early years of building homes (back when the world was flat), one person could build a pretty serviceable home, too.

Today it's a different story. In order to develop the kinds of complex systems today's business world demands, a team approach is necessary. Why? Knowledge has become so specialized that one person can't know all the facets of a business, understand a problem, design a solution, translate that solution into a program, deploy the program onto hardware, and make sure the hardware components all work together correctly.

The team has to consist of analysts to communicate with the client and understand his or her problem, designers who construct a solution, programmers who code the solution, and system engineers who deploy the solution. A development process has to take all these roles into account, utilize them properly, and allot the proper amount of time to each stage of the effort. The process must also result in a number of work-products that indicate progress and form a trail of responsibility.

Finally, the process must ensure that the stages of the effort aren't discrete. Instead, feedback must take place among the stages to foster creativity and increase the ease of building new ideas into the effort. Bottom line: It's easier to make a change to the blueprint and then make the change to the house, rather than change the house while you build the physical structure.

In arriving at a process, the temptation is to construct a set of stages that result in massive amounts of paperwork. Some commercially available methodologies do this, leaving project managers to fill out endless forms. The paperwork becomes an end unto itself.

One reason for this is the erroneous idea that a one-size-fits-all methodology is possible. Every organization is unique. An organization has its own culture, standards, history, and people. The development methodology that's right for a multinational conglomerate will probably fail in a small business, and vice versa. In trying to shoehorn a methodology to fit an organization, the misconception is that massive paper trails will somehow help.

So here's the challenge. A development process must

- Ensure the development team has a firm understanding of the problem it's trying to solve
- Allow for a team that consists of an array of roles
- Foster communication among the team members who occupy those roles
- Allow for feedback across stages of the development effort
- Develop work-products that communicate progress to the client, but eliminate superfluous paperwork

Oh, by the way, it would be a good idea if the process produces a finished product within a short timeframe.

> You'll notice that I use the words "process" and "methodology" inter-changeably here. Although it's possible to find some differences between the two, I'd rather not split hairs. It's been my experience that the word "methodology" has acquired a bad odor. Mixing "process" into the discussion, I feel, somewhat alleviates that.

GRAPPLE

To meet the multifaceted challenge of creating a development process, I present the Guidelines for Rapid APPLication Engineering (GRAPPLE). The ideas within GRAP-PLE aren't original. They're a distillation of the ideas of a number of others. The Three Amigos created the Rational Unified Process, and prior to that, each Amigo had his own process; the ideas in those processes are similar to GRAPPLE. Steve McConnell's book, *Rapid Development* (Microsoft Press, 1996), contains a number of best practices that pertain to...well...rapid development.

The first word in GRAPPLE's name, *Guidelines*, is important: This isn't a methodology written in stone. Instead, it's a set of adaptable, flexible ideas. Think of it as a simplified skeleton of a development process. I present it as a vehicle for showing the UML within a context. With a little tweaking here and there, GRAPPLE can work in a variety of organizations (but maybe not all). It leaves room for a creative project manager to add his or her own ideas about what will work in a particular organization, and to subtract the built-in steps that won't.

Before I discuss GRAPPLE, here's a question you might be asking: "Why are you telling me about this in a book about the UML?"

Here's the answer. If I don't tell you about a development process and provide a context for using the UML, all I've done is show you how to draw diagrams. The important thing is to show why and when you'd use each one.

In Part II, "A Case Study," you'll go through a test case that applies GRAPPLE and the UML.

RAD³: The Structure of GRAPPLE

GRAPPLE consists of five *segments*. I use "segments" rather than "stages" to get away from the idea that one "stage" has to be complete before the next one starts. (I resisted the temptation to call them "pieces." "Five easy pieces" was just too cute.) Each segment, in turn, consists of a number of *actions*. Each action produces a *work-product*, and each action is the responsibility of a particular *player*.

In many cases, the project manager can combine the work-products into a report that he or she presents to the client. The work-products, in effect, serve the same purpose as a paper trail without bogging down the project in paperwork.

To adapt GRAPPLE, a project manager could add actions to each segment. Another possibility is to drill down a level deeper, and subdivide each action into subactions. Still another possibility is to reorder the actions within each segment. The needs of an organization will dictate the course to follow.

GRAPPLE is intended for object-oriented systems. Thus, the actions within each segment are geared toward producing work-products of an object-oriented nature.

The segments are

1. Requirements gathering
2. Analysis
3. Design
4. Development
5. Deployment

This acronymizes nicely to RADDD, or RAD[3]. After the third segment, the project manager combines the work-products into a design document to give to the client and the developers. When all the RAD[3] segments are complete, all the work-products combine to form a document that defines the system.

Before all these segments start, you assume the client has made a business case for the new system. You also assume the members of the development team, particularly analysts, have read as much relevant documentation as possible.

Let's examine each segment more closely, with an eye toward showing the parts of the UML that fit into each one.

Requirements Gathering

If you were to try and assign a relative importance to each segment, this one is a good candidate for *numero uno*. If you don't understand what the client wants, you'll never build the right system. All the use case analysis in the world won't help if you don't understand the essentials of the client's domain and the problem he or she wants you to solve.

Discover Business Processes

It's a good idea to begin the development effort by gaining an understanding of the client's business processes, specifically the one(s) you're trying to enhance with the proposed system. To gain this understanding, an analyst interviews the client or a knowledgeable client-designated person and asks the interviewee to go through the relevant process(es) step-by-step.

An important outcome is that the analyst gains a working vocabulary in a subset of the client's terminology. The analyst uses this vocabulary when interviewing the client in the next action.

The work-product is an activity diagram or a set of activity diagrams that captures the steps and decision points in the business process(es).

Perform Domain Analysis

This action is like the example of the conversation with the basketball coach. It can take place during the same session as the preceding action. The objective is to gain as solid an understanding as possible of the client's domain. Note that this action and the preceding one are about concepts, not about the system you're going to build. The analyst has to get comfortable in the client's world, as he or she will ultimately be the client's emissary to the development team.

The analyst interviews the client with the goal of understanding the major entities in the client's domain. During the conversation between the client and the analyst, another team member takes notes (optimally, on a laptop computer equipped with a word processing package), and an object modeler constructs a high-level class diagram. If you can have more than one team member take notes, by all means do so.

The object modeler listens for nouns and starts by making each noun a class. Ultimately, some nouns will become attributes. The object modeler also listens for verbs, which will become operations of the classes. At this point, a computer-based modeling tool becomes extremely valuable.

The work-product is a high-level class diagram and a set of meeting notes.

> **To Tape or Not to Tape?**
>
> Should you tape these interviews or should you just rely on your meeting notes? This is a question that crops up frequently. When you tape an interview, the temptation is to not listen as closely, or take notes as rigorously. (After all, you can always listen to the tape later.) If you do decide to tape, my advice is to forget the tape recorder, and take notes as though the recorder weren't there.
>
> Tape recording can be a useful tool when you're training a new object modeler. An experienced modeler can compare the new modeler's diagrams with the taped discussion and check for completeness.

Identify Cooperating Systems

Seventeenth-century poet John Donne wrote, "No man is an island, entire of itself." If he were writing today, it would have been "No *person* is a land-mass surrounded entirely by water, entire of him- or herself." He might also have written "No *system* is an island…," and so on.

Donne would have been right on all counts. Today's business systems don't typically emerge in vacuums. They have to work with others. Early in the process the development team finds out exactly which systems the new system will depend on, and which systems will depend on it. A system engineer takes care of this action, and produces a deployment diagram as the work-product. The diagram shows the systems as nodes, with lines of internode communication, resident components, and intercomponent dependencies.

Discover System Requirements

This one is extremely important. You might have guessed that, because it has "requirements" in its name. In this action, the team goes through its first Joint Application Development (JAD) session. Several more occur throughout the course of GRAPPLE.

A JAD session brings together decision-makers from the client's organization, potential users, and the members of the development team. A facilitator moderates the session. The facilitator's job is to elicit from the decision-makers and the users what they want the system to do. At least two team members should be taking notes, and the object modeler should be refining the class diagram derived earlier.

The work-product is a package diagram. Each package represents a high-level area of system functionality (for example, "assist with customer service"). Each package groups a set of use cases (for example, "retrieve customer history" and "interact with customer").

The complexity of the system determines the length of the session. It's almost never less than half a working day, and can last as long as a full workweek. The client's organization has to make a commitment to invest the necessary time.

Why use a JAD session to develop the system requirements? Why not interview each individual? As you'll recall, I said the last part of the challenge for a development process is to turn out a system in a short timeframe. Individual interviews can take weeks, or even longer if people's schedules conflict. Waiting for individual interview results eats up time, and with it, the potential competitive advantage of quickly completing the system. Individual interviews will probably contain conflicting views, and more time gets wasted as the team tries to resolve the conflicts. Grouping everyone together creates a whole that exceeds the sum of the parts, and the interplay among JAD participants results in a symbiosis that's beneficial for everybody.

Present Results to Client

When the team finishes all the Requirements actions, the project manager presents the results to the client. Some organizations might require the client's approval at this point, in order for development to proceed. Other organizations might require a cost estimate based on the results. The work-product, then, will vary according to the organization.

Analysis

In this segment, the team drills down into the results of the Requirements segment and increases its understanding of the problem. In fact, parts of this segment begin during the Requirements segment, as the object modeler begins refining the class diagram during the Requirements JAD session.

Understand System Usage

This action is a high-level use case analysis. In a JAD session with potential users, the development team works with the users to discover the actors who initiate each use case from the Requirements JAD session, and the actors who benefit from those use cases. (An actor, remember, can be a system as well as a person.) A facilitator moderates the session, and two team members take notes. After a few projects, the facilitator for this session will likely evolve into a use case analyst.

The team also tries to develop new use cases. The work-product is a set of use case diagrams that shows actors and any stereotyped dependencies («extends» and «includes») between use cases.

Flesh Out Use Cases

In this action, the development team continues its work with the users. The objective is to analyze the sequence of steps in each use case. This JAD session can be a continuation of the previous JAD session. Beware: This is usually the most difficult JAD session for the users. They're probably not accustomed to breaking down an operation into constituent steps and exhaustively enumerating all those steps. The work-product is a text description of the steps in each use case.

Refine Class Diagrams

During the JAD sessions, the object modeler listens to all the discussions and continues to refine the class diagram. At this point, the object modeler should be filling in the names of associations, abstract classes, multiplicities, generalizations, and aggregations. The work-product is a refined class diagram.

Analyze Changes of State in Objects

The object modeler further refines the model by showing changes of state wherever necessary. The work-product is a state diagram.

Define Interactions Among Objects

Now that the team has a set of use case diagrams and a refined class diagram, it's time to define how the objects interact. The object modeler develops a set of sequence diagrams and collaboration diagrams to depict the interaction. State changes should be included. These diagrams form the work-product for this action.

Analyze Integration with Cooperating Systems

Proceeding in parallel with all the preceding steps, the system engineer uncovers specific details of the integration with the cooperating systems. What type of communication is involved? What is the network architecture? If the system has to access databases, a database analyst determines the architecture (physical and logical) of those databases. The work-products are detailed deployment diagrams and (if necessary) data models.

Design

In this segment, the team works with the results of the Analysis segment to design the solution. Design and Analysis should go back and forth until the design is complete. Some methodologies, in fact, combine Analysis and Design into one stage.

15

Develop and Refine Object Diagrams

Programmers take the class diagram and generate any necessary object diagrams. They flesh out the object diagrams by examining each operation and developing a corresponding activity diagram. The activity diagrams will serve as the basis for much of the coding in the Development segment. The work-products are the object diagrams and the activity diagrams.

Develop Component Diagrams

Programmers play a major role in this action. The task here is to visualize the components that will result from the next segment and show the dependencies among them. The component diagrams are the work-product.

Plan for Deployment

When the component diagram is complete, the system engineer begins planning for deployment and for integration with cooperating systems. He or she creates a deployment diagram that shows where the components will reside. The work-product is a diagram that's part of the deployment diagram developed earlier.

Design and Prototype User Interface

This involves another JAD session with the users. Although this is part of Design, this session can be a continuation of the prior JAD sessions with users—an indication of the interplay between Analysis and Design.

The user interface should allow for completion of all use cases. In order to perform this action, a GUI analyst works with the users to develop paper prototypes of screens that correspond to groups of use cases. The users position post-it notes that represent screen components (pushbuttons, check boxes, drop-down lists, menus, and so on). When the users are satisfied with the positioning of the components, developers build screen prototypes for the users' approval. The work-products are screen shots of the screen prototypes.

Design Tests

Use cases enable the design of tests for the software. The objective is to assess whether or not the developed software performs as it's supposed to—that is, it does what the use cases specify. Preferably, a developer or test specialist from outside the development team uses the use case diagrams to develop test scripts for automated test tools. The test scripts constitute the work-product.

Begin Documentation

It's never too early to begin documenting the system for the end-users and for system administrators. Documentation specialists work with the designers to begin storyboarding the documentation and arriving at a high-level structure for each document. The document structure is the work-product.

Development

Here's where the programmers take over. With enough analysis and design, this segment should go quickly and smoothly.

Construct Code

With the class diagrams, object diagrams, activity diagrams, and component diagrams in hand, the programmers construct the code for the system. The code is the work-product from this action.

Test Code

Test specialists (not the developers) run the test scripts to assess whether or not the code is doing what it should. The test results are the work-products. This action feeds back into the preceding action and vice versa, until the code passes all levels of testing.

Construct User Interfaces, Connect to Code, and Test

This action draws on the user-approved prototype user interfaces. The GUI specialist constructs them and connects them to the code. Further testing ensures that the interfaces work properly. The functioning system, complete with user interfaces, is the work-product.

Complete Documentation

During the Development segment, the documentation specialist works in parallel with the programmers to ensure timely delivery of all documentation. The documentation is the work-product for this action.

Deployment

When development is complete, the system is deployed on the appropriate hardware and integrated with the cooperating systems. The first action in this segment, however, can start long before the Development segment begins.

Plan for Backup and Recovery

The system engineer creates a plan for steps to follow in case the system crashes. The plan, the work-product for this action, specifies what to do to back up the system and to recover from the crash.

Install Finished System on Appropriate Hardware

The system engineer, with any necessary help from the programmers, deploys the finished system on the appropriate computer(s). The work-product is the fully deployed system.

15

Test Installed System

Finally, the development team tests the installed system. Does it perform as it's supposed to? Does the backup and recovery plan work? Results of these tests determine whether further refinement is necessary, and the test results make up the work-product.

Celebrate

Self-explanatory. The team invents ad hoc work-products for this action.

The GRAPPLE Wrap-up

If you step back and look at the segments and actions in GRAPPLE, you'll see that the movement is from general to specific—from the unrefined to the refined. It begins with a conceptual understanding of the domain, moves to high-level functionality, drills down into use cases, refines models, and designs, develops, and deploys the system.

You'll also notice that more actions were in the Analysis and Design segments than in the Development segment. This is, pardon the pun, by design. The idea is to spend as much time as you can in up-front analysis and design, so that coding proceeds smoothly. It might seem like heresy, but in the ideal world, coding is just one small part of system development. The more you analyze, the closer you come to the ideal.

GRAPPLE, as I said, is a simplified skeleton of a development process. I didn't touch on the details of important issues like levels of testing. I also left out some important nuts and bolts: Where and how does the team maintain the work-products-in-progress? How does the team handle the all-important issue of configuration management?

I didn't address these topics because they're tangential to our discussion of the UML. The short answer for these nuts-and-bolts issues is to embrace the technology. Work-products (finished or in-progress) can reside in a repository that lives on the organization's LAN. One option is to have a hierarchy of directories that the team members can access. A safer option is to install a centralized repository package that tracks checkout and check-in of work-products, and only permits one person at a time to check out an editable copy of an item. This is the foundation of a solution for configuration management. Repository technology is advancing steadily, and several choices are available.

The next hour begins Part II, a case study that applies the UML and GRAPPLE.

Summary

A development methodology structures the segments and activities in a system development project. Without a methodology, chaos would reign, developers wouldn't understand the problem they were trying to solve, and systems wouldn't meet the needs of their users. Early methodologies forced a "waterfall" sequence of analyze, design, code, and deploy.

This kind of sequential methodology can compartmentalize development, so that a development team might not take advantage of the increased understanding that results during the life of a project. It also typically allots the major share of project time to coding, and thus takes valuable time away from analysis and design.

This hour presented GRAPPLE (Guidelines for Rapid APPLication Engineering), a skeleton development process. GRAPPLE consists of five segments: Requirements gathering, Analysis, Design, Development, and Deployment. Each segment consists of a number of actions, and each action results in a work-product. UML diagrams are work-products for many of the actions.

Part II applies GRAPPLE and the UML to a case study.

Q&A

Q Is the "waterfall" method ever appropriate?

A If the scope of the proposed system is very small (admittedly, a subjective call), you might get away with a sequential methodology. For modern object-oriented system development, however, a methodology that encourages the continuing interplay among segments of development is likely to produce a better result.

Q In the preceding answer, you mention object-oriented system development. Suppose the proposed system isn't object-oriented?

A Even with non–object-oriented systems (as in the case of many mainframe-based projects) the ideas you learned in this hour are appropriate. JAD sessions, up-front analysis and design, and interplay among development segments will still work. You would have to adapt GRAPPLE (by, for instance, eliminating classes and class modeling), but that's the idea—it's a set of flexible guidelines rather than a methodology written in stone.

Workshop

Now that you know about methodologies, test your knowledge with these quiz questions. Appendix A, "Quiz Answers," supplies the answers.

Quiz

15

1. What are some typical concerns of a client?
2. What is meant by a development *methodology*?
3. What is the "waterfall" method? What are its weaknesses?
4. What are the segments of GRAPPLE?
5. What is a JAD session?

PART II
A Case Study

Hour

HOUR 16

Introducing the Case Study

Now that you've had some UML experience and exposure to a skeleton development methodology, you're going to see how the UML is applied in a development effort. This hour begins Part II, a case study that applies the UML in the context of the GRAPPLE process. You're going to cover

- The scenario for the case study
- Discovering and modeling business processes
- Tips on interviewing

The noted multinational (and fictional) conglomerate LaHudra, Nar, and Goniff, Inc. has surveyed the world of restaurants and come to some startling conclusions: People like to eat out, but they don't enjoy some parts of the experience.

"You know," said LaHudra, "I could have predicted the results from our survey. When I go out to eat, I hate it when I give the waiter my order and he disappears for an hour. Go out to a classy place, and you expect better treatment than that."

204

"That's true," said Nar. "Sometimes I change my mind after I order and I want to get a hold of the waiter. Or I have a question…or something…and I can't find the guy."

Goniff chimed in: "I agree. But still, the dining-out experience is a lot of fun. I like it when someone waits on me. I like the idea of a kitchen staff preparing a meal for me. Our survey results show that most people feel that way, too."

"Isn't there some way we can retain the essential experience but enhance it somehow?"

"How?" asked Nar.

"I know how!" said LaHudra. "With technology."

And that's when they decided to have one of their corporate software development teams build the restaurant of the future.

GRAPPLEing with the Problem

The development team members are all strong proponents of GRAPPLE. They understand that most of the project time will be devoted to analysis and design. That way, coding will take place quickly and efficiently, and the likelihood of a smooth installation and deployment will increase.

The effort has to start with requirements gathering, and with an understanding of the restaurant domain. As you'll recall from the last hour, the Requirements gathering segment consists of these actions:

- Discover business processes
- Perform domain analysis
- Identify cooperating systems
- Discover system requirements
- Present results to client

In this hour, we'll cover the first action.

Discovering Business Processes

LaHudra, Nar, and Goniff don't do anything in a small way. They're ready to take on the world of restaurants, and they've put together a new LNG Restaurants Division. They've hired a number of experienced restaurateurs, waiters, chefs, and maintenance people.

All they're waiting for is the technological backbone for the restaurant of the future. Then they'll launch their first restaurant, complete with the technology to increase the pleasure of dining out.

The development team members are lucky. They're starting with a blank piece of paper. All they have to do is understand the business processes and the domain and they're on their way.

The Business Process analysis starts with an analyst interviewing a restaurateur. During the interview, a note-taker is sitting by, typing away at a laptop. At the same time, a modeler is working at a whiteboard, drawing and modifying an activity diagram that the analyst, the note-taker, and the restaurateur can all see.

In the subsections that follow, we'll go through an interview for each business process in a restaurant. The goal is to produce activity diagrams that model the processes.

Serving a Customer

"Thanks for taking the time to do this," said the analyst.

"My pleasure," said the restaurateur. "What exactly do you want to know?"

"Let's start with a single business transaction. What happens when a customer walks into a restaurant?"

"It works like this. If the customer has a coat on, we help him or her off with it, store it in our cloakroom, and give the customer a coat-check ticket. We can do that for a hat, too. Then we..."

"Just a second. Let's backtrack. Suppose there's a waiting line. Don't they get in line first, or leave their name up front, or..."

"No. We try to make them feel as comfortable as possible right off the bat. Then we worry about lines, if there are any.

"If, in fact, there's a waiting list, we ask the customer whether or not they made a reservation. We always try to honor those in a timely way and seat people with reservations as quickly as possible. If there's no reservation, they leave their name and then they have the option of going to our cocktail lounge and having a drink before dinner. They don't have to do that, of course. They can sit and wait in a well-appointed waiting area."

"Interesting. They haven't even sat down yet to order a meal, and several decision points have already been reached."

Let's stop for a moment and take stock of where we are. The activity diagram of the business process now looks something like Figure 16.1.

Back to the interview.

The analyst's job is to proceed with the business process.

"Okay. After the waiting list customer's turn comes up, or the reservation-customer has arrived, it's time to seat that customer, right?"

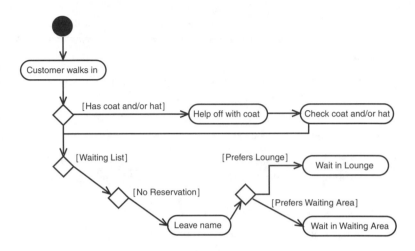

FIGURE **16.1**

The beginning stages of the activity diagram for the restaurant business process, "Serving a customer."

"Right. But, now that I think of it, it's not quite that simple. The table has to be ready. It has to be clean, of course, so a busser gets rid of the tablecloth from the previous customer, and sets the table. When it's ready, the maitre d' walks the customer to the table, and calls for a waiter."

"'Calls for'?"

Notice what the analyst does here. The restaurateur has used a new term (new within the context of the interview), and the analyst pursues the definition.

Knowing when and how to do this is part of the art of interviewing, and experience is the best teacher.

"Yes. That's not too involved because waiters have their designated serving areas and they generally know when a table is ready. They sort of hover in the area, and they usually see the maitre d' gesturing for them."

"What happens next?"

"Well, the waiter takes over from here. He shows each diner a menu, and asks them whether they want to order drinks while they decide. Then he calls over an 'assistant' who brings a tray of bread and butter and pours a glass of water for each person in the party. If someone orders a drink, the waiter goes and gets it."

"Just a second. You said 'he.' Is the person who waits on tables always a man?"

"No. I just say that out of force of habit. Sorry."

"Okay. How about if we use the neutral term 'server?' I also notice that the customer has a couple of opportunities to order a drink."

"That's true. If a customer is waiting for a table and they're in the lounge with a drink, they can bring the drink to the table if they haven't finished it by the time the table is ready. By the way, we always reserve the right to refuse service to someone who's obviously had one too many."

> The interviewer isn't just a passive listener after asking a question. Here, the analyst has put together a common theme from some earlier answers and asked a question based on something cropping up a few times (the opportunity to order a drink). The answer contains a piece of business logic, a rule that the business follows in a particular situation. In this case, the business logic pertains to refusing service to an inebriated customer.

"Glad to hear it. We're back at the table with the diners deciding on a menu choice."

"Yes. We always have some daily specials that aren't on the menu, and the waiter...uh, server...recites those to the customers."

"You know what I've noticed happens a lot? People ask the server what they recommend, and the servers usually seem pretty honest—they'll tell you if one dish is better than another. Is that something you encourage?"

"Yes, I do. Certainly our servers eat at our restaurant, and they have their opinions on what they like and don't like. If they really, really don't like a particular dish, we want them to tell the chef before they tell the customer, but I don't mind if they express a preference. Of course, you don't want your servers telling the customers the food stinks, but expressing a preference for one dish over another is okay."

"Understood. All right, let's summarize. The customer and...well, it's actually a party isn't it?...The party leaves their coats, sits in the lounge, waits for a table, gets seated, possibly orders drinks, gets served bread and water, and looks at the menu."

> It's a good idea to stop and summarize from time to time. It helps you check your understanding, gives you the opportunity to use the domain's terminology, and usually gives the interviewee a comfort level that you've been listening intently to him or her.

"Right. The server comes back with a drink, and the customers drink while they read the menu. The server allows them five to ten minutes to make a selection, and then comes back. The server comes back sooner, of course, if they've made up their minds sooner."

"How does he know to come back sooner?"

"Well, they have to somehow get his attention. He's usually in the area of the table, unless he's back in the kitchen getting an order or talking with the chefs for some reason."

"Area?"

"Yes. Each server is assigned an area that consists of a number of tables. One area is designated as the smoking area, the rest are for non-smokers."

"How do you determine who serves in what area?"

"We rotate the servers through all the different areas."

"Let's get back to the serving process. The diners make their selections, the server writes them down, and then…"

"And then notifies the chef. The server does that by writing the selection on a form he gives the chef."

"What's on the form?"

"The table, the selection, and—this is extremely important—the time."

"Why is that so important?"

"Because the kitchen is usually (we hope) a very busy place, and the chef often has to prioritize his efforts in terms of the time an order arrives."

"Can that get complicated?"

"Actually, it gets a little more complicated down the line."

"How so?"

"Most meals consist of an appetizer before the main course. Most people like to have the main course hot. So the chef prepares the appetizer—many are already made, like some of the salads—and the server brings it out to the party. The challenge is to bring out the main course for everyone in the party at the same time, and have it hot. I say 'challenge' because people at the table typically finish their appetizers at different times. The whole thing has to be coordinated."

"Hmmm…this sounds like a separate process. Let's have it be a whole different discussion—from the chef's point of view."

"Okay. That sounds like a good idea."

"We're at the point where the chef is cooking the main course. By the way, how does our diagram look to you?" (See Figure 16.2.)

"I think you've got it. Anyway, the chef cooks the main course and the server picks it up when the people in the party are finished with the appetizer. The server brings it to the table. The people eat their meals, and the server comes over at least once to check on things."

The analyst has made an important decision—to put off the discussion of a sequence that will probably turn out to be a separate process. Recognizing when to do this comes with experience.

A good rule of thumb is, if the interviewee uses words such as "complex" and "complicated," or answers "yes" when you ask if something's about to get complicated, you're probably facing a set of steps that will require its own model. Let the interviewee talk a bit before making the decision on this.

16

FIGURE 16.2

The intermediate stages of the activity diagram for the restaurant business process "Serving a customer."

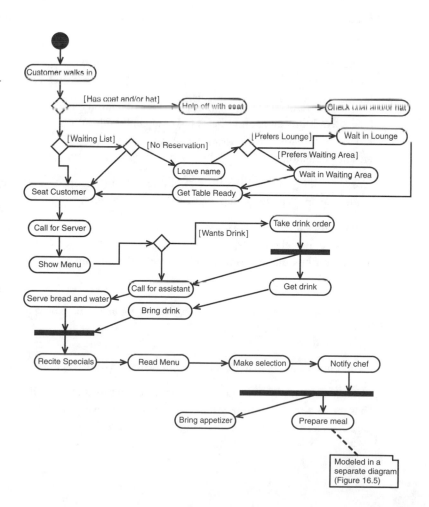

"Suppose a customer isn't satisfied with something about the meal?"

"Then we do our best to make sure they are, even if it costs us some money. It's better to lose a little money than to lose a customer."

"Nice concept."

"Thanks. When the diners finish their meals, the server comes by and asks whether they want dessert. If they do, the server provides a dessert menu, and takes their orders. If not, he asks if they want coffee. If they do, he brings coffee and cups, and pours it for them. If they don't want anything, he brings the check. After a few minutes, he comes by and collects cash and/or credit cards. He brings change and/or credit card receipts, the customers leave a tip, pick up their coats, and leave."

"Is that it?"

"Not quite. The server calls a busser over to clean the table, set it, and get it ready for the next party."

"Since that doesn't involve the customer, I'm going to consider that a separate process—albeit a brief one. I wanted to ask you a couple of questions. First, how does the server know when the people are finished?"

"He stays in his area, and glances over at each table. With experience, he knows about how long it takes to eat a meal, so he can anticipate when to be near the table. You have another question?"

"Yes. Earlier you said the server might be back in the kitchen talking to the chef for some reason. Why does that happen?"

"Sometimes a customer wants to know how long it will be before the meal comes out. In cases like that, the customer summons the server, who goes back and asks the chef. When he finds out, he comes back and tells the customer."

 The interviewer makes sure to ask any remaining questions at the end.

"You know, I never realized all the things that go into serving a customer in a restaurant."

"Funny you should say that. Until you asked me to spell out all the steps, I never thought that much about it. I think your diagram captures everything I said, and it's a useful picture for clarifying my own thinking." (See Figure 16.3.)

Figure 16.3

The full activity diagram for the restaurant business process, "Serving a customer."

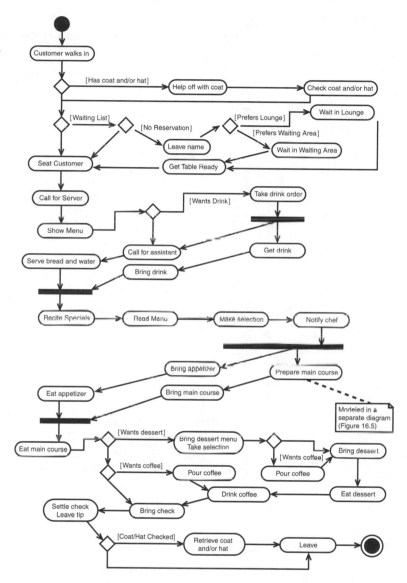

16

As you learned in Hour 11, "Working with Activity Diagrams," you can turn an activity diagram into a swimlane diagram. When you model a business process, this is a good thing to do because the swimlane diagram shows how each role figures into the process. Figure 16.4 is a swimlane diagram for the business process "Serving a customer."

Figure 16.4

A swimlane diagram for "Serving a customer."

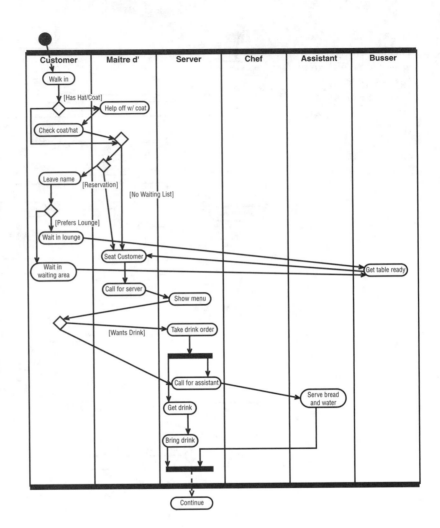

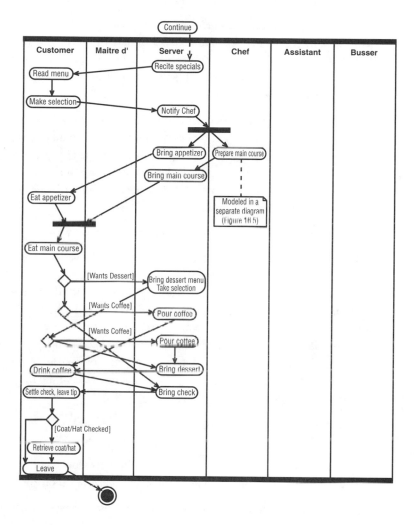

Preparing the Meal

Remember that first separate business process the interview revealed? Let's rejoin the analyst and the restaurateur and explore the process of "Preparing the meal."

"When we were talking before," said the analyst, "you mentioned that most meals provide an appetizer before the main course, and that most people prefer the main course hot. You mentioned the challenge of bringing out the main course for everyone in a party at the same time, and having it hot, and you mentioned the importance of coordination. Could you elaborate?"

"Certainly," said the restaurateur. "People in a party almost always finish their appetizers or salads or soups at different times. We have to coordinate to bring out hot main courses to everyone. The coordination takes place between the server and the chef. The chef receives the order from the server and starts preparing the appetizers and cooking the main course. When the appetizers are finished, the server comes back to the kitchen, gets them, and brings them out to the table."

"And the server knows the appetizers are done because…?"

"Because he checks the kitchen from time to time. Now, here's where the coordination comes in: The chef, after giving the appetizer to the server, relies on the server to let him know when everyone in the party is almost finished with their appetizers before he puts the final touches on the main course. The server stays in his or her designated area, and keeps an eye on the table. At the appropriate time, the server goes back to the kitchen, tells the chef the party is just about ready for the main course, and the chef finishes preparing it. A skillful chef, working with a group of assistants, balances the meal preparation for a number of parties at once. The goal is to have the main course ready as soon as everyone in the party is ready for it."

"Does it always happen exactly on time?"

"No, not always. But with a little experience and common sense, you get it right more often than not. What sometimes happens is that one slow eater in a group isn't quite ready when we bring out the main course, but that's a minor glitch."

"Got it. What do you think of our diagram for this process?" (See Figure 16.5.)

As was the case with the previous business process, a swimlane diagram is appropriate, as Figure 16.6 shows.

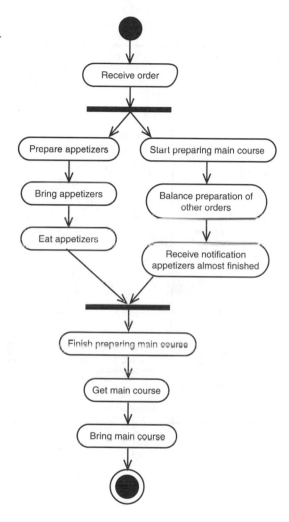

FIGURE 16.5

An activity diagram for "Preparing a meal."

16

FIGURE 16.6

A swimlane diagram for "Preparing a meal."

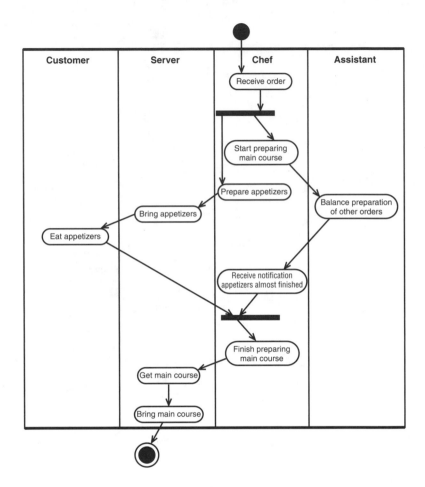

Cleaning the Table

"Let's get back to that other separate process—the one where the busser cleans the table," said the analyst.

"That one involves a little coordination, too. The server makes sure everyone has left, and then calls for the busser to come and take care of the table. On a busy night, this has to happen quickly. We don't have as many bussers as we have servers, so sometimes this is a haphazard process. The bussers aren't always nearby, so the server might have to hunt around for one."

"I think I know what you mean by 'take care of the table,' but how about getting a little more specific?"

"Sure. In the restaurants I run, we have a new tablecloth for every party. So the busser has to remove the used tablecloth, bundle it up, and bring a fresh set of silverware and cloth napkins to the table. He folds the napkins, and arranges the silverware and a plate for each position at the table. Then he brings the bundled-up tablecloth to a room in back of the kitchen. We pack them up and send them to the laundry the next day."

Figure 16.7 shows the activity diagram for this process.

FIGURE 16.7

An activity diagram for "Servicing a table."

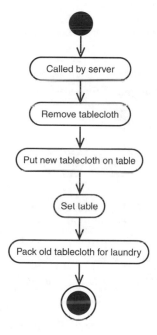

Lessons Learned

If you're an aspiring analyst, remember these lessons from this "interview":

- It's good to stop and summarize from time to time to test your understanding, practice with the terminology, and make the interviewee comfortable.

- Always get the interviewee to explain any terminology that you think is unfamiliar. Don't worry about looking unknowledgeable. The reason you're there is to acquire knowledge and learn the terminology. After all, you're going to have to use the new vocabulary when you get into the domain analysis.

- Every so often, you'll be able to ask a question based on a theme you discern in the answers to some preceding questions. Keep your mind and ears open for opportunities to ask questions like this. Business logic often emerges in the answers.

- Take note when rules of business logic come out. Maintain a record of these rules. They'll probably come in handy later. (You never know—someday you might want to build an automated decision tool that relies on these rules.) Of course, a running record should appear in the meeting notes.

- If you sense part of the process becoming complicated and convoluted, consider setting off the complication as a separate business process. It will be easier to model, and the resulting model will be clearer than if you try to lump everything together into one process.

- Get the interviewee's feedback on the activity diagram. Make any modifications that he or she suggests.

You've been through a lot in this hour, and you got a look at some valuable techniques. As you gain experience, you'll come up with some techniques of your own.

In the next hour, you'll learn about domain analysis.

Summary

This hour introduced the scenario for the case study that applies the UML in a development effort. In the scenario, the fictional conglomerate LaHudra, Nar, and Goniff decides to incorporate computer technology into the restaurant of the future. As an analyst, your job is to understand the business processes involved, understand the domain, and gather the requirements—actions in the first segment of GRAPPLE.

The newly created LNG Restaurants Division supplies you with the domain experts you'll require to understand the business processes.

The content of this hour was largely devoted to the dialog in an interview, and how that might proceed. Interspersed notes provided hints about how to do the interview. The objective was to show you how to map the interview results into a UML model.

In the next hour, you'll learn about analyzing a domain.

Q&A

Q Is it always the case that the actions within a segment proceed in the order that you listed them?

A No. Sometimes it might make sense to go in a different order. For example, you might want to discover system requirements before you identify cooperating systems. Also, bear in mind that some of the actions might not even be necessary for some projects, and some actions can take place in parallel with others. The "G" in GRAPPLE means "Guidelines." It doesn't stand for "Gee, I always have to do it exactly like this."

Q **Is it necessary to have a single interviewer for finding out the business processes from a client or an expert? Will two work better than one?**

A Usually it's a good idea to have one person at a time talk to the expert, so that he or she doesn't feel confronted by an inquisition. You might consider changing interviewers halfway through a session. The second interviewer might have originally been one of the note-takers and can switch roles with the first interviewer.

Q **Are there any special considerations for interview notes?**

A Make sure you have the date, time, place, and participants carefully listed at the beginning. You never know when you'll need that information and you don't want to have to rely on memory for it. Also, within the notes try to capture as much as you possibly can. It's almost like being a court stenographer. If you try to outline as you go along, you're going to miss something.

Q **Won't you miss something if you try to get everything?**

A Absolutely—which is why you're better off with more than one note-taker. One is sure to pick up what another one misses. Remember, the notes you take will be part of a document you give to the client. The more complete the notes, the easier to trace the evolution of an idea.

Workshop

To really get the hang of all this, follow along with our quiz questions and exercises. The answers are in Appendix A, "Quiz Answers."

Quiz

1. Which UML diagram is appropriate for modeling a business process?

2. How can you modify this diagram to show what the different roles do?

3. What is meant by "business logic"?

Exercises

1. Try applying the principles from this hour to a different domain. Suppose LaHudra, Nar, and Goniff have engaged you to head up a development team to build a system for their corporate library. Start the Requirements gathering segment by understanding and modeling the business processes involved. For this one, you'll have to rely on your own knowledge of libraries. Hold on to your notes for your solution because you'll use this library example in the exercises for the hours that follow in Part II.

2. Go back over the interviews in this hour. What pieces of business logic emerged?

HOUR 17

Performing a Domain Analysis

In this hour, you'll continue with the conceptual analyses in the Requirements Gathering segment of GRAPPLE. You'll cover

- Analyzing the interview
- Developing the initial class diagram
- Creating and labeling associations between classes
- Finding multiplicities
- Deriving composites
- Filling out the classes

The first two actions in GRAPPLE are concerned with the domain rather than with the system. Nothing in the preceding hour referred to the proposed system, and nothing in this hour will either. Indeed, in the scenario thus far, no specific system has been proposed. We only have a nebulous assignment from LaHudra, Nar, and Goniff to use technology to enhance the dining-out experience.

The objective in the last hour and in this one is to achieve an understanding of the domain. That means we have to know the specific processes we're trying to enhance and the nature of the world those processes operate in. In our scenario, uncovering the business processes has jump-started the development team's knowledge. As a result, the team members have a vocabulary they can use to communicate further with the LNG Restaurants Division. This is of utmost importance because the team now has a foundation for growing and evolving its knowledge over the course of the project.

Analyzing the Business Process Interview

The development team will have additional interviews with the restaurant experts, but first they work within the context of the business-process interview. The objective is to produce an initial class diagram. An object modeler does this by either working with the team during the interview or by going over the results of the interview. At this point the modeler looks for nouns, verbs, and verb phrases. Some of the nouns will become classes in the model, some will become attributes. The verbs and verb phrases can become either operations or the labels of associations.

Let's examine the results of the interview from the previous hour. What nouns and verbs did the restaurateur use?

Here are the nouns:

> customer, coat, cloakroom, coat-check ticket, hat, line, waiting list, reservation, name, cocktail lounge, drink, dinner, waiting area, table, busser, tablecloth, maitre d', waiter, serving area, diner, menu, assistant, tray, bread, butter, glass, water, person, party, server, menu choice, selection, daily special, restaurant, chef, dish, kitchen, order, smoking area, form, time, appetizer, main course, dessert, dessert menu, coffee, cup, check, cash, credit cards, change, credit card, receipt, tip, silverware, napkin, room, laundry.

Notice that we use each noun in its singular form.

The verbs and verb phrases are

> has, help, store, give, get in line, honor, seat, leave, sit, wait, come up, get rid of, set, walk, call for, hover, see, gesture, show, ask, order, decide, call over, bring, pour, order, go, get, wait, bring, finish, reserve, refuse, recite, ask, recommend, encourage, like, tell, express, look, come back, drink, read, allow, make a selection, get attention, get an order, talk, assign, designate, determine, notify, write, give, prioritize, consist of, prepare, bring, finish, coordinate, cook, pick up, eat, come over, check on, make sure, cost, lose money, lose a customer, come by, ask, want, provide, take an order, pour, collect, leave, call, clean, get ready, glance, anticipate, talk, come out, summon,

go back, find out, tell, provide, prefer, finish, coordinate, receive, check, rely, stay, keep an eye on, clean, make sure, take care of, hunt around for, remove, bundle up, fold, arrange, pack up, send.

When we first note all the nouns and verbs, we keep our minds open and include everything. Would a modeler ultimately use all these words in the model? No. Common sense dictates which ones to keep and which ones to eliminate. Further interaction with the restaurateur will also help.

Developing the Initial Class Diagram

Let's put ourselves in the role of the modeler and start developing the class diagram. Here's where the aforementioned common sense comes into play. We'll start by eliminating some of the nouns.

Recall from the interview that "waiter" and "server" are synonymous. Thus, we can eliminate one of these terms. The interviewer and the interviewee decided on "server," so we eliminate "waiter." "Customer" and "diner" are synonymous, so we can eliminate another noun. Let's stick with "customer." "Person" seems a little too generic, so we can eliminate that one, too. "Menu choice" and "selection" seem to say the same thing, so let's eliminate one of them. "Selection" seems more descriptive (but this is a matter of opinion), so let's keep that one.

Can we eliminate any others? Some nouns are more appropriate as attributes rather than classes. In our list, "name," "time," and "reservation" fit that category. Another noun, "laundry," isn't physically part of the restaurant, so we can eliminate it.

Here's the other side of the coin: It's also possible to add a class or two. If we examine the interview, we'll see that the restaurateur referred to "designated areas" and "rotating the servers." Who does the "designating" and "rotating?" Clearly another class, "manager," belongs in our list. That class might not have emerged during the original interview, simply because the analyst was focusing on the customer, the server, the chef, and the busser.

 Adding a class (and as you'll see later, adding abstract classes) reflects the evolution of understanding as the effort proceeds.

After filtering out the synonyms and attributes, and adding the new class, here's our list of nouns-that-can-become-classes:

17

customer, coat, cloakroom, coat-check ticket, hat, line, waiting list, cocktail lounge, drink, dinner, waiting area, table, busser, tablecloth, maitre d', serving area, menu, assistant, tray, bread, butter, glass, water, party, server, selection, daily special, restaurant, chef, dish, kitchen, order, smoking area, form, appetizer, main course, dessert, dessert menu, coffee, cup, check, cash, credit card, change, credit card receipt, tip, silverware, napkin, room, manager, reservation.

We use these classes to build the class diagram in Figure 17.1, capitalizing the first letter of each class name. If the class name has more than one word, we'll put all the words together and capitalize the first letter of each constituent word.

FIGURE 17.1
The initial class diagram for the restaurant domain.

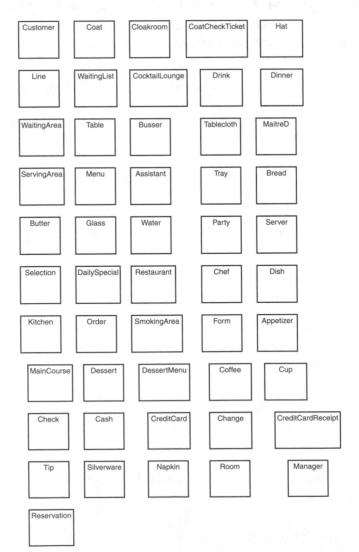

Grouping the Classes

Now we'll try to form some meaningful groups. One group consists of people: customer, party, busser, maitre d', assistant, chef, server, and manager. This group could stand some subdivision because all of its members except the customer and the party are employees. So we're left with customer, party, and the employee group.

Another group consists of food items: drink, dinner, bread, butter, water, daily special, dish, appetizer, main course, dessert, and coffee.

A third group consists of utensils: glass, silverware, tray, cup, napkin, and tablecloth.

The fourth group holds payment items: coat-check ticket, check, cash, change, credit card, credit card receipt, and tip.

Another group consists of areas within the restaurant: waiting area, smoking area, cocktail lounge, cloakroom, kitchen, serving area, table, and room. "Room" refers to the room that holds the tablecloths (and presumably other items) that the restaurant sends out to the laundry. To make the last one more descriptive, let's call it "laundry room."

Finally, we can group restaurant forms together: menu, dessert menu, coat-check ticket, check, and form. The last one is the form the server gives the chef when the order goes into the kitchen. To be more descriptive, let's call it "order form."

Notice that a couple of these last items fall into two groups (forms and payment items). This, as we'll see, is acceptable.

What do we do with these groups? Each group name can become an abstract class—a class that generates no instances of its own, but serves as a parent for subclasses. Thus, the abstract class RestaurantArea has CocktailLounge, ServingArea, Table, WaitingArea, Cloakroom, and Kitchen as its children.

We can modify the class diagram from Figure 17.1 and produce the diagram in Figure 17.2.

Forming Associations

Next, we'll create and label associations among some of the classes. The verbs and verb phrases can help us with the labeling, but we won't limit ourselves to the ones from the interview. Labels that are somewhat more descriptive might suggest themselves.

One strategy is to focus on a few of the classes and see how they associate with one another, and then move on to another group until we've exhausted the set of classes. After that, we'll develop aggregations and composites. Then, we'll incorporate verbs and verb phrases as class operations.

17

FIGURE 17.2

Abstract classes partition the class diagram into meaningful groups.

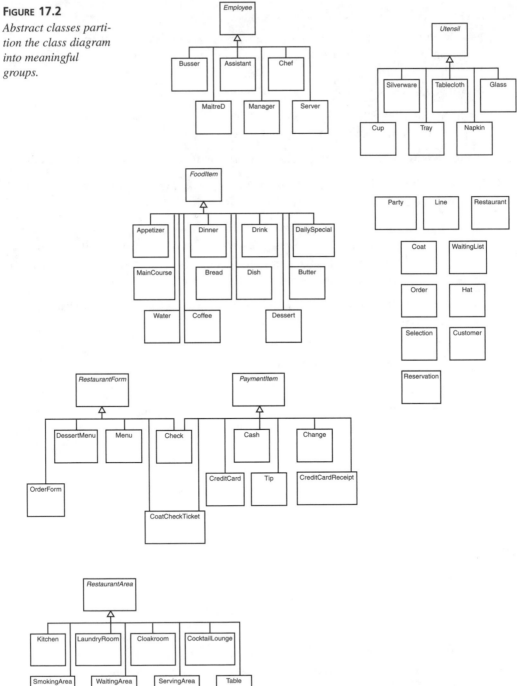

Associations with the Customer

Let's begin with the Customer class. Which classes associate with Customer? Reservation is an obvious one. Another one is Server. Some others are Menu, Meal, DessertMenu, Dessert, Order, Check, Tip, Coat, and Hat. Figure 17.3 shows the associations.

FIGURE 17.3

Initial associations with the Customer class.

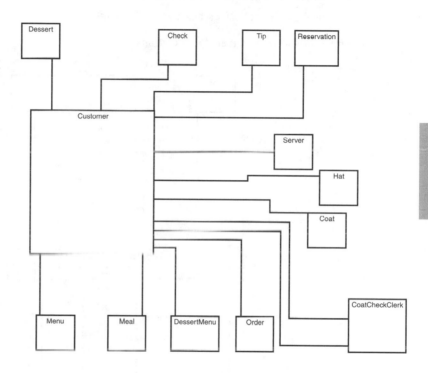

At this point, we can make some decisions. Is it necessary to include Coat and Hat? After all, we're focusing on serving a meal. After some discussion, we would probably conclude that these classes should stay in the model because our field of interest includes the whole dining-out experience. This leads us to add another class, CoatCheckClerk because someone has to check the coat and hat for the customer.

Let's label the associations by generating phrases that characterize the associations. Here are some phrases that immediately come to mind:

- The Customer makes a Reservation
- The Customer is served by a Server
- The Customer eats a Meal
- The Customer eats a Dessert
- The Customer places an Order
- The Customer selects from a Menu

- The Customer selects from a DessertMenu
- The Customer pays a Check
- The Customer leaves a Tip
- The Customer checks a Coat with a CoatCheckClerk
- The Customer checks a Hat with a CoatCheckClerk

Figure 17.4 shows the labeled associations.

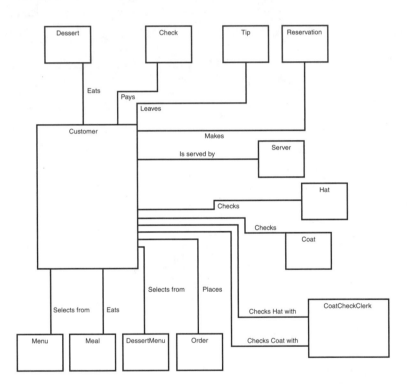

FIGURE 17.4

Labeled associations with the Customer class.

Now we turn our attention to multiplicities. A multiplicity, remember, is part of an association: It indicates how many instances of class B associate with a single instance of class A.

In most of the bulleted phrases, the Customer is involved with one instance of the other class. The second phrase is different from the others. It has a passive voice ("is served by") rather than the active voice in the other phrases (for example, "pays" and "leaves"). This suggests that something different might be happening with this association. If we turn it around and examine the association from the Server's point of view ("The Server serves a Customer"), it's apparent that a Server can serve many Customers.

The final two phrases map to a kind of association we haven't encountered before:

- The Customer checks a Coat with a CoatCheckClerk
- The Customer checks a Hat with a CoatCheckClerk

How do we model this?

NEW TERM This kind of association is called a *ternary association*. "Ternary" indicates that three classes are involved. You model this kind of association by connecting the associated classes with a diamond, and you write the name of the association near the diamond, as in Figure 17.5. In a ternary association, the multiplicities indicate how many instances of two classes are involved when the third class is held constant. In this example, one Customer can check more than one Coat with one CoatCheckClerk.

FIGURE 17.5
A ternary association.

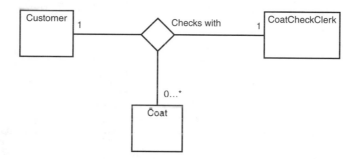

In the next subsection, you'll see another way to handle this.

It's possible to have more than three classes in an association. For the sake of generality, the UML refers to *n*-ary associations.

Figure 17.6 shows all labeled Customer associations with the multiplicities included.

Associations with the Server

Let's use that Customer-Server association as a segue into associations with the server. One way to model many of the Server associations is to treat them as ternary:

- The Server takes an Order from a Customer
- The Server takes an Order to a Chef
- The Server serves a Customer a Meal
- The Server serves a Customer a Dessert
- The Server brings a Customer a Menu

- The Server brings a Customer a DessertMenu
- The Server brings a Customer a Check
- The Server collects Cash from a Customer
- The Server collects a CreditCard from a Customer

FIGURE 17.6

Including the multiplicities in the associations with the Customer class.

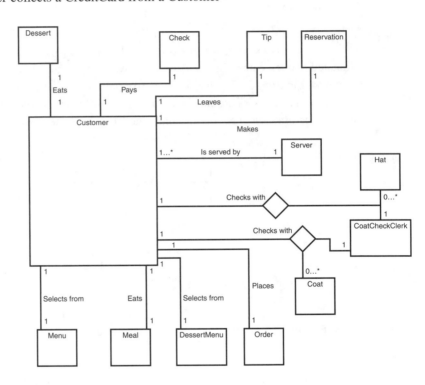

This will undoubtedly clutter up the model and make it difficult to comprehend. A more efficient way is to examine these associations, use the minimum number of labels, and attach appropriate association classes.

The Server's job is apparently to take things and bring things. "Collect" is a kind of "take" and "serve" is a kind of "bring." We can label these Server associations, then, as "take" or "bring." We attach an association class, and in that class we specify what is taken or brought. To do that, give the association class an attribute called *item* and make it an enumerated type. The possible values of the attribute are the possible items that the Server can bring or take.

Figure 17.7 shows this in action.

FIGURE 17.7

Using association classes in the Server associations.

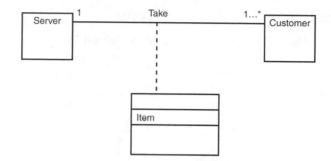

The Server also associates with an Assistant and with a Busser, as Figure 17.8 shows.

FIGURE 17.8

Additional associations with the Server.

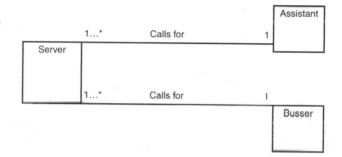

Associations with the Chef

The Chef associates with Assistants, with the Server, and with the Meal, as in Figure 17.9.

FIGURE 17.9

Associations with the Chef.

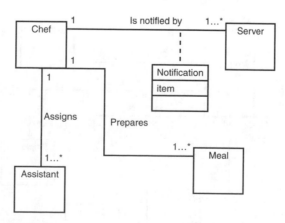

Associations with the Busser

The Busser has a few duties, as indicated in Figure 17.10.

FIGURE **17.10**

Associations with the Busser.

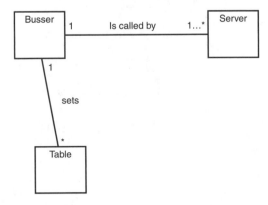

Associations with the Manager

The Manager is the new class we derived during the domain analysis. This class associates with many of the others, and we would develop these phrases:

- The Manager operates the Restaurant
- The Manager monitors the Employees
- The Manager monitors the Kitchen
- The Manager interacts with the Customer

Figure 17.11 models these associations.

FIGURE **17.11**

Associations with the Manager.

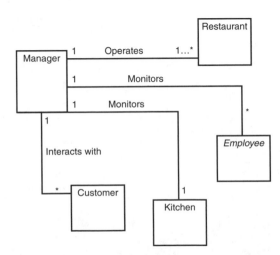

A Digression

One school of thought is that you should eliminate nouns that are roles in associations and just have a general class such as Employee. In the association, you would put the role name near the appropriate end of the association.

In some contexts (such as a payroll system), that works well. In this one, it probably won't. Consider these associations:

- The Server brings the Customer
- The Server takes from the Customer
- The Server brings the Chef
- The Server takes from the Chef
- The Server summons the Busser

The diagram looks like Figure 17.12.

FIGURE 17.12

Modeling with the Employee class.

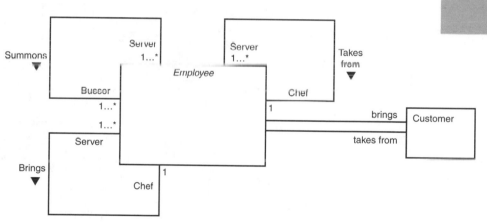

As you can see, the class icons in the diagram become dense and unclear, and we haven't even included the association classes.

In all things modeling-related, let comprehensibility be your guide.

Forming Aggregates and Composites

We've been forming and naming abstract classes and associations, and another organizational dimension awaits. The next step is to find classes that are components of other classes. In this domain, that shouldn't be difficult. A Meal, for instance, consists of an Appetizer, a MainCourse, a Drink, and a Dessert. The Appetizer and the Dessert are optional. Also, the components are in a specific order, and we want that order preserved in our model.

Here are some other composites:

- An Order consists of one or more MenuSelections
- A Restaurant consists of a Kitchen, one or more ServingAreas, a WaitingArea, a CocktailLounge, and a LaundryRoom
- A ServingArea consists of one or more Tables
- A Party consists of one or more Customers

In each case, the component is a member of only one aggregate, so Figure 17.13 models all these as composites.

FIGURE 17.13

Composites in the restaurant domain.

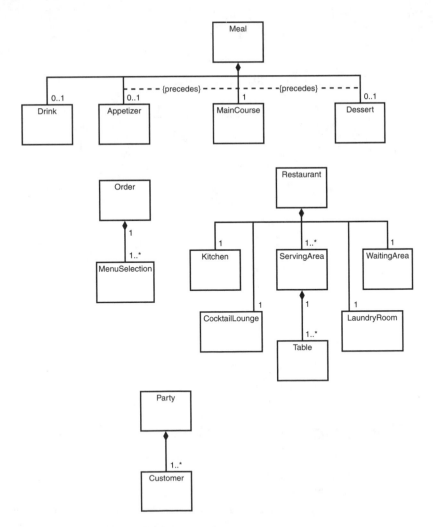

Filling Out the Classes

Further interviews and sessions will prove helpful for fleshing out our classes. Bear in mind that from here on in, an object modeler will sit in on all sessions, work with a computer-based modeling tool, and refine the model on the fly. We can begin the refinement now by adding some attributes and operations.

Our most important classes appear to be Customer, Server, Chef, Manager, and Assistant. Check is another important class.

The Customer

What are the obvious attributes for Customer? Here are a few:

- name
- arrivalTime
- order
- serveTime

How about the operations? Our verb list can guide us (but not limit us). Some Customer operations are

- eat()
- drink()
- beMerry (just kidding!)
- order()
- pay()

Figure 17.14 shows the Customer class.

FIGURE 17.14

The Customer class.

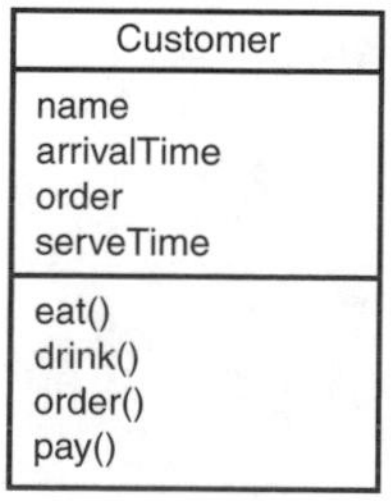

Customer
name
arrivalTime
order
serveTime
eat()
drink()
order()
pay()

The Employee

Server, Chef, Manager, and Assistant are all children of the abstract class Employee. Thus, we assign attributes to Employee and the child classes inherit them. Some of these attributes are

- name
- address
- socialSecurityNumber
- yearsExperience
- hireDate
- salary

For the Assistant, things get a little more complicated. First, we'll need a separate attribute called *worksWith* because an Assistant can help either the Server or the Chef. This attribute will be an enumerated type.

Operations will be specific to each child class. For the Server, these operations seem appropriate and can be seen in Figure 17.15:

- carry()
- pour()
- collect()
- call()
- checkOrderStatus()

For the Chef:

- prepare()
- cook()
- prioritize()
- createRecipe()

For the Assistant:

- prepare()
- cook()
- serveBread()
- serveWater()

The Manager operations include

- monitor()
- operateRestaurant()
- assign()
- rotate()

FIGURE 17.15

*The Employee class
and its children.*

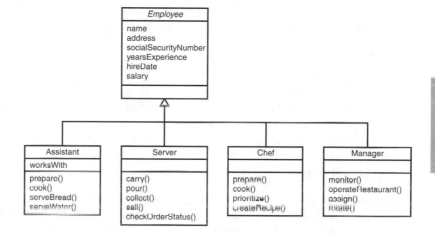

The Check

The Check is obviously an important class because it contains the information on collecting money for the meal. Its attributes are

- mealTotal
- tax
- total

Because total is the sum of mealTotal and tax, it's a derived variable. Our model (see Figure 17.16) reflects this. The Check's operation is computeTotal(mealTotal,tax).

FIGURE 17.16

The Check class.

General Issues About Models

At this point, you've gathered a lot of information. Here are a few hints to help you keep it all organized.

Model Dictionary

When you're putting together interview results, business processes, and domain analyses, keep a model dictionary. This is a glossary of all the terminology in the model. It will help you maintain consistency and avoid ambiguity.

For example, in our restaurant domain, the term "menu" is prominent. This term means one thing to a restaurateur, and something else to a GUI developer. "Server" is another term fraught with danger: a restaurateur thinks "waiter" or "waitress," a system engineer thinks something else entirely. If you have definitions everyone agrees on, or if you are at least aware of the potential for confusion, you'll avoid a lot of problems down the road. Most modeling tools allow you to build a dictionary as you create your model.

Diagram Organization

Another hint pertains to diagram organization. It's not a good idea to have every detail of your class model in one huge diagram. You'll need a master diagram that shows all the connections, associations, and generalizations, but it's best to elide attributes and operations from this picture. You can turn the spotlight on selected classes by putting them in separate diagrams. Modeling tools typically enable you to organize your diagrams by linking them appropriately.

Lessons Learned

What have we learned from going through the domain analysis?

- The business process interview provides the foundation for the domain analysis
- The nouns in the business process interview provide the candidate classes
- Eliminate nouns that are attributes, nouns that are synonymous with other nouns in the list, and nouns that represent classes out of the domain's scope
- Be alert for opportunities to add classes that might not have emerged during the business process interview
- Use some of the verbs or verb phrases from the interview as labels for associations
- Group classes together and use the group names as abstract classes
- Group classes into aggregates and/or composites

- Rename the classes for clarification
- Some associations may be ternary (that is, involve three classes)
- Use common sense to name associations and to set multiplicities

In the next hour, you'll move out of the conceptual realm and move into system-related issues.

Summary

This hour continued the conceptual analysis that began in the previous hour. The business process interview results provide the foundation for the domain analysis. The nouns, verbs, and verb phrases in the interview are the candidates for the initial class diagram that defines the restaurant domain. Common sense tells you which ones to use and which ones to eliminate. It's possible that you'll add classes as you do your analysis.

The object modeler adds substance to this diagram by deriving abstract classes, associations, and multiplicities. Deriving aggregates and/or composites helps organize the model. Additional interviews and sessions will be necessary to completely flesh out the model, but it's possible to begin adding attributes and operations at this point.

Q&A

Q How will I know which classes to eliminate from the candidate class list?

A By using common sense, eliminate redundant class names and be aware of names that are attributes. Eliminate class names that are out of the scope of the domain you're analyzing. Remember that you can add classes, too.

Workshop

This workshop tests the all-important skill of domain analysis—as embodied in the creation and development of a class diagram. The answers are in the domain of Appendix A, "Quiz Answers."

Quiz

1. How do we make use of the nouns in the interview with an expert?
2. How do we use the verbs and verb phrases?
3. What is a "ternary" association?
4. How do you model a ternary association?

Exercises

1. Revisit the Customer's ternary associations with the CoatCheckClerk. Use an association class to model these associations in a more efficient way.

2. If you've closely followed the interview and the domain analysis, you might come up with some classes that didn't appear in either. One is the Cashier. Form an association between the Server and the Cashier. Use an association class if necessary. If you can think of some other classes, incorporate them into the domain analysis.

3. Our Restaurant composite includes only "physical" classes—areas such as the Kitchen and the Cocktail Lounge. You might argue that a Restaurant also consists of people. Revisit the Restaurant composite and include the employees in the diagram. Does including the employees turn the composite into an aggregate?

4. In addition to attributes and operations, I pointed out in Hour 3, "Working with Object-Orientation," that you can represent a class's responsibility. For the Server class, add a responsibility panel and fill it in with a description of the Server's responsibility.

5. Continue with the Library domain from the first exercise in Hour 16, "Introducing the Case Study," and develop a class diagram.

HOUR 18

Gathering System Requirements

The preceding two hours dealt with conceptual issues about the domain. You derived business processes and generated class diagrams. Now it's time to get to the system. In this hour, you'll cover

- Envisioning the system
- The Joint Application Development (JAD) session
- Organizing system requirements
- The use of use cases

Messrs. LaHudra, Nar, and Goniff are impressed. They've seen the output of their development team and they know the effort is headed in the right direction. Everyone seems to have a good understanding of the restaurant domain—so good, in fact, that the restaurateurs in the LNG Restaurants Division say the diagrams have crystallized their own thinking about restaurant operations.

Now it's time for the team to work on the technical backbone for the restaurant of the future. They've got business processes and class diagrams. They can begin coding, right? Wrong. They're not even close to writing a program. First, they have to develop a vision of the system.

Most projects begin with statements like "Construct a database of customer information and make it user-friendly so that clerks can use it with a minimum of training" or "Create a computer-based helpdesk that resolves problems in under a minute." Here, the development team has started with the vague mission to "Use technology to build the restaurant of the future." They have to envision this technology-based restaurant so they can start figuring out how restaurant personnel will work in it. They're working at a level that a development team usually doesn't get to, but LaHudra, Nar, and Goniff have faith in them.

The team will use its business process knowledge and newly acquired domain knowledge to see where an infusion of technology enhances the dining-out experience. Let's listen in on a team meeting. The players are an analyst, a modeler, a restaurateur, a server, a chef, and a system engineer. A facilitator runs the meeting.

FIGURE **18.1**

The business process diagram for "Serving a customer."

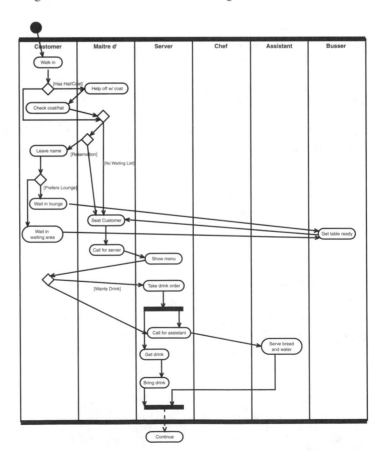

Developing the Vision

Facilitator: "Looking at our business process diagrams, I think we can all see a number of places where computer-based technology will help. I'll keep a running list here on the whiteboard. Who wants to start?"

The facilitator distributes copies of Figure 18.1, the business process diagram for "Serving a customer," and Figure 18.2, the business process diagram for "Preparing a meal."

Analyst: "Yes, apparently the restaurant business, like almost any other, depends on the movement of information. If we can speed that movement along—something technology is really good at—we'll meet our goal."

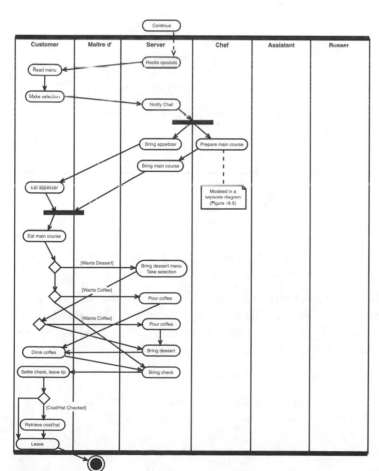

FIGURE **18.2**

The business process diagram for "Preparing a meal."

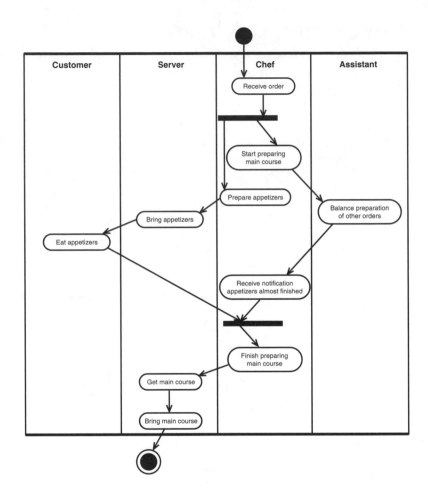

Restaurateur: "I'm not sure I understand. What do you mean by 'the movement of information?' I always thought my business was about the movement of food."

System Engineer: "I think I can help. When the customer places an order, he's giving information to the server…by the way, let's all agree that a 'server' is someone who waits on tables, not a major piece of hardware in a client/server system…and when the server relays the order to the chef, he's moving the information along."

Facilitator: "Where else do we see information move?"

Server: "I think I'm seeing the picture. When a customer asks me to track down where his order is and I ask the chef, that's information movement, isn't it?"

Analyst: "Absolutely."

Chef: "Movement, shmovement. No offense, but I'm never all that thrilled when a server comes in and asks me how long it's going to take until I'm finished preparing a meal. It takes as long as it takes, and I can't be bothered."

Facilitator: "Maybe we can figure out a way to minimize that aggravation. Any other points of information movement?"

> Here, the facilitator tries to smooth things over with the chef, so that he'll stay involved.

Restaurateur: "How about when the server recites the daily specials? Or when he answers a question about something on the menu?"

Facilitator: "Definitely."

Chef: "Sometimes I answer questions, too. People send the server back to the kitchen to ask about a particular recipe. I either relay the info through the server, or if it's not too busy, I come out and talk to the customer. They love that."

Server: "I'll tell you about a kind of information movement I'm never happy about. A customer places an order, I go back and pass it along, and then fifteen minutes later when I'm back at the kitchen for something else, I hear we're out of the ingredients for that order. I have to go back and ask the customer to order something else. That usually irritates the customer—and it irritates me because it cuts into my tip."

Analyst: "I wonder if we should add that to the business process..."

Facilitator: "Maybe. I think you'll agree that's a separate meeting."

> The facilitator tries to keep the meeting focused. Notice how the facilitator avoids saying the maddening "Yes, but..."

Analyst: "Yes. I didn't mean to take us off-track."

Facilitator: "Let's see where we are. According to my list here, information transfer takes place when

- The customer places an order
- The server relays the order to the chef

- The customer asks the server to track the status of an order
- The server recites the daily specials
- The server answers a question about something on the menu
- The chef answers questions about a recipe."

As in the business process interview, it helps when the facilitator stops and summarizes.

Analyst: "I know it's not in any of our business process diagrams, but doesn't the customer sometimes have a question about something on the check? When the server answers that, we're talking about information movement."

Facilitator: "We sure are. Anything else from the business processes?"

System Engineer: "I think I see one. How about all that coordination that takes place between the server and the chef? You know, when they make sure that the main course comes out hot after everyone in the party finishes their appetizers? That's quite a bit of information moving around."

Analyst: "I agree. The information is flowing a couple of different ways there."

Restaurateur: "You've only given us two business process diagrams. I recall we created one more."

Facilitator: "You're right. Here's the one for 'Servicing a table.'" (See Figure 18.3.)

FIGURE 18.3
The business process diagram for "Servicing a table."

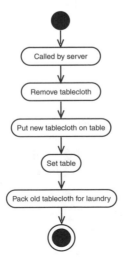

Analyst: "It looks like there's only one instance of information transfer going on here, but I bet it's an important one: The server calls for the busser to let him or her know that it's time to clean up the table."

Restaurateur: "Yes, that's extremely important. You can't seat a new party until their table is ready. If the cleanup doesn't always start and end as soon as possible, we'll have a lot of hungry—and angry—customers stacking up in the lounge and the waiting area."

Modeler: "I've been working on my class diagrams while I've been listening to all of you. Can I ask a question? Would it be a good idea if our system—whatever it's going to look like—allowed us to assess our overall efficiency in serving our customers?"

Restaurateur: "Sure. That way we'd know where and how to improve. What did you have in mind?"

Modeler: "In our Customer class, we have an attribute called arrivalTime and an attribute called serveTime. I want to add a derived attribute called waitDuration, which would be the difference between arrivalTime and serveTime. What do you think?"

Restaurateur: "That's a nice idea. Then we'd know how we're doing with our customers."

Analyst: "Yes, you would. You'd have a lot of data to play with—like waitingTime as a function of the time of day, or as a function of how many servers were working at the time, things like that."

Modeler: "Here's another possibility. Suppose we have another attribute called departureTime, and a derived attribute called mealDuration that would be the difference between serveTime and departureTime?"

Facilitator: "With apologies to our friend the chef here, I'd say you're really cooking. Any other ideas?"

Modeler: "As long as we're working with time-based attributes, how about some attributes in the Server class, the Waiter class, and the Chef class that tell the manager how long each employee is taking to get the job done?"

Restaurateur: "Uhhh...No. That whole idea of monitoring performance doesn't sit well with employees—or with me, for that matter. Not that they want to slack off—they don't—they just don't want to feel like Big Brother's looking over their shoulder with a stopwatch, and that their jobs are in jeopardy if they don't save a second here and a second there. If you keep everybody happy, you'll run a better restaurant and customers will sense that, too."

Chef: "I agree. As I said before, when you're preparing a meal it takes as long as it takes. I don't want to look at a bunch of printouts and have a manager tell me I have to take 4.5 minutes less to prepare a Trout Almandine."

Server: "And I don't want to hear about taking too long to come back with dessert menus when the customers have finished the main course. There's just too much going on."

Modeler: "Okay. I'll scrap that idea. In fact, now that you mention it, I ought to remove 'monitor' as an operation from the Manager class. In the meantime, here's what the Customer class looks like now." (See Figure 18.4.)

FIGURE 18.4

The updated Customer class.

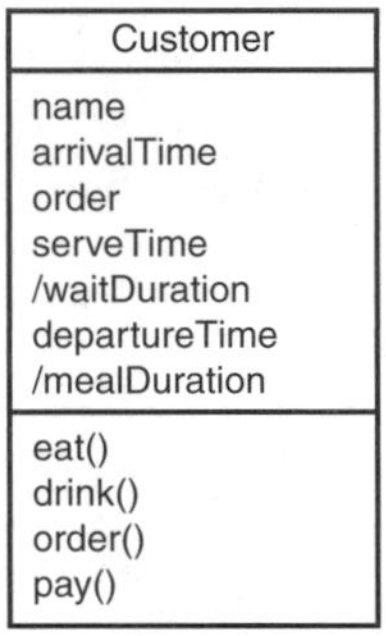

Customer
name arrivalTime order serveTime /waitDuration departureTime /mealDuration
eat() drink() order() pay()

The modeler's ideas show that she is constantly updating the class diagrams.

The discussion between the modeler, the restaurateur, and the server shows a crucial point: Having business people participate in system development is an absolute must. Without input from the restaurateur and the server, the development effort would have spent time and money implementing some performance-monitoring features that ultimately would be self-defeating. Employees would have reacted negatively, causing repercussions for the system and eventually for the restaurant.

Facilitator: "From what I'm hearing, it sounds like we can distinguish between two kinds of speedup. One involves speeding up information transfer, and the other involves speeding up how each employee performs a task. The sense of the group seems to be that the second one is an annoyance, but the first one is good. Am I right?"

(All agree)

Analyst: "Now that we've settled that, can we move on to some ideas about what the system should specifically do?"

Facilitator: "Sure. Ideas, anyone?"

Server: "When I'm moving all this information, I sure cover a lot of ground in the course of an evening. Sometimes I have to work an area that's far from the kitchen. Schlepping around back and forth is what takes time, not to mention shoe leather."

Analyst: "Sounds like we have to come up with something that eliminates, or at least alleviates, the schlepp factor. Then we'll speed up information transfer."

Facilitator: "Schlepp factor?"

Analyst: "Yes. Our system has to somehow keep the servers from walking around so much. Obviously they have to walk to the kitchen to get the order and bring it back to the table, but suppose that's the only time they went back there? And suppose they go back to the kitchen just in time to get the order?"

System Engineer: "I think we're onto something. How about if we had something like a local area network that connects the servers to the kitchen? And the servers to the bussers? Then the information would move around very quickly."

Analyst: "I hate to be overly analytical about this, but…a local area network? They'd be tripping over wires to get to the terminals. Instead of walking constantly to the kitchen, the servers would be running around to get to a terminal. That just sounds like technology for the sake of technology. What does that save?"

System Engineer: "If we do it the way you just said it, I agree we'd save nothing. We might even make matters worse. But that's not what I had in mind."

Analyst: "Well, then? The suspense is killing me."

System Engineer: "Suppose each server and busser carries a terminal around with him— a handheld PC. And suppose we set up a network that involves no wires. We can have a desktop terminal in the kitchen and one in the manager's office. By the way, another possibility for the server and the busser is a Palm device, or maybe a Pocket PC, but the handheld has a slightly bigger screen and a keyboard, and those features might give us a little more flexibility in the long run."

Analyst: "Hmmm… I like your style. The system you're talking about would resolve a number of issues. Like when the party decides on their orders, the server could tap them into his handheld PC and the order would go to a terminal in the kitchen. That eliminates the step, and the steps, of walking from the serving area to the kitchen."

Server: "I love it. How about when the party is almost finished with their appetizers, I let the kitchen know by pressing something on the handheld PC? That saves me from having to go back and tell the chef to finish preparing the main course."

Chef: "Then I'd get the message in the kitchen. In fact, all my assistants would get the message at the same time, and we could have the messages on a big screen or two or three. I wouldn't have to keep track of which assistant was cooking what meal and tell them how far along they ought to be. They could take that responsibility for themselves."

18

System Engineer: "And when the order is finished, you folks in the kitchen could send a message to the server's handheld PC to let him know. He doesn't have to keep coming back and checking. Incidentally, we can refer to a handheld PC as just a 'handheld.'"

Server: "That's beautiful. I could also send a signal to a busser to come clean up a table. I wouldn't have to run around and hunt for one. That would speed everything up."

Restaurateur: "How are you all going to make this happen?"

System Engineer: "Let's not worry about that right now."

Facilitator: "So we're all set, then? Our system will be a wireless local area network with handheld computers for the servers and bussers, and desktop computers in the kitchen and the manager's office. We're just missing one thing."

Analyst: "What's that?"

Facilitator: "A cool name for the system."

Chef: "How about 'MASTER CHEF'?"

Facilitator: "What do the letters stand for?"

Chef: "I dunno. I just like MASTER CHEF."

Analyst: "How about Wireless Interactive Network for Restaurants? It comes out as WINER."

Facilitator: "I'm not sure about the connotation."

System Engineer: "How about keeping it short and sweet: 'Wireless Interactive Network'—WIN."

Chef: "I like it."

Analyst: "Me, too. It's hard to argue with 'WIN.'"

Facilitator: "Can we all agree on WIN? Okay. I think our work here is done."

Setting Up for Requirements Gathering

The team passes the results of their meeting to the corporate bigwigs. LaHudra can't believe his good fortune in stumbling into a great new area. Nar is overwhelmed by it all. Goniff sees visions of dollar signs dancing before his eyes. They give the team the go-ahead to proceed.

Now that the team has a vision for the system, can the programmers program and the systems engineers engineer? Absolutely not. The team must center the WIN system around the users' needs, not around nifty technology. Although they have a few insights from the team meeting, they still haven't exposed the WIN concept to a group of employees and managers to get feedback and ideas from the users' point of view.

The next GRAPPLE action does just that. In a Joint Application Development (JAD) session, the team will gather and document system requirements. With these in hand, they will be able to make some estimates about time and money.

The JAD session takes place in a conference room. Led by a facilitator, it's called a "joint" session because it includes members of the development team along with potential system users and domain experts. The development team members in this meeting are two analysts who are doubling as note-takers, a modeler, two programmers, and a system engineer. The potential users are three servers, two chefs, two restaurateurs, and two bussers.

The objective of this meeting is to produce a package diagram that shows all the major pieces of functionality for the system. Each package will represent one piece, and contain use cases that detail what the functionality piece is all about.

Let's go to the session.

The Requirements JAD Session

Facilitator: "First, I want to thank you all for coming to our session. These sessions can take a lot of time, but they can also be a lot of fun. What we're trying to do is gather the requirements for a system called WIN—Wireless Interactive Network.

"The WIN concept is pretty straightforward. The way we envision it, servers carry hand-held computers and use them to communicate with the kitchen and with bussers. Bussers also carry these computers and use them for communication. The kitchen will have a desktop terminal and one or more screens. The manager will also have one in her office. Here's a picture of what I'm talking about." (See Figure 18.5.)

"We hope to install WIN in LNG Restaurants, and we want it to help you do your jobs. In order for that to happen, we need you to tell us what you want the system to do. In other words, if the system were in place, what would you use it to do?

"We'll be asking that question over and over again. At the end of the session, we'll have an organized set of requirements that everyone will be happy with. Think of it as a high-level organized wish list. We'll use those requirements as a step toward building a blueprint that programmers will use to create the system. One thing I'd like you to keep in mind: We need insights and ideas from every one of you, no matter what your job title is."

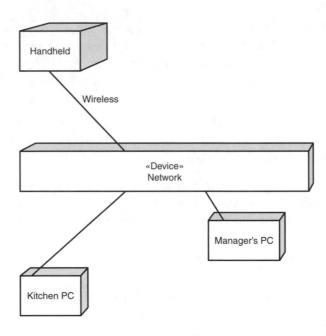

FIGURE **18.5**
The WIN system.

Analyst1: "Can we start by figuring out what the major pieces of functionality should be?"

Facilitator: "Sure can. Group, how should we proceed?"

Restaurateur2: "Well, I wasn't in on the preliminary discussions, but I think this is a good idea. Can we organize it according to, say, areas in the restaurant? You know, the serving areas need one set of requirements, the kitchen needs another, the waiting area another, and so forth?"

Facilitator: "That's a possibility."

Analyst2: "When I look at the business process diagrams, it seems to me we already have an organization."

Programmer1: "What's that?"

Analyst2: "By job. The chef has to do one set of things, the server has to do another, and so on."

Facilitator: "Sounds good. Can we agree on organizing by job?"

(All agree)

Facilitator: "All right! From the business process diagrams, and the class diagrams, the jobs we have are Server, Chef, Busser, Assistant, and Manager."

Restaurateur2: "Didn't you leave out a couple? How about coat-check clerk and bartender?"

Restaurateur1: "Ooh. How did we skip those?"

Facilitator: "I'll add those to our list, and I'll use the UML package symbols to keep track." (See Figure 18.6.)

FIGURE **18.6**

The packages of functionality for WIN.

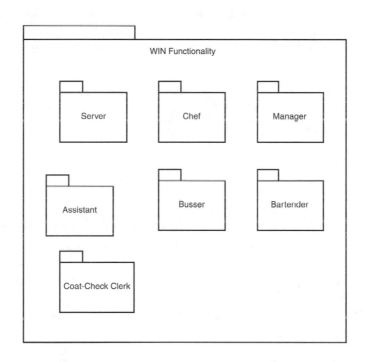

Modeler: "I'm on it. I just added some information to our class diagrams. The CoatCheckClerk class was in already. I elaborated on it and added the Bartender."

Restaurateur2: "I wondered what you've been doing there on your laptop. Could you show us these, uh, 'classes'?"

Modeler: "Sure. Here they are." (See Figure 18.7.)

FIGURE **18.7**

The CoatCheckClerk class and the Bartender class.

CoatCheckClerk
checkCoat() checkHat() printTicket()

Bartender
takeDrinkOrder() prepareDrink() printBarTab()

Restaurateur2: "Interesting. Maybe when we take a break you can explain to me what it all means."

Facilitator: "Now that we have the major pieces, does anyone have a preference as to where to start?"

Server1: "How about with the Server part?"

Facilitator: "Sounds good. All right, what kinds of functionality would you want to see in this package? Remember, group, just because we're doing a piece that happens to not coincide with your particular job, you can still participate. Everyone's insights are welcome."

Server2: "I'd like to be able to take an order on my little computer and pass it to the kitchen."

Facilitator: "Okay. What else?"

Server1: "Can I find out the status of an order?"

Chef2: "Can I notify a server when the order is done?"

Facilitator: "Yes and yes. You'll notice that I'm writing these in as labeled ellipses. We refer to these as 'use cases.' We'll be asking some of you to come back and help us analyze those use cases, but that's another meeting."

The Outcome

The JAD session continued on for the rest of the day. When the participants were finished, they had a set of requirements that appear as use cases arranged in the packages.

For the server package, the use cases were

- Take an order
- Transmit the order to the kitchen
- Change an order
- Receive notification from kitchen
- Track order status
- Notify chef about party status
- Total up a check
- Print a check
- Summon an assistant
- Summon a busser
- Take a drink order

- Transmit drink order to lounge
- Receive acknowledgment
- Receive notification from lounge

For the chef package, the use cases were

- Store a recipe
- Retrieve a recipe
- Notify the server
- Receive a request from the server
- Acknowledge server request
- Enter the preparation time
- Assign an order

The use cases for the busser were

- Receive a request from the server
- Acknowledge a request
- Signal table serviced

The use cases for the assistant were

- Receive a request from the server
- Receive a request from the chef
- Acknowledge a request
- Notify request completed

For the bartender:

- Enter a drink recipe
- Retrieve a drink recipe
- Receive notification from the server
- Receive a request from the server
- Acknowledge a request
- Notify request completed

And for the coat-check clerk:

- Print a coat check
- Print a hat check

Figure 18.8 shows how all this looks in the UML.

FIGURE **18.8**
*The functionality
package diagram.*

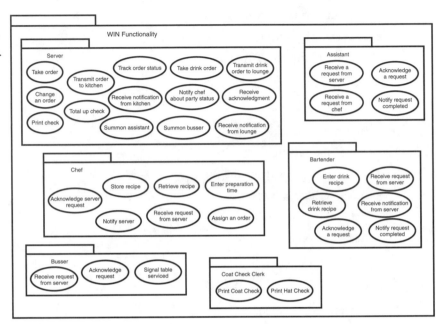

The modeler kept evolving the class diagrams by adding the two classes and associations as in Figure 18.9.

FIGURE **18.9**
*The newly added
class information.*

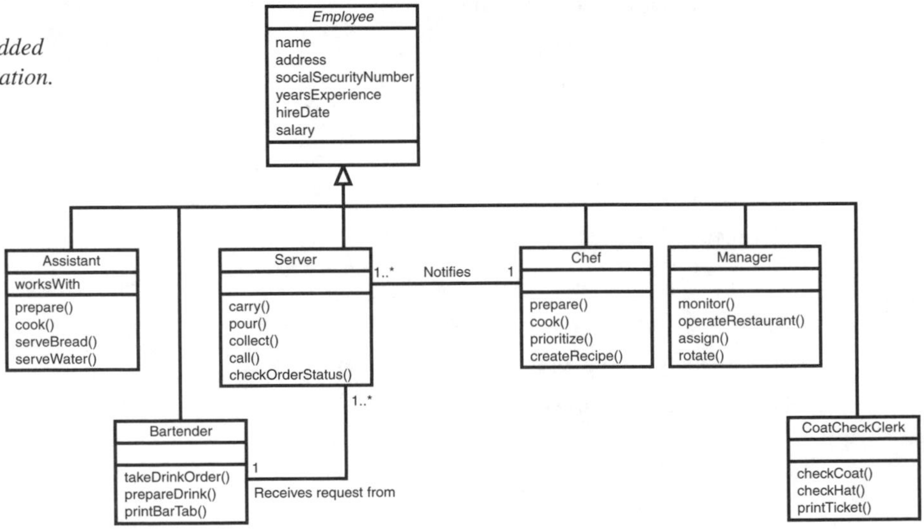

Now What?

The design document the team will deliver to its client is growing by leaps and bounds. It includes business processes, class diagrams, and a set of functionality packages.

Now does the team start coding? No way. In the next hour, they start analyzing the contents of the packages.

Summary

In the context of a team meeting, the development team has generated a vision for the computer-based system in the restaurant of the future. The team members decided that speeding up information movement is the key to the success of the system, and they've come up with ways for technology to do that.

In a JAD session, the development team meets with potential users and domain experts to gather the requirements for the system. The result is a package diagram in which each package represents a major piece of functionality. Use cases inside a package elaborate on the functionality.

18

Q&A

Q Can some of the JAD session participants be the same people who participated in the earlier team meeting?

A Yes. In fact, that's advisable. They might remember crucial details that might not come through clearly in the meeting notes.

Q I notice that Messrs. LaHudra, Nar, and Goniff don't participate in these meetings. Does anyone from that level ever take part in meetings and JAD sessions?

A These particular individuals don't. In some organizations, however, upper management participates actively at least for part of a session. It's hard to get a high-level executive for an entire JAD session.

Q Is it always the case that you'll organize system functionality by roles, as we did for this domain?

A No, not always. This just turned out to be convenient for this domain. In fact, we could probably come up with an alternative way of doing it for the restaurant world if we really put our minds to it. Another type of system might demand a different kind of cut. For example, a helpdesk might have Call Receiving, Problem Resolution, and Call Return as the packages. Again, within each package, you'd have a set of use cases.

Workshop

Test your knowledge of requirements gathering and find the answers in Appendix A, "Quiz Answers."

Quiz

1. How are we representing system requirements?

2. Does class modeling stop after the domain analysis?

3. What is the "schlepp factor"?

Exercise

1. Continue on with the Library domain from the exercises in Hours 16 and 17. What are the major packages of functionality? What are the constituent use cases?

HOUR 19

Developing
the Use Cases

Now that you've seen what's involved in requirements gathering, you're going to move on to analyzing the requirements and fleshing them out into a system. In this hour, you'll cover

- The care and feeding of use cases
- Specifying descriptions, preconditions, and postconditions
- Specifying steps
- Diagramming the use cases

The use cases from the package diagram in Hour 18, "Gathering System Requirements," give a good picture of what the system will have to do. The team will have to analyze and understand each one. They've moved gradually from understanding the domain to understanding the system. The use cases have provided the bridge.

If you're getting the idea that the system development project is use case–driven, you have a good understanding of the whole process.

Notice that at no point in the JAD session did the development team discuss how the system would accomplish all the activities specified in the panoply of use cases. The idea was just to enumerate all the possible use cases. As the use cases are fleshed out in this hour, notice how the components of the WIN system start to materialize. At this point in the development effort, the system begins to take center stage.

We'll put ourselves in the shoes of the development team and deal with part of this collection of use cases.

The Care and Feeding of Use Cases

To analyze the use cases, we have to run another JAD session. The discussion in this JAD session is intended to derive an analysis for each use case.

A word of caution: The use case JAD session is usually the most difficult one, as it calls for the participants—potential users of the finished system—to become analysts. In their own niche, each one is a domain expert, and you have to tap into their expertise. Typically, they're not used to either verbalizing or analyzing what they know. They probably haven't been part of a system design effort before, and they may be uncomfortable with trying to specify what a system should do to help them carry out their work.

In order to alleviate the strain, it's best to organize the JAD session so that the team deals with one group at a time—for instance, just the Servers. That way, the others won't sit idly by as the Servers analyze their use cases. The overall domain experts, the restaurateurs, can show up to lend a hand with all the groups. A cross-section of the users would be appropriate when dealing with the Customer package.

The use cases are numerous. Just to keep this hour manageable, we'll focus on the first nine use cases for the Server package. After you see how these analyses are done, you'll be able to do the remaining Server use cases, as well as the use cases for the other packages. (See the exercises in the Workshop at the end of this hour.)

The Use Case Analysis

Remember (from Hour 7, "Working with Use Case Diagrams"), each use case is a collection of scenarios, and each scenario is a sequence of steps. For each scenario in each use case, we'll want to show

- A brief description of the scenario
- Assumptions for the scenario
- The actor who initiates the use case

- Preconditions for the use case
- System-related steps in the scenario
- Postconditions when the scenario is complete
- The actor who benefits from the use case

> In your analysis, you can also include any exception conditions or alternative flows. I've kept the scenarios simple for this example, however.

No specific way of laying out a use case analysis is "correct." The items listed typically provide a complete picture of a use case.

> In your design document (the document you give your client and the programmers), each of these use case analyses will have a separate page. You'll probably want to include a diagram of the use case, complete with actors, on this page.

The system-related steps in the scenario are extremely important. They'll show how the system is supposed to work. When the JAD session participants tell us these steps, they're telling us, in effect, what the system will ultimately look like. After this JAD session, we should have a good idea about the components of the system.

The assumptions are important, too. In the list of assumptions, you can list design considerations, as you'll see.

This is what I meant by the system development project being "use case–driven." The use cases will ultimately create the path to the system.

The Server Package

The Server class seems to figure in the greatest amount of activity—which isn't surprising, because the Server interacts with virtually every other class.

The Server use cases are

- Take an order
- Transmit the order to the kitchen
- Change an order

- Receive notification from kitchen
- Track order status
- Notify Chef about party status
- Total up a check
- Print a check
- Summon an Assistant
- Summon a Busser
- Take a drink order
- Transmit a drink order to lounge
- Receive acknowledgment
- Receive notification from lounge

Take an Order

Let's begin with "Take an order." We'd rely on experienced servers to give us a description, assumptions, preconditions, steps, and postconditions. The package and subpackage already indicate the initiating actor (Server) and the benefiting actor (Customer).

A good one-sentence description might be, "The server enters the customer's order into the handheld device and transmits it to the kitchen." The assumptions are that a customer wants a meal, the customer has read the menu, and the customer has made a selection. Another assumption is that the server's handheld has a user interface dedicated to order entry.

The preconditions are that a customer has been seated and has read the menu. The postcondition is that the order is entered into WIN.

The steps in the use case are

1. On the handheld computer, the server activates the user interface for order entry.
2. The order-entry user interface appears.
3. The server enters the customer's menu selection into WIN.
4. The system transmits the order to the kitchen PC.

Although we've assumed an order entry interface exists, we haven't yet specified how that interface will look or how the physical act of entering the order will proceed. We don't know yet what the kitchen PC's user interface will look like, nor have we said anything about the technical details of transmitting an order.

The point is that as we state our design assumptions, we're starting to get a handle on what the system is supposed to do, and we'll start to crystallize our thoughts on how to do it. The steps in the use cases force us to come up with assumptions about the components of the system. Remember that the use cases are intended to show how the system looks to a user.

Transmit the Order to the Kitchen

Ready for another? This one will be included in (that is, "used by") at least two use cases—the previous one and "Change an order."

The description is, "Take an order entered into the handheld, put it on the wireless network, and send it to the kitchen PC." The assumptions are that we'll have a means of communicating the order (via a wireless network), and again, that we have an order-entry interface. Do we have to repeat this assumption? We do. Each use case will eventually appear on a separate page in the design document, which will serve as a reference about the system. For clarity, the assumptions should appear on each use case, even if we have to repeat them from use case to use case.

The precondition is an order entered into a handheld. The postcondition is that the order has arrived in the kitchen. The benefiting actor is the customer.

The steps are

1. A button-click in the order-user interface indicates "Send to kitchen."
2. WIN transmits the order over the wireless LAN.
3. The order arrives in the kitchen.
4. The order-entry user interface on the handheld indicates that the order arrived in the kitchen.

Obviously, we have to change our use case diagram for the customer subpackage. It has to show the «include» dependency between this use case and "Take an order" and between this use case and "Change an order." Figure 19.1 shows the updated use case diagrams for the Server package.

19

FIGURE 19.1

The updated use case diagrams for the Server package.

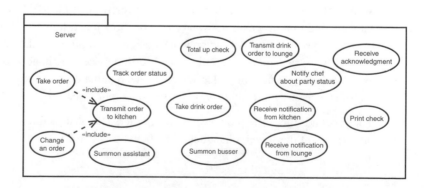

Change an Order

While we're on the subject, let's move to "Change an order." The description is, "Modify an order already entered into WIN." The assumption is that an order has already been placed and sent to the kitchen and that, subsequently, the customer wants to change that order. We also assume that WIN has a database of orders showing the server who entered each order and the table the order came from, that the server can access the database from the handheld, that WIN can make transmissions from the handheld to the kitchen PC and back, and that the handheld has a user interface screen for changing an order.

The precondition is the previously placed order. The postcondition is that the modified order has arrived in the kitchen. The benefiting actor is the customer.

The steps in this use case are

1. On the handheld computer, the server activates the user interface screen for changing an order.
2. The user interface brings up a list of existing orders in the kitchen placed by this server.
3. The server selects the order to be changed.
4. The server enters the modification to the order.
5. The system transmits the order to the kitchen PC.

Step 5 includes the previous use case "Transmit the order to the kitchen."

Track Order Status

As you might recall, earliest discussions about the restaurant of the future included finding out when a customer's order will come out of the kitchen. This use case does just that. Implementing it in the system will go a long way toward facilitating the server's job.

The description is, "Track the status (time to completion) of an order already entered into WIN." The assumption is that an order has already been placed, has been sent to the kitchen, and that the customer wants to know how much longer it will take for the food to arrive. We repeat two of the previous design assumptions: a database of orders and the capability to transmit messages back and forth between the handheld and the kitchen PC. We also assume a user-interface screen on the handheld for tracking orders and a user-interface screen on the kitchen PC for the same purpose.

The precondition is the previously placed order. The postcondition is that the order status has arrived at the server's handheld. The benefiting actor is the customer.

The steps are

1. On the handheld computer, the server activates the user-interface screen for tracking an order entry.

2. The user interface brings up a list of existing orders in the kitchen that this server has placed.

3. The server selects the order to be tracked.

4. The system transmits a tracking message to the kitchen PC.

5. The kitchen PC receives the message.

6. The chef brings up the tracking order interface on the kitchen PC.

7. The chef enters a time estimate for the order's completion.

8. The system transmits the time estimate back to the server's handheld.

Notify Chef About Party Status

Starting with this use case, I'll use subheadings within these subsections to indicate the aspects of the use case analysis, and bullets to set off phrases within those subheadings— with two exceptions: I'll still number the steps, and I won't use bullets for the description.

Description

Via the network, the server tells the chef that a customer is almost finished with the appetizer.

Assumptions

- The server is in the customer's serving area.
- The server can gauge the customer's progress.
- The system has a user-interface screen for customer status.
- The system transmits messages from handheld to kitchen PC and vice versa.

Preconditions

- The customer is partially finished with the appetizer.

Postconditions

- The chef has initiated the final stages of completing the main course.

Steps

1. On the handheld computer, the server activates the interface screen for customer status.

19

2. The user interface brings up a list of the tables in the server's serving area.

3. The server selects the table of interest.

4. The server sends an "almost finished with appetizer" message about this table to the kitchen PC.

5. The kitchen PC receives the message.

6. The server receives an acknowledgment from the kitchen PC.

This last step uses the "Receive acknowledgment" use case, which is in the Server package. Figure 19.2 shows a diagram for the "Notify chef about party status" use case.

FIGURE 19.2
The use case diagram for "Notify chef about party status."

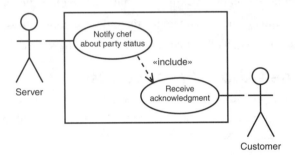

Benefiting Actor

- Customer

Total Up a Check

Description

Add up the items in the order.

Assumptions

- There is a database of orders accessible to the server's handheld.
- Each item in the order is attached to its price.

Preconditions

- The party has completed its meal.

Postconditions

- The bill is totaled.

Steps

1. The server brings up a list of active orders on the handheld.
2. The server selects the appropriate order.
3. The server clicks a button on the handheld to total the check.
4. The system calculates the total from the prices in the order.

Benefiting Actor

- Customer

Print a Check

Although this one may seem trivial, it's an important part of the transaction.

Description

Print the totaled check.

Assumptions

- A (wireless) networked printer in the serving area

Preconditions

- A totaled check

Postconditions

- A printed check

Steps

1. The server clicks a button on the handheld to print the check.
2. The networked printer in the serving area prints the check.
3. The server clicks a button on the handheld to remove this order from the list of active orders.

Benefiting Actor

- Customer

Summon an Assistant
Description

Request an assistant to clean the table for the next customer.

19

Assumptions

- The system allows wireless communication between two mobile employees.
- The system has a user interface screen for sending a message to an assistant.

Preconditions

- An empty table that has to be cleaned and reset

Postconditions

- The assistant has come to the table to clean and reset.

Steps

1. The server activates the interface for sending a message to an assistant.
2. The server receives an acknowledgment from the assistant.

As in the use case "Notify chef about party status," the last step uses the "Receive acknowledgment" use case.

Benefiting Actor

- Assistant

Analyzing this use case, as well as the use cases in the Assistant package, might lead us to believe that splitting the Assistant class into two classes, AssistantServer and AssistantChef, is a good idea. (It just makes things cleaner.) Could they be children of an abstract Assistant class? They could, but we probably wouldn't gain much from setting up this abstract class.

Creating these two new classes necessitates revisiting the domain analysis. We have to rework the class diagrams, particularly the diagram for Employee, as Figure 19.3 shows.

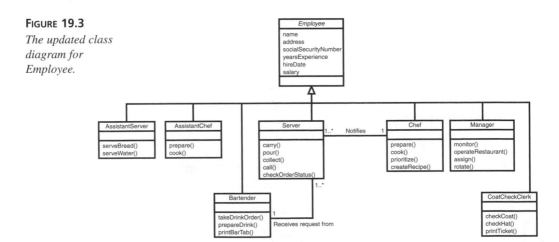

FIGURE 19.3
The updated class diagram for Employee.

We would also have to update our package diagrams to include an Assistant Server package and an Assistant Chef package.

This is an example of how the segments of GRAPPLE feed each other. The knowledge gained during use case analysis has helped us evolve the domain analysis.

Remaining Use Cases

The remaining use cases in the Server package are roughly analogous to the ones we've analyzed. I leave it to you as an exercise to finish the analyses for this package. (See Exercise 1 in the Workshop.)

Components of the System

One important aspect of the use case analysis is that you begin to reveal the components of the system. Before we leave this hour, let's take note of the components that have emerged through our analysis of the use cases in the Server package. You'll find them in the "Assumptions" section of each use case analysis. (Additional components will become apparent when you do the exercises.)

On the software side, it's obvious that a number of user interface screens are necessary. WIN will need handheld-based user interfaces for order entry, order change, order status tracking, customer status, and sending messages to an assistant. For good measure, something like an interface "home page" will be necessary to keep all these other interface screens organized. WIN will also need a user interface on the kitchen PC to enable the chef to track an order.

It also seems that we'll need a database to contain all the orders. Each record will contain the table, the order, the time the order went in, the server, whether the order is active, and more.

On the hardware side, we'll need a wireless network, handheld computers for the mobile employees (servers, assistant servers, and bussers), and a desktop PC in the kitchen and another in the lounge. We'll need a networked printer in each serving area. We'll probably need a palmtop and a printer for the coat-check clerk, too.

A rather involved design document is starting to take shape. In the next hour, you'll delve even further into the use cases.

Summary

It's not enough to list all the use cases. A development team has to understand each one in great detail in order to begin to understand the system. In this hour, accordingly, you went through the intricacies of use case analysis.

19

A use case analysis involves specifying a description of the use case, deriving the pre-conditions and postconditions, and specifying the steps. One important aspect of the use case analysis is that the components of the system begin to emerge.

Q&A

Q In the initial segment of GRAPPLE, I notice you skipped over the action "Identify cooperating systems." Why is that?

A As you'll remember, this development team started with a blank piece of paper. No cooperating systems existed. The next system that someone devises for LNG Restaurants, however, might have to access WIN in some way.

Q In this hour, you modified the use case diagrams and the class diagram. Does this usually happen?

A Yes. You can never be hesitant about making changes as your knowledge evolves. The original list of use cases captured all the knowledge at one point in the effort, and it represents a snapshot at that point. The modified diagrams represent the development team's latest thinking.

Workshop

The workshop for this hour tests your knowledge on fleshing out use cases. To see the fleshed-out answers, turn to Appendix A, "Quiz Answers."

Quiz

1. What are the parts of a typical use case diagram?
2. What does it mean for a use case to "include" (or "use") another use case?

Exercises

1. Draw the use case diagram for "Summon an Assistant."
2. Analyze the remaining use cases in the Server package, and draw use case diagrams.
3. Analyze the use cases in the Chef package, and draw use case diagrams.
4. Do the same for the Bartender, Assistant, and Busser packages.

HOUR 20

Getting into Interactions and State Changes

In this hour, you get deeper into the use cases analyzed in the preceding hour. You'll use them as a foundation for understanding the parts of the system and how they interact. The topics you'll cover are

- Listing the working parts of the system
- Modifying use cases
- Analyzing interactions among the working parts

The use-case analysis in the last hour goes a long way toward making the WIN system a reality. The analysis still isn't far enough along to begin coding the system, however.

Analyzing the use cases has helped conceptualize the working parts of the system. Although we now know a lot about the use cases, we still have to model how those working parts will interact with one another and how (and when) they change state. Passing this information to the programmers will make their jobs a lot easier. They will have a vision of how to code classes and make them work together.

The Working Parts of the System

One way to start is to enumerate the system components suggested in each package of use cases. Although we didn't explicitly analyze all the use cases in all the packages in the last hour, we can still extract the system components those use cases assume. In a real development effort of course, a development team would have analyzed all the use cases before moving on.

The Server Package

At the end of the last hour, we enumerated the software parts of the system based on our analysis of the first nine use cases in the Server package: On the handhelds, WIN will need user interface screens for order entry, order change, order-status tracking, customer status, and message sending. A user interface main screen will also be necessary. Our analysis revealed the need for an order-tracking user interface screen on the kitchen PC. WIN will require a database to hold all the orders.

The use cases we didn't analyze might also suggest system components. To refresh your memory, those use cases were

- Summon a busser
- Take a drink order
- Transmit drink order to lounge
- Receive acknowledgment
- Receive notification from lounge

The use cases suggest some straightforward components. The first one tells us something in the Server's user interface (like a dedicated screen) has to enable the server to summon a busser. The second tells us that a screen is necessary for taking a drink order (analogous to the screen for taking a meal order). The user interface has to be able to receive an acknowledgment (to show, for example, that a busser has received a request) and to receive a message from the lounge that a drink is ready.

Given the job of a server, it's not surprising that the main components in this package are user interface screens concerned with order taking and with message sending and receiving.

The Chef Package

The use cases in the Chef package are

- Store a recipe
- Retrieve a recipe
- Notify the server

- Receive a request from the server
- Acknowledge server request
- Enter the preparation time
- Assign an order

What components do these use cases suggest? Again, they follow in a straightforward manner.

The Busser Package

The use cases for the busser were

- Receive a request from the server
- Acknowledge a request
- Signal table serviced

The Assistant Server Package

As you'll recall, we decided in the last hour to split the Assistant package into Assistant Server and Assistant Chef. The use cases for the Assistant Server would be

- Receive a request from the server
- Acknowledge a request
- Notify request completed

The Assistant Chef Package

The use cases for the Assistant Chef would be

- Receive a request from the chef
- Acknowledge a request
- Notify request completed

One might argue that a separate computer for an Assistant Chef isn't necessary because he or she works in close proximity with a Chef in the kitchen. If the kitchen is very large, however, electronic communication might be a good idea.

The Bartender Package

The use cases for the Bartender are

- Enter a drink recipe
- Retrieve a drink recipe

20

- Receive notification from the server
- Receive a request from the server
- Acknowledge a request
- Notify request completed

These use cases are analogous to the Chef package's use cases, and the software components they suggest are analogous to the Chef's components. The hardware is analogous, too: Behind a bar, a desktop would make more sense than a handheld would.

We'll need a database of drink recipes and user interface screens that allow easy access to this database for entering and retrieving a recipe. The bartender's user interface has to show a notification from a server (that a customer's table is ready) and a request from a server for a drink. The bartender has to be able to send an acknowledgment that a request was received and also to notify the server that a drink is ready.

The Coat-Check Clerk Package

The Coat-Check Clerk's use cases are

- Print a coat check
- Print a hat check

The software components in the coat-check clerk's handheld should include a user interface screen that enables printing the appropriate check. The check should include the time and a description of the article. We will probably also want the system to have a database of checked items.

Interactions in the System

At this point in the project, the task is to show how the system components interact in order to complete each use case. We'll model the interactions for a couple of the use cases in the Server package. The set of use cases is too big for us to look at all of them; but, in a real-world project, a development team does just that.

Remember what I said earlier: Behind every use case lurks a sequence diagram.

Take an Order

Let's start with the "Take an order" use case. From Hour 19, "Developing the Use Cases," the steps are

1. On the handheld computer, the server activates the user interface for order entry.
2. The order entry user interface appears.
3. The server enters the customer's menu selection into WIN.
4. The system transmits the order to the kitchen PC.

In the model we developed in the last hour, this use case includes "Transmit the order to the kitchen," whose steps are

1. A button-click in the order user interface indicates "Send to kitchen."
2. WIN transmits the order over the wireless LAN.
3. The order arrives in the kitchen.
4. The order-entry user interface on the handheld indicates that the order arrived in the kitchen.

A sequence diagram will show this interaction nicely. (So will a collaboration diagram, which I ask you to create in Exercise 1.) Preparing the diagram forces us to focus our thinking in several ways.

First, when the server takes the customer's order, the server, in effect, creates something— an order! That order is an object in the WIN system. (It's also an instance of a class, Order, from our domain analysis in Hour 17, "Performing a Domain Analysis.") The chef will use it as a guideline for initiating and carrying out a set of actions. The server will total up a check that corresponds to it. The customer will pay the check. This created order, then, is an important item.

Also, if you examine the use cases "Change an order" and "Track order status," (as we will in a moment) you'll see references to a list of orders. This list has to come out of a database of orders—a database I alluded to at the end of Hour 19. How does the order get into that database? It has to happen in the course of this use case.

20

We can focus our thinking in still another way. In the included use case, the term "kitchen" is a little vague. As we're modeling software components, we have to refine what we mean here. Envisioning how this all might work leads us in a common-sense way to conclude that the order must somehow show up in the chef's user interface in the kitchen PC. How it does that is not our concern at this point, of course.

After we think these ideas through, the "Take an order" use case looks like this:

1. On the handheld computer, the server activates the user interface for order entry.
2. The order entry user interface appears.
3. The server enters the customer's menu selection into WIN.
4. WIN creates an order.
5. Include (Transmit an order to the kitchen).
6. The system enters the order into the database of orders.

 "WIN" and "the system" are synonymous.

Notice the shorthand in Step 5 that indicates the inclusion of the "Transmit an order to the kitchen" use case.

The "database of orders" challenges our thinking on the hardware side. This database has to reside on a computer, but we haven't specified one. One possibility is to have a central machine that holds this database and make it accessible to all other machines on the network.

While we're at it, we should expand the "Transmit the order to the kitchen" use case and include the modification about the chef's user interface. Because it has a step that specifies a message on the server's handheld indicating receipt of the order by the kitchen, we should add a step that has the system send a message from the kitchen PC to the handheld. The steps, then, are

1. A button-click in the order user interface indicates "Send to kitchen."
2. WIN transmits the order over the wireless LAN.
3. The order arrives in the chef's user interface in the kitchen PC.
4. WIN sends a message from the kitchen to the handheld user interface indicating receipt of the order.
5. The order entry user interface on the handheld indicates that the order arrived in the kitchen.

These use case modifications are just two more examples of the way one phase of a project can influence another. In this context, preparing our sequence diagrams helped refine our thinking about the use cases at the base of those diagrams.

Figure 20.1 shows the sequence diagram that captures our thinking for this use case. Just to recap what you learned earlier about sequence diagrams, the objects laid across the top of the diagram represent the components in this use case. The Order object is created during the use case, and for that reason, it's lower than the other two, and the message pointing to it has a «create» stereotype. The dashed line descending from each object is that object's "lifeline," and time proceeds vertically downward. The little rectangles on the lifelines are called "activations." Each activation represents the period of time during which an object is performing an action.

FIGURE 20.1

The sequence diagram for "Take an order."

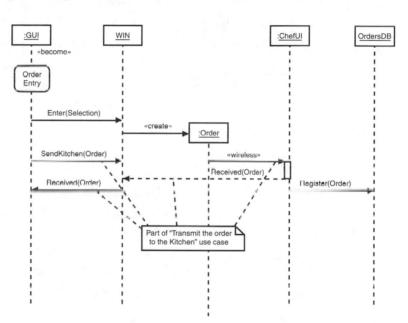

Note the state change on the first lifeline. It's intended to clarify how the user interface sets up to handle a particular kind of activity. We could include all the possible state changes as separate state diagrams, but this would be overkill. Putting them on the sequence diagrams (at least in this domain) appears to be more economical.

20

In a sequence diagram, a message arrow with a dashed line represents a return message.

Change an Order

Let's try another one. From the last hour, the steps in the "Change an order" use case are

1. On the handheld computer, the server activates the user interface screen for changing an order.
2. The user interface brings up a list of existing orders in the kitchen placed by this server.
3. The server selects the order to be changed.
4. The server enters the modification to the order.
5. The system transmits the order to the kitchen PC.

Again, preparing the diagram helps us refine our thinking and modify the use case slightly. After Step 4, we'd no doubt want the system to create a modified order. After Step 5, the system should enter the modified order into the database of orders.

The new use case should thus be

1. On the handheld computer, the server activates the user interface screen for changing an order.
2. The user interface brings up a list of existing orders in the kitchen placed by this server.
3. The server selects the order to be changed.
4. The server enters the modification to the order.
5. WIN creates a new order based on the modification to the existing order.
6. Include(Transmit an order to the kitchen PC).
7. The system enters the modified order into the database of orders.

Again, we use the shorthand to indicate the included use case. Figure 20.2 shows the sequence diagram that corresponds to this use case. As in Figure 20.1, we show a change of state.

Track Order Status

Let's look at one more case before we finish. The "Track order use case" consists of these steps:

1. On the handheld computer, the server activates the user interface screen for tracking an order entry.
2. The user interface brings up a list of existing orders in the kitchen placed by this server.

3. The server selects the order to be tracked.

4. The system transmits a tracking message to the kitchen PC.

5. The kitchen PC receives the message.

6. The chef brings up the tracking order interface on the kitchen PC.

7. The chef enters a time estimate for the order's completion.

8. The system transmits the time estimate back to the server's handheld.

FIGURE 20.2

The sequence diagram for "Change an order."

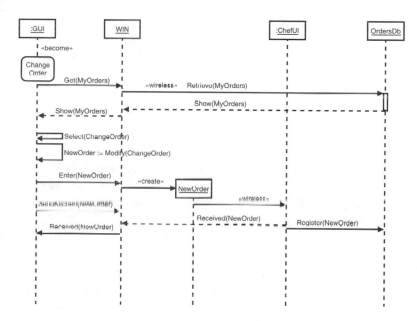

In keeping with the modifications we made earlier, we'd probably want to change Step 5 to "The message arrives in the chef's user interface in the kitchen PC." We might also want to interview a chef or two and ask how he or she comes up with the time estimate in Step 7. Perhaps we can develop a software package that would help.

Figure 20.3 does the honors for this use case.

Implications

Seeing all the results so far, Messrs. LaHudra, Nar, and Goniff are ecstatic.

"This is going to change the entire nature of the restaurant business," said Nar.

"I agree we're onto something," said LaHudra, "but what do you mean 'change the entire nature of the restaurant business'?"

20

FIGURE 20.3

The sequence diagram for "Track an order."

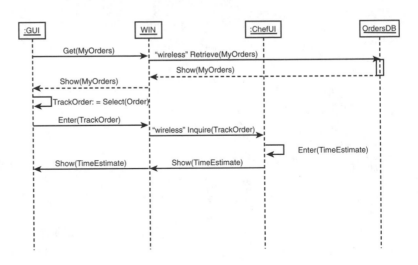

"Yes, what do you mean?" asked Goniff.

"Well, if you think about it," Nar continued, "the whole job of the server is going to change, and so is the job of the chef. The servers won't be running around as much as they do now. They'll be information resources for the customers because they'll always be in their designated serving areas. They'll go to the kitchen and the bar only when they have to. Through their handheld computers, they'll become monitors of the order-preparation process and managers of their areas. They'll be more like lifeguards than traditional waiters. In fact, they'll be able to actually sit down while they work in their areas, because 'work' won't involve running around so much anymore."

"And the chefs?"

"They'll become more managerial, too. They'll use their computers to assign orders to assistant chefs, and coordinate what goes on in a kitchen. This will be great for large kitchens and large restaurants, now that we're moving information around instead of people."

"Hmmm... That has a nice ring to it," said LaHudra. "Apparently, when you move information more, you can get away with moving people less. Not bad."

"Not bad at all," said Goniff, already plotting the next expansion of the business.

Summary

After the use case analysis, a development team turns its attention to the system components the use cases suggest. What are they? How do they interact? This hour showed how to answer these questions in the context of developing the WIN system.

The objective of this effort is to provide information to the programmers—information that facilitates their efforts. The results of this analysis should make it easy for programmers to code the system objects and how those objects communicate with one another.

After you model interaction among components, the system is much closer to becoming a reality. As you model the interactions, you may find that it's appropriate to modify the use cases at the base of these interactions.

Q&A

Q You've shown modification of use cases in several places here. Realistically, does that happen in a project?

A It absolutely does. Granted, the examples here may seem a bit contrived: For instance, in reality we probably would have known about the database in the first use case before we ever got this far. The point is to show you that as our knowledge evolves, the model evolves along with it.

Q Why would the original use cases fail to capture all the nuances in the first place?

A Because they're the results of JAD sessions with system users, not system developers. You'll notice all the additions and changes were system-related, not business-related. After you finish the sessions with the potential users and have a chance to analyze the use cases, it's not uncommon that modifications like these emerge.

Workshop

Here's where you get your chance to spread your wings on modeling interactions among system components. After you have answered the questions, interact with Appendix A, "Quiz Answers," to find the answers. Incidentally, you might want to use the components listed in this hour to help you go above and beyond the listed exercises and make additional sequence diagrams and collaboration diagrams.

Quiz

1. How do you represent an object that's created during the course of a sequence diagram?

2. How is time represented in a sequence diagram?

3. What is a "lifeline"?

4. In a sequence diagram, how do you show an "activation," and what does it represent?

20

Exercises

1. Develop a collaboration diagram equivalent to the sequence diagram for the Server use case "Take an order."

2. Create a sequence diagram for the use case "Take a drink order."

3. Select at least one use case in the Chef package and develop a sequence diagram. Use the list of components mentioned in this hour. Are any additional ones necessary?

4. Use your imagination on this one: The use cases in the Coat-Check Clerk package seem pretty simple. Can you embellish each one by adding a step or two? Would any additional components be helpful? Draw a sequence diagram for one of these use cases.

HOUR 21

Designing Look, Feel, and Deployment

In this hour, you'll move into two important aspects of system design: the user interface and system deployment. Here are the topics you'll cover:

- Some general principles of GUI design
- The GUI JAD session
- From use cases to user interfaces
- UML diagrams for GUI design
- Mapping out system deployment

You've come through a lot of use case–driven analysis. In this hour, you're going to look at two aspects of system design. Both are ultimately traceable to use cases, and both are extremely important to the final product. Graphical user interfaces (GUIs) determine system usability. Deployment turns the system's planned physical architecture into a reality.

Some General Principles of GUI Design

User interface design, equal parts art and science, draws upon the vision of the graphic artist, the findings of the human factors researcher, and the intuitions of the potential user. After much experience with WIMP (Windows, Icons, Menus, Pointing Device) interfaces, some general principles have emerged. Here are some of the major ones:

1. Understand what the user has to do. User interface designers typically perform a *task analysis* to understand the nature of the user's work. Our use case analysis roughly corresponds to this.

2. Make the user feel in control of the interaction. Always include the capability for the user to cancel an interaction after it's started.

3. Give the user multiple ways to accomplish each interface-related action (like closing a window or a file) and forgive user errors gracefully.

4. Because of cultural influences, our eyes are drawn to the upper-left corner of a screen. Put the highest priority information there.

5. Take advantage of spatial relationships. Screen components that are related should appear near one another, perhaps with a box around them.

6. Emphasize readability and understanding. (Words for all of us to live by!) Use active voice to communicate ideas and concepts.

7. Even though you might have the capability to include upwards of umpteen gazillion colors on a screen, limit the number of colors you use. Limit that number severely. Too many colors will distract the user from the task at hand. By the way, it's a good idea to give the user the option of modifying the colors.

8. If you're thinking of using color to denote meaning, remember it's not always easy for a user to see an association between a color and a meaning. Also, bear in mind that some users (about 10% of adult males) have color confusion, and may find it difficult to distinguish one color from another.

9. As is the case with color, limit your use of fonts. Avoid italics and ornate fonts. "Haettenschweiler" is a font name that's fun to say, but doesn't always promote ease of use.

10. Try to keep components (like buttons and list boxes) the same size as much as possible. If you use different-size components, a multiplicity of colors, and a variety of fonts, you'll create a patchwork that GUI specialists call a "clown-pants" design.

11. Left-align components and data fields—line them up according to their left-side edges. This minimizes eye movements when the user has to scan the screen.

12. When the user has to read and process information and then click a button, put the

buttons in a column to the right of the information or in a row below and to the right of the information. This is consistent with the natural tendency (in our culture) to read left to right. If one of the buttons is a default button, highlight it and make it the first button in the set.

These dozen principles aren't the only ones, but they give you an idea of what's involved in designing a GUI. The challenge is to convey the proper information in an uncomplicated, straightforward, intuitive visual context.

If you're creating Web pages, check out GUI honcho Jakob Nielsen's highly informative www.useit.com for more information on user interface design.

Figure 21.1 shows what happens when you put some of these principles into action. Figure 21.2 shows what happens when you don't.

FIGURE 21.1

Applying GUI design principles.

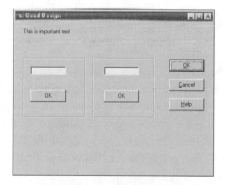

FIGURE 21.2

The result of not applying GUI design principles.

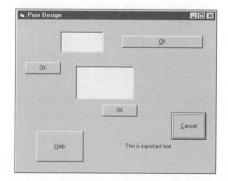

21

The GUI JAD Session

Although this doesn't directly connect to the UML, it's a good idea to talk about how potential users determine the GUI. Once again, a Joint Application Development (JAD) session is in order.

For this session, you recruit potential users of the system. For WIN, we'd recruit servers, chefs, assistant servers, assistant chefs, bussers, and coat-check clerks. The development team players should include programmers, analysts, modelers, and a facilitator. The objective is to understand the users' needs and implement an interface based on their ideas—an interface that enables the system to integrate smoothly into business processes. The old way of developing a system—writing a program from scratch, molding the behavior of the users so they can interact with it, and modifying business processes to accommodate it—is extinct.

To keep the session efficient, you'd schedule the users in groups according to the roles. You'd plan the length of each session according to the number of use cases in each role's package. This is just a rough guideline, of course, as some use cases are more complex than others. Remember, too, that new use cases might emerge as you design the GUI.

The users' participation in the session is a two-part affair. In the first part, they derive the user interface screens. In the second, they approve prototypes generated by the development team.

How do the users derive the screens? The facilitator suggests a use case to start from, and the users discuss ways to implement that use case via the system. When they're ready to start talking at the level of a specific screen, the users work with paper mockups. The facilitator provides a large sheet of easel paper in landscape view (long dimension as the horizontal) to represent the screen. Post-it notes represent the GUI components (for example, pop-up menus, buttons, combo boxes, list boxes). The users' task is to work as a group to position the components appropriately.

When they reach agreement on which components should be on a screen and where those components should be located, development team members create prototype screens. As they work, they use appropriate GUI principles outlined in the preceding section. Then, they present those screens on computers, and the users make any necessary modifications.

The point of all this, of course, is to have users (rather than developers) drive the process as much as possible. That way, the system will work optimally in the real world of everyday business activities.

From Use Cases to User Interfaces

Use cases describe system usage. Therefore, the user interface has to serve as a means of implementing the use cases.

Think of a use case's sequence diagram as one view of a use case. If we could "rotate" that view in three dimensions so that the leftmost part of the sequence diagram sticks out of the page and faces us, we'd be looking at the user interface that takes the user into the sequence. (See Figure 21.3.)

FIGURE 21.3

"Rotating" the sequence diagram orients the user interface toward us.

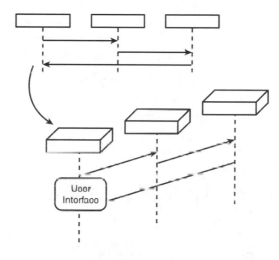

Let's examine the use cases in the Server package and show how they map into the WIN user interface. Here are those use cases once again:

- Take an order
- Transmit the order to the kitchen
- Change an order
- Receive notification from kitchen
- Track order status
- Notify chef about party status
- Total up a check
- Print a check
- Summon an assistant
- Summon a busser

21

- Take a drink order
- Transmit drink order to lounge
- Receive acknowledgment
- Receive notification from lounge

The Server interface has to accommodate all these use cases.

One way to begin is to partition the set of use cases into groups. Three groups are sufficient. One group deals with orders ("Take an order," "Change an order," "Track order status," "Take a drink order"). Another group deals with checks ("Total up a check," "Print check"). A third is concerned with sending and receiving messages ("Notify chef about party status," "Summon an assistant," "Summon a busser," "Transmit drink order to lounge," "Receive acknowledgment," "Receive notification from lounge").

We might want to start with a main screen that takes the server to screens for all the other groups of use cases. We'd want to be able to navigate from one group to any other group. Within a group, we'd want to navigate to any use case within the group. Figure 21.4 shows a first cut at the main screen. This will have to go on a handheld, so it will probably be scaled down in some ways.

FIGURE 21.4

First cut at a Server main screen.

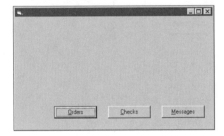

Our JAD session might arrive at the convention that navigation within a group will be done by buttons on the right of the screen, while navigation between groups will be accomplished by buttons at the bottom of the screen. Figure 21.5 shows a first cut at one of the Server interface screens—the screen for the orders-related use cases.

FIGURE 21.5

Screen for orders-related use cases.

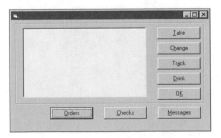

This screen opens in the Take Order mode. The large white box will be a scrollable copy of the dinner menu with check boxes that the server clicks to indicate the customer's selections. (When we deal with the interface, we have to remember we're dealing with the world of restaurants and be extra careful about how we use the word "menu.") Clicking OK creates the order and sends it to the kitchen PC. Clicking a button on the right brings its associated capabilities to the screen.

Clicking a bottom-row button brings up a separate group of capabilities. The Message button, for example, brings up the screen in Figure 21.6. By the way, the user interface doesn't have to be just visual. This interface incorporates a sound signal to notify the server that a message has arrived. He or she clicks the Read button to read a scrollable list of messages.

FIGURE 21.6
Screen for message-related use cases.

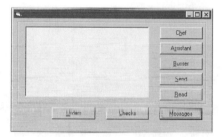

UML Diagrams for GUI Design

The UML makes no specific recommendations regarding diagrams for GUI designs. In an earlier hour, however, we hinted at a possibility: Recall from Hour 8, "Working with State Diagrams," that I presented an example that dealt with state changes in a GUI. Although that example drilled deeper into the mechanics of GUIs than we have to at this point, it suggests that state diagrams are useful when we discuss user interfaces.

In Hour 24, "Shaping the Future of the UML," we present some ideas on how to extend the UML to model GUIs.

You'd use a state diagram to show the flow of a user interface. Figure 21.7 shows how the high-level screens in the Server interface connect with one another.

21

FIGURE 21.7

A state diagram for high-level screen flow in the Server interface.

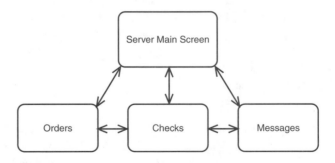

Because a particular screen consists of a number of components, a class diagram of a composite is appropriate for modeling a screen. Figure 21.8 shows a composite diagram that corresponds to the screen in Figure 21.5.

FIGURE 21.8

A composite diagram that corresponds to the screen in Figure 21.5.

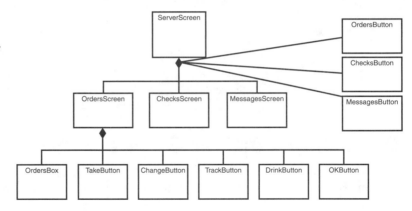

Mapping Out System Deployment

After the GRAPPLE analysis segment has produced the general concept of the WIN system, a system engineer will start thinking about how the physical architecture should look. He or she will start considering alternative network topologies and how to implement them in a wireless way, and will start figuring out which software components belong on which nodes in the network. This design segment doesn't have to wait for analysis to be complete. Its actions can proceed in parallel with actions in other GRAPPLE segments, such as the design of the GUI.

The key is for the project manager to track all the actions in all the segments.

The Network

Remembering the different types of LANs available (from Hour 13, "Working with Deployment Diagrams"), the system engineer has a number of choices. The objective is to pick the one that integrates most smoothly with wireless connectivity for the handheld computers.

To understand some of the decisions the system engineer has to make, let's delve a little into Wireless LANs (WLANs). It's usually the case that a radio transceiver called an *access point* sits at a fixed location and connects to a LAN (of the standard, everyday-garden-variety wired type). The access point receives messages from—and transmits messages to—the wireless devices, and changes received messages into a form the wired network understands. Multiple access points increase the WLAN's range and the number of users that can access it.

How do users access the WLAN? In WIN, they'll make the connection via wireless-LAN adapters integrated with their handheld computers. No matter how many access points are incorporated into the network, each handheld will associate with just one access point and its area of coverage, which is called a *microcell*. (It's similar to a cell that works with cellular phones.)

The system engineer has to decide on how many access points to have in the restaurant, what kind of wireless-LAN adapter to integrate with the handhelds, and the type and layout of the wired network.

If any of this has interested you in WLANs, visit www.wlana.com, the Web site of the Wireless LAN Association (WLANA). WLANA is a consortium of corporations that market components for WLANs.

Let's suppose the system engineer decides on a thin ethernet for the LAN (see Hour 13).

The Nodes and the Deployment Diagram

We've already enumerated the nodes in our system. The servers, assistant servers, and bussers will have handheld computers. The choice of a handheld (running the Windows CE operating system) is a good one for this project. As the System Engineer mentioned in Hour 18, "Gathering System Requirements," the screen size (larger than that of a Palm device or Pocket PC) and the keyboard add some flexibility. This could be important later if LaHudra, Nar, and Goniff decide to expand the application. The programmers can use well-known development tools to create the software and port it to the mobile computers.

21

For network connectivity, the development team can fit each handheld with a WLAN PC card. One such card is the Proxim RANGELAN2. Proxim also makes an access point into the LAN. Like the Proxim WLAN PC card, the access point is called RANGELAN2.

The kitchen, cloakroom, and cocktail lounge will have desktops. Each desktop will connect to a printer. In addition, each serving area will have a desktop connected to a printer so the server can print checks and retrieve them without walking too far. (A server's print server, so to speak.)

To illustrate the deployment, the System Engineer delivers the deployment diagram shown in Figure 21.9.

FIGURE 21.9
Deployment diagram for WIN.

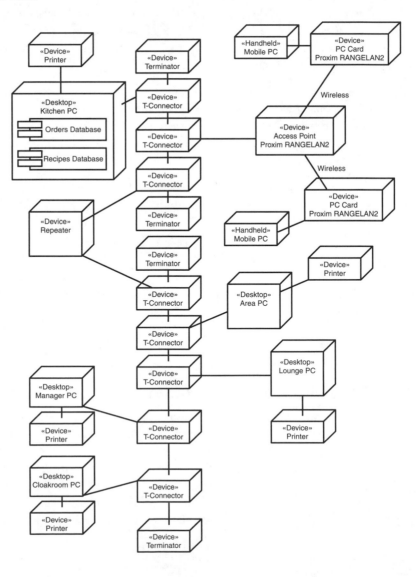

Next Steps

The development team has traveled the road from use cases to user interfaces to WLANs. What's next?

First, the analysts clean up the model. They look through the model dictionary and clear up any ambiguities. They make sure that all terminology is used consistently throughout all diagrams, and that problems with terms like "menu" and "server" haven't crept in. When all appropriate analysis and design parts of GRAPPLE are complete, the team compiles its results into a design document and hands off copies to the client and to the programmers.

It then falls to the programmers to start turning the design into code. (The coding part is beyond the scope of this book.)

The code will be tested, rewritten according to the results of the tests, and retested—a process that will continue until the code passes all tests. The use case analysis forms the basis for the tests.

Document specialists begin creating documentation for the system, and they create training materials as well. A good document creation effort should proceed like a good system development effort—with careful planning, analysis, and testing—and should begin early in the development process.

With a solid analysis and design and an informative, well-organized design document, these next steps should proceed smoothly all the way through deployment.

The main idea is to focus intense efforts on analysis and design so that the developer confronts as few challenges as possible during implementation and the result of the project is a system that fully meets the client's needs.

...And Now a Word from Our Sponsor

Messrs. LaHudra, Nar, and Goniff couldn't be more thrilled with the way the development effort has gone. The development team has kept them posted throughout the process and has given them UML-based blueprints that show where the project is headed. They're even happy with the System Engineer's strategic thinking on which mobile device to use.

The whole effort has fired up their imaginations, impelling them to look for new ways to harness technology—both inside and outside the restaurant world. They've come to the realization that most business processes involve the movement of information. To the extent that technology accelerates that movement, it provides a potentially huge competitive advantage.

21

Empowering a Sales Force

Outside the restaurant world, the three entrepreneurs see the potential of reusing the wireless LAN ideas for a mobile sales force inside a huge work area. Reuse shouldn't be difficult, as all the modeling information is intact.

One application of this idea might be in the gigantic home supply stores that cater to do-it-yourself types. (Places where "hardware" has a different connotation than the one in this book.) Salespersons on the floor of that kind of store would benefit from a handheld device that accesses product information through a wireless LAN. A system like this would help the salesperson answer questions about where the product is located in the store, whether or not it's in stock, and how someone would use it.

This has some intriguing implications for both salesperson and customer. The customers would always be sure they're getting the latest and most accurate information from the salespeople. A new salesperson trained on how to use the system could quickly start working with minimal training about the stock.

LaHudra, Nar, and Goniff will soon invade the world of home improvement.

Although LaHudra, Nar, and Goniff are obviously trailblazers, they're no longer alone in their visions for mobile devices and wireless LANs. For additional developments in this field, see "Handhelds Nudge PCs" in the May 14, 2001 issue of *Internet Week*. If you can't get a hard copy, you might find an archived version at www.internetweek.com.

Some visionaries in the mobile device industry are pushing the envelope with slightly larger devices. Weighing about three pounds, tablet PCs are keyboardless, portable touchscreen machines with display sizes that range from 10 to 12 inches. (They're also called "Web pads" because they typically offer Internet connectivity.) Manufacturers like Sony, Siemens, Sonicblue, AirSpeak, and Microsoft are marketing these computers to mobile workers in a variety of industries.

In fact, as I write this, tablet PCs are invading the restaurant world. One restaurant is using a tablet PC as a digital wine list that links wirelessly to information about its wines. The next time you hear a sommelier describe a wine as "somewhat impetuous, with an amusing insouciance and a brisk bouquet," he or she might just be relying on a tablet PC and a wireless LAN.

Expanding in the Restaurant World

This mobile sales force idea isn't enough for LaHudra, Nar, and Goniff. They want to do nothing less than use technology to revolutionize the restaurant business. They believe they can build WIN-based restaurants in major cities throughout the world. They feel the technology will expedite the dining experience and make it more convenient for everyone to eat out.

Goniff, ever on the lookout for new ways to make a buck, had been thinking about this for a while (at least since the end of Hour 20!).

"Fellas," said he to his partners, "if we build restaurants in all the major cities, we can take technology to the next step and move information all over."

"How so?" asked Nar, always a little slow on the uptake.

"Think about it. If we're international, we can go on the Web and…"

LaHudra interjected: "Just a second. We're already on the Web. We get hits all day on www.lahudranargoniff.com, don't we?"

"Let me finish, LaHudra. We can use the Web to get people to come into all these restaurants. We'll use the Web to give them a free sandwich."

"What???!!!" asked Nar and LaHudra simultaneously, and incredulously.

"Work with me on this. We devote a page of our Web site to our restaurants division. Someone hits that page, supplies his name and a bunch of other information, and gets to select the sandwich of his choice. If our database shows he hasn't done this before, he gets to go to another page where he can print out a coupon for a sandwich. He takes the coupon into the nearest restaurant. He gets the sandwich, eats it, loves it, and comes back as a paying customer."

"Nice, but the Web goes everywhere," said Nar. "Suppose somebody doesn't live near one of our restaurants and still wants the sandwich?"

"Wait! I know!" said LaHudra. "They can use their credit card to pay a nominal shipping fee on the Web site, and our closest restaurant will send it right to their house in an inexpensive cold container. They can put the sandwich in the microwave and warm it up. That way, they can have a LaHudra-Nar-Goniff experience wherever they are. Then, when they happen to travel to a city that has one of our restaurants, they're likely to eat there."

"By the way, what about that 'other information' they entered when they printed the coupon?" asked Nar.

21

"I'm way ahead of you," said Goniff. "We use that information to e-mail them promotional information about our other businesses, according to their demographics—if they indicate it's OK to do that, of course.

"Now where's that development team? We've got work to do."

Summary

When your project moves into the Design segment, two items to focus on are the user interface and the system deployment. Both are ultimately use case-driven, and both are extremely important.

User interface design depends on artistic vision and scientific research. A number of principles of user interface design have emerged after years of work with WIMP interfaces. This hour presented some of them. Keep them in mind as your development team designs GUIs.

Use cases drive the design of the user interface. The system has to enable the user to complete every use case, and the user interface is the gateway into the use cases.

In parallel with a number of project efforts, the team's system engineer maps out the physical architecture. The architecture is use case-driven because system usage ultimately determines the physical nature and layout of the system. The system engineer provides a UML deployment diagram that shows the nodes, the software components that live in each node, and the internodal connections. Although deployment issues show up late in the GRAPPLE process, there's no reason to hold back on starting to think about deployment. As shown in this hour, fundamental issues can arise that require resolution.

After the system is modeled, the modeling information can be reused in a variety of contexts. The model can fuel a multitude of new business ideas.

Q&A

Q **After the users have developed a paper prototype, is it really necessary to go to the trouble of creating a screen and showing it to them? After all, they've created the paper screen and positioned the paper components. Can't they just wait to see the screen on the working system?**

A You absolutely have to show the users a real screen—"real" in the sense that it's on a computer. First of all, users are likely to see things on the screen they didn't see on paper. Another reason—related to the first—is that the dimensions of post-it notes only approximate the dimensions of onscreen components (relative to the larger sheet that represents the screen). Placing the post-its results in some distortion of the spatial relationships among the onscreen components. The screen is likely to look somewhat different from the paper prototype. Also, screen shots become valuable parts of your design document.

Q I know this isn't directly related to the UML, but one of the GUI principles you mentioned is to give a user multiple ways to accomplish interface-related actions. Why is that important?

A This is important because you can't predict all the contexts in which a user will perform an action. Sometimes the user will be using a keyboard-intensive application, and a keystroke combination will be more appropriate than a mouseclick. Sometimes the user will be using the mouse, and a mouseclick is more appropriate. Providing both ways of accomplishing the same thing makes the interaction that much easier for the user.

Q Speaking of questions not directly related to the UML, why the "active voice" GUI principle?

A Studies show that people have an easier time understanding the active voice than the passive. Also, the active voice typically requires fewer words and thus takes up less precious screen real estate than the passive voice does. Users (as well as publishers and editors) appreciate it if your directions say "Click the Next button to continue" rather than "The Next button should be clicked by you in order for the process to be continued."

Workshop

This workshop tests your knowledge of issues related to designing a system's look and feel and to mapping out the system's physical architecture. Design your answers well, and then interface with Appendix A, "Quiz Answers."

Quiz

1. What is a task analysis?
2. Which analysis that we've already done is roughly equivalent to a task analysis?
3. What is a "clown-pants" design?
4. Give three reasons for limiting the use of color in a GUI.

Exercises

1. Use a UML state diagram to model the chef's user interface.
2. Use pencil and paper to design at least one of the screens for the chef's user interface. Start by grouping the use cases, and then stick to the JAD session conventions. If you have access to Visual Basic or another visual screen design tool, try using it to complete this exercise.

21

3. Play the role of System Engineer and research alternatives (other than the selected PC card and access point) for implementing the WLAN with handheld devices.

4. Suppose the development team had decided to use palmtops instead of handhelds. Play the role of System Engineer again and list all the implications of this choice. Research potential ways of implementing the WLAN with Palm OS-based devices or with Pocket PCs. Modify Figure 21.9 accordingly.

HOUR 22

Understanding Design Patterns

Now that you've learned the fundamentals of the UML and you've seen how to use it in the context of a development project, we end Part II with a look at applying the UML to support a hot area—design patterns. In this hour, you'll cover

- Parameterization
- Design patterns
- Applying a design pattern
- Using our own design pattern
- The advantages of design patterns

In the preceding 21 hours, you covered a variety of topics. From class diagrams to sequence diagrams, from state diagrams to JAD sessions, the goal was to get you ready to apply the UML in frequently occurring, real-world situations.

Now we change our direction a bit. In this hour, I'll delve into an application of the UML that is becoming increasingly popular. This application, the representation of design patterns, captures the essence of solutions that have worked repeatedly in real-world projects and situations.

Parameterization

In Hour 2, "Understanding Object-Orientation," I mentioned that a class is a template for creating objects. I said you could think of a class as a cookie-cutter that stamps out new objects. An object, you'll recall, is an instance of a class.

To further refresh your memory, let's return once again to our washing machine example. Specifying the washing machine class—or to be notationally correct, the WashingMachine class—as having the attributes brandName, modelName, serialNumber, and capacity, and the operations addClothes(), addDetergent(), and removeClothes() gives us a way to create new objects in the washing machine class. Each time we want to create an object, we assign values to the attributes.

NEW TERM   As it happens, the UML enables you to move a step higher. It gives you a mechanism for creating classes in a way that's analogous to creating objects. You can set up a class so that when you assign values to a subset of its attributes, you've created a class rather than an object. This kind of class is called a *parameterized class*. Its UML representation appears in Figure 22.1. The perforated box in the upper-right corner holds the parameters to which you assign values in order to generate the class. Just for the record, these are called *unbound parameters*. When you assign values to them, you *bind* them to those values. The T in the perforated box is a classifier that indicates the class is a template for creating other classes.

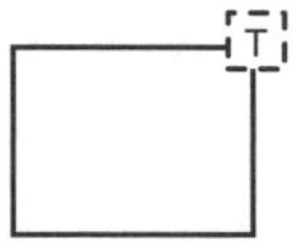

FIGURE 22.1

The UML icon for a parameterized class.

Here's an example. Suppose you set up LivingThing as a parameterized class. The unbound parameters could be genus and species, along with regular attributes name, height, and weight as shown in Figure 22.2.

If you bind genus to "homo," and species to "sapiens," you create a class called "Human." The class name is bound to T. Figure 22.3 shows one way of representing the binding. This particular style is called *explicit binding*, because it explicitly shows the generated class in a dependency relationship with the parameterized class and provides the generated class with its own name.

FIGURE 22.2

LivingThing as a parameterized class.

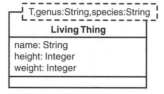

FIGURE 22.3

Explicitly binding the LivingThing parameterized class.

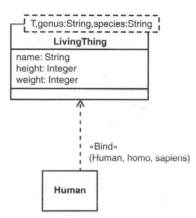

Another binding style is called *implicit binding*. You don't show the dependency relationship, and the bindings appear in an angle-bracketed list in the name of the generated class. Figure 22.4 shows this.

FIGURE 22.4

Implicitly binding the LivingThing parameterized class.

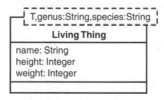

In either case, you can then assign values to name, height, and weight to create objects in the Human class.

Design Patterns

It's possible to expand on the parameterization idea. Any UML classifier can be parameterized. In fact, a group of collaborating classifiers can be parameterized, and that leads us off in an intriguing direction.

After several decades of increasingly widespread use, object orientation has resulted in a number of robust solutions to frequently recurring problems. These solutions are called *design patterns*, and they've been getting a lot of play lately. Because design patterns have grown out of the object-oriented world, they're easy to conceptualize, diagram, and reuse. Because we now have the UML, we have a common modeling language to explain and disseminate them.

The first book to popularize design patterns is entitled, unsurprisingly, *Design Patterns* (Addison-Wesley, 1995). Its authors—Erich Gamma, Richard Helm, Ralph Johnson, and John Vlissides—have become widely known as the "Gang of Four."

A design pattern is essentially a solution—a design—that has emerged through practical experience with a number of projects, and development teams have found it to be applicable in a variety of contexts. Each design pattern describes a set of communicating objects and classes. The set is customized to solve a design problem in a specific context.

In their book, the Gang of Four cataloged and characterized 23 fundamental design patterns. They partitioned these patterns into three categories according to each pattern's *purpose*: (1) *Creational* patterns that concern themselves with the process of object creation, (2) *Structural* patterns that deal with the composition of objects and classes, and (3)*Behavioral* patterns that specify how classes or objects interact and apportion responsibility. They further partition their design patterns in terms of whether they apply to objects or classes. They refer to this criterion as *scope*, and most patterns' scope is at the object level.

Each design pattern has four elements: (1) a *name* that enables us to describe a design problem in a word or a phrase, (2) a *problem* that defines when to apply the pattern, (3) a *solution* that specifies the elements that make up the design and how they collaborate, and (4) the *consequences* of applying the pattern.

Now we come to that "intriguing direction" I mentioned earlier: Within a model, we can represent a design pattern as a parameterized collaboration in the UML. The design pattern is expressed in a general way, with generic names for the collaborators. Assigning domain-specific names makes the pattern applicable to a specific model. The parameterized collaboration helps you visualize the specificity within the context of the pattern.

Chain of Responsibility

Let's examine one design pattern, and you'll see what I mean.

The Chain of Responsibility is a behavioral pattern that applies to a number of domains. This pattern deals with the relationship between a set of objects and a request. You apply this pattern when more than one object can handle a request. The first object in the chain gets the request and either resolves it or moves it along to the next object in the chain, until one can handle it. The original requesting object doesn't know which object will handle its request. The object that ultimately handles the request is said to be an *implicit receiver*.

Restaurants are set up this way, and so are car dealerships when they finance auto purchases. In a restaurant, a customer typically doesn't send a request directly to a chef and isn't usually acquainted with the chef the request is going to. Instead, the customer gives an order to a server, the server gets it to the chef, who might fulfill the order or pass it along to an assistant chef. (That's how it happens at the LaHudra, Nar, & Goniff restaurants, anyway.) In an automobile dealership, the dealer passes a loan application to several financial institutions until one decides to offer a loan

Professional sports leagues implement this pattern when a team places a player on waivers. The team with the worst record gets a chance to claim the player. If it decides not to take the player, the team with the next worst record has a chance, and so forth. The team placing the player on waivers doesn't explicitly know which team will claim him. (See Exercise 1.)

Now that you've seen the Chain of Responsibility design pattern in a few contexts, you're ready to understand it in the abstract. The participants in this pattern are a Client, an abstract Handler, and concrete Handlers that are children of the abstract Handler. The Client initiates a request. If a (concrete) Handler can take care of that request, it does so. If not, it passes the request along to the next concrete Handler. Figure 22.5 shows how this structure looks.

The idea behind this pattern is to free an object from having to know which other object fulfills its request. It gives you additional flexibility when you assign responsibilities to objects. The downside is that the pattern gives no guarantee that the request will be handled by any object. For example, a ballplayer placed on waivers might not be claimed by any team in the league.

Note the reflexive association on the abstract Handler class. The Gang of Four intended to show that you have the option of having the Handler implement the successor link. (In some contexts, the objects know how to find their own successors.) I decided to represent that implementation with an association class as in Figure 22.5, to allow the further option of adding attributes to the successor.

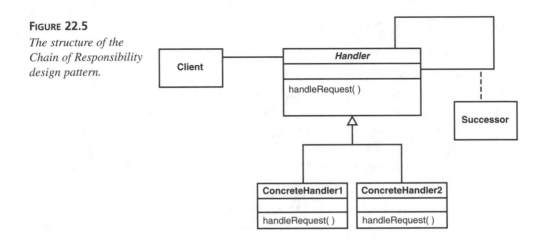

FIGURE 22.5

The structure of the Chain of Responsibility design pattern.

Chain of Responsibility: Restaurant Domain

In the restaurant domain, the abstract Handler is the Employee class, and concrete Handlers are the server, the chef, and the assistant chef. The customer is the Client, who might initiate a request, like placing an order, and doesn't know who will ultimately fulfill it.

Substituting domain-specific names into Figure 22.5 gives us Figure 22.6.

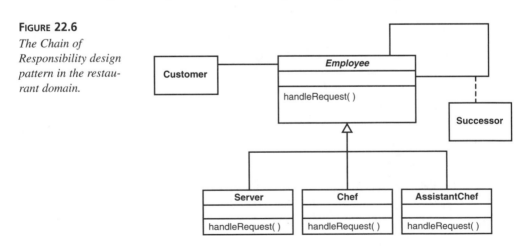

FIGURE 22.6

The Chain of Responsibility design pattern in the restaurant domain.

Figure 22.6, while a useful diagram, doesn't show us how the domain-specific names fit into the pattern. To show the context, we use a parameterized collaboration as in Figure 22.7.

FIGURE 22.7

A parameterized collaboration for representing the Chain of Responsibility in a restaurant.

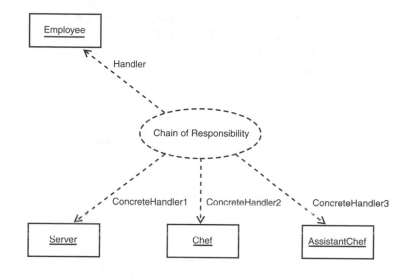

In Figure 22.7, the dashed oval represents the collaboration that is the design pattern, hence the name inside the oval. The surrounding boxes represent the collaborators. The dependencies show the collaboration depends on the collaborators. The label on a dependency tells the role the depended-on collaborator satisfies within the pattern. The collaboration has been parameterized with the addition of the domain-specific class names.

Chain of Responsibility: Web Browser Event Models

When developing interactive Web pages, a designer has to consider the event model of the browser that will open it. In Internet Explorer (IE), you write JavaScript or VBScript code for reacting to an event like a button click. This code, called an "event handler," specifies the changes, if any, that occur when the button is clicked.

In an HTML document, you can divide a page into areas called DIVs, and subdivide a DIV into forms. You can position a button inside a form. Does this sound strangely like a composite? That's because it is. Each element is a component of the document, and some components are components of other components. Gamma, Helm, Johnson, and Vlissides list the Composite as one of their design patterns, and note that it's often used in conjunction with the Chain of Responsibility pattern. The component-composite relationship implements the successor links. When I showed you the class diagram for the Chain of Responsibility, I mentioned parenthetically that in some contexts the objects know how to find their own successors. This is one of those contexts.

When the button is positioned in a form inside a DIV whose document opens in IE, the button-click event starts with the button, is passed along to the form, then to the DIV, and finally to the containing document. Each of these elements can have its own button-click event handler to react to the click event.

If a document-resident script dynamically specifies which element's event handler fires, the script is an instance of the Chain of Responsibility design pattern. Figure 22.8 shows the class diagram, and Figure 22.9 shows the parameterized collaboration for this design pattern applied to the IE event model.

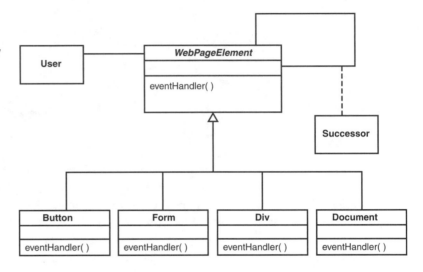

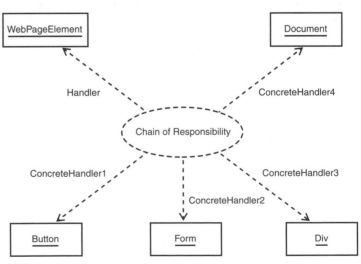

Netscape Navigator has an event model, too. Its model is the exact opposite of IE's. In Navigator, the highest-level element (the document) gets the event first and passes it along until it ends up at the element from which it originated. How would you change the class diagram in Figure 22.8 to model the Navigator event model? (See Exercise 2.)

IE refers to its event model as *event bubbling*. Navigator refers to its event model as *event capturing*.

22

Our Own Design Patterns

While the Gang of Four became justly famous for their catalog of design patterns, they didn't mean to imply that their patterns were the only ones possible. On the contrary, their intent was to encourage the overall discovery and use of patterns.

Just to give you an idea of how these patterns emerge, remember our work in Hour 11, "Working with Activity Diagrams." During that hour, you saw an example dealing with Fibonacci numbers and an exercise concerning triangle numbers.

What were the common features? Each one started with an initial value or set of values, followed a rule to accumulate numbers, and ended with the *n*th number in a series.

Let's refer to this pattern as "Series Calculator." Although we could implement this as one object, let's make it a set of collaborating objects to illustrate some concepts about design patterns.

The Series Calculator has three participants, InitialValue (which can hold one or more values), AccumulationRule, and FinalValue. Figure 22.10 shows the class diagram for this pattern. The starting value is in the attribute *first*. If a second starting value is necessary, as in the case of Fibonacci numbers, it's specified in an attribute called *second*. Sometimes, as in the case of factorials, the pattern will need a value for the *zero*th term. The algorithm for AccumulationRule is implemented in the operation accumulate(). The number of terms to calculate is in the attribute *n*th in AccumulationRule.

FIGURE 22.10

The class structure for our Series Calculator design pattern.

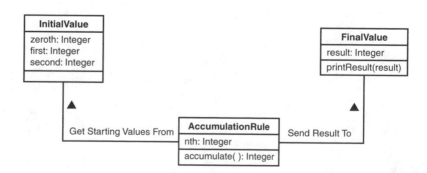

In the collaboration, AccumulationRule gets the starting value(s) from InitialValue, applies the rule the requisite number of times, and sends the result to FinalValue to be printed. Figure 22.11 shows the interaction.

FIGURE 22.11
The interaction within the Series Calculator design pattern.

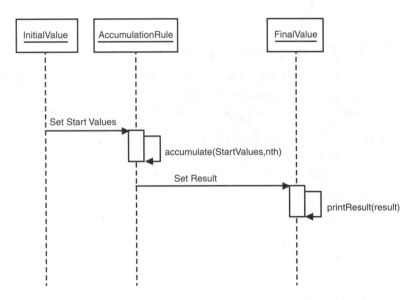

To apply this design pattern to the triangle numbers series, we adopt some triangle-numberish names for the classes and show the parameterized collaboration in Figure 22.12. (This collaboration, of course, avoids the "trivial" solution I pointed out at the end of Exercise 3 in Hour 11.)

FIGURE 22.12
The parameterized collaboration for a Triangle Number calculator.

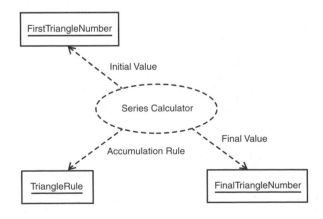

For good measure, we show the parameterized collaboration for a Factorial calculator in Figure 22.13.

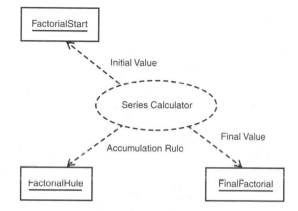

FIGURE 22.13
The parameterized collaboration for a Factorial calculator.

The Advantages of Design Patterns

Design patterns are useful in a number of different ways. First, they promote reuse. If you've expressed a solid design as a pattern, you've made it easy for you and others to work with it again. Also, they give you a clear, concise way of speaking and thinking about a set of classes or objects that work together to solve a problem. This increases the likelihood that you'll use the pattern as a component of a design. Finally, if you use patterns in your design, you'll probably find it easy to document the system you build.

Summary

A parameterized class has unbound parameters. Binding these parameters results in the creation of a class. You can parameterize any UML classifier. A parameterized collaboration serves as the representation of a design pattern—a solution that's useful in a variety of domains.

One design pattern, the "Chain of Responsibility," deals with objects passing a request from one to another until one object can handle it. This pattern comes from the best-known book on design patterns.

Our own design patterns emerge from work we did in Hour 11 on activity diagrams. We can create a design pattern for a calculator that computes the nth value in an arithmetic series. This pattern's participants are InitialValue, AccumulationRule, and FinalValue.

Design patterns afford a number of advantages. They enable designers to easily reuse proven solutions, incorporate solid components into designs, and clearly document the systems they create.

Q&A

Q How difficult is it to "discover" design patterns?

A It's not a question of difficulty—it's more a matter of experience. As you progress in your career as an analyst and a designer, you'll see certain regularities occur again and again. After a while, you'll think in terms of those regularities. Studies show that experts in a particular domain think in terms of patterns and apply those patterns in most situations they encounter. It's the basis of their seemingly smooth, effortless performance.

Q Are patterns only useful for design?

A No. Patterns can emerge anywhere in the development process, or in any field of endeavor. The Gang of Four was inspired by the work of an architect who discerned recurring patterns in the designs of buildings.

Workshop

The quiz questions and exercises in this workshop get you thinking about some of the UML's advanced features. Advance to Appendix A, "Quiz Answers," for the answers.

Quiz

1. How do you represent a parameterized class?
2. What is "binding" and what are the two types of binding?
3. What is a "design pattern"?
4. What is the "Chain of Responsibility" design pattern?

Exercises

1. Apply the class diagram for the Chain of Responsibility design pattern to the waiver process that takes place in professional sports leagues.
2. Change the class diagram in Figure 22.8 so that it visualizes the Netscape Navigator event model. As I pointed out earlier this hour, an event in Navigator starts at the document level and is passed along until it winds up at the element from which it originated. The originating element may be buried several levels deep in the HTML document.

PART III
Looking Ahead

Hour

Hour **23**

Modeling Embedded Systems

As was the case in Hour 22, "Understanding Design Patterns," you're going to see the UML applied to another hot area in this hour. This time, you'll learn about computer systems that don't sit on desks, laps, or palms. Instead, they're embedded deep inside venues like planes, trains, and automobiles. Here are the topics you'll cover:

- What embedded systems are
- Embedded systems concepts
- Modeling an embedded system in the UML

LaHudra and his intrepid partners, Nar and Goniff, have been raking in the profits from their LNG Restaurants Division. Service is so good and the meals so tasty that people are coming from miles around to sample the delicious fare in an efficient and friendly atmosphere.

Two flaws have marred their otherwise good fortune. As they read over the monthly reports, the ominous trends stood out. "Take a look at this," said Nar, handing the print-outs to Goniff and LaHudra. "We're making a boatload of money, but we should be making more. The waiters…uhm…servers seem to be dropping more than their fair share of dishes."

"Yes, I noticed that, too," said Goniff. "Every time they drop a dish full of food, the chef has to prepare another meal. And, we have to pay for a new dish."

"Does it really make a difference if a few of our waiters have butterfingers?" asked LaHudra.

"It most certainly does," replied Goniff. "A couple of dishes here, a couple there, pretty soon we're talking real money. But something else about the servers is bothering me even more."

"What's that?" asked Nar.

"These reports show they call in sick a lot. It's a good thing we've got all this technology in the restaurants. It helps us when we have to work shorthanded—we can usually get by with the servers who do show up covering larger service areas than they typically do."

"Let's find out what's wrong," said LaHudra.

The Mother of Invention

The three partners interviewed several of the servers who had frequently called in sick over the previous two months, and they made an astounding discovery: the dropped dishes and the sick days were related. The servers had been handling and grasping their handheld computers so much that their wrists began to weaken. Just as loose lips sink ships, weak wrists drop dishes. What's more, their wrists had often become so painful they couldn't come in to work.

"Can't we help these people somehow?" asked a disconsolate Nar.

"And in the process, maybe help ourselves?" countered an opportunistic Goniff.

"Maybe there's some way we can help them strengthen their grip and their wrists," said LaHudra.

"Well, what should we do," asked Goniff, "buy each of them a grip strengthener?"

"We could do worse," said LaHudra, "but I don't know how effective those little hand grippers really are. It might take forever for our people to strengthen their wrists by using them."

"Still, the idea is a good one," said Nar. "Maybe we just need a better grip strengthener than the ones you can buy in a store."

"Really? How would we make a better grip strengthener?" LaHudra asked.

He didn't have long to wait for an answer. Nar was on one of his patented rolls.

"As I recall, lots of people believe that the best and most efficient form of exercise is one that creates the greatest challenge when your muscles are working their hardest. If we can create a gripper that increases its resistance as the forearm muscles work harder, I bet we can strengthen our servers' wrists in half the time they'd need with a regular gripper."

"Exactly how do we do that?" wondered the perpetually pragmatic LaHudra.

"The same way we revolutionized the restaurant business," said Nar, "with technology."

"Wait a second," said LaHudra, "we did what we did in the restaurants by adding computers. Do you seriously mean to tell me that we're going to add a computer to a grip-strengthening device?"

"Why not?" said Nar.

"Why not indeed," Goniff chimed in. "I'm with you, Nar. And when we've finished creating this gizmo, we can market it. I've got the perfect name: How about the LNG 'GetAGrip'?"

"I think I'm going to like it," said LaHudra, cautiously.

"I like it already," bubbled Nar, enthusiastically. "Where's that development team?"

Fleshing Out the GetAGrip

The WIN development team reassembled. Their new mission was to implement the vision of the GetAGrip, a "smart" wrist/forearm strengthening device that provides variable resistance during the repetitions of an exercise: The more the muscles work, the harder it should be to squeeze the GetAGrip.

In the course of realizing the vision, the team did some research to find out how to measure how hard a muscle is working. They learned about electronic signals from active muscle fibers. These signals, called EMGs (short for *electromyographic* signals), are the basis for fascinating devices that allow handicapped people to manipulate electronic equipment.

This isn't an excursion into science fiction. In the early '90s, neuroscientist David Warner at the Loma Linda University Medical Center placed electrodes on a boy's face and connected them to a computer. The boy, completely paralyzed from the neck down in an auto accident, was able to move objects on the computer screen by tensing some of his facial muscles.

To learn more about this exciting area, read Hugh S. Lusted and R. Benjamin Knapp's article, "Controlling Computers with Neural Signals," in the October, 1996 issue of *Scientific American*.

The team concluded that they could capture these EMGs via a small, inexpensive "surface electrode" placed on the forearm, pass the captured EMGs through a computer, and then use them as a basis for the computer to adjust resistance in a hand-gripping device. This involves real-time data capture and analysis because the adjustments have to occur as soon as the muscle contracts.

One design possibility is to put the surface electrode on the forearm, connect it to a desktop computer, and have the desktop analyze the EMGs and make the necessary resistance adjustments in the hand gripper. The upside of this design is that it makes it possible to display all kinds of data onscreen, print informative progress reports, and analyze trends. The downside, however, is that the exerciser is tethered to a computer.

Another possibility is to embed a computer chip directly into the gripping device so that the exerciser is free to move around while he or she uses the GetAGrip. Figure 23.1 shows how this design would look. In each repetition of the exercise, the exerciser grips the squeeze bar and moves it toward the base bar.

The upside of the embedded design is that the exerciser can use a device like this almost anywhere (if the computer is battery powered). The downside, of course, is the loss of all the potential information that a desktop could store and display.

JAD sessions revealed that everyone would be much happier with the second design, and this takes us into the wonderful world of embedded systems.

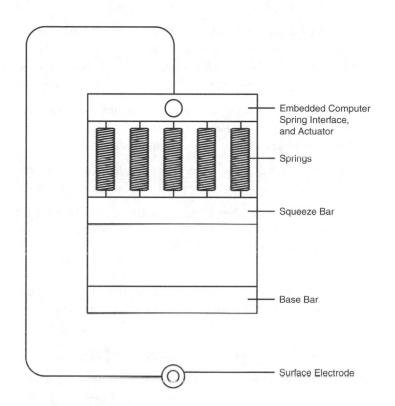

FIGURE 23.1

The embedded system version of GetAGrip.

Embedded Computer Spring Interface, and Actuator

Springs

Squeeze Bar

Base Bar

Surface Electrode

23

What Is an Embedded System?

By now, you know that computers are everywhere. What you might not know is just how much territory "everywhere" encompasses. The computers you see all around you are just the tip of the iceberg. Many of them lurk below the surface, in places you can't easily see. They're inside appliances, cars, airplanes, factory machinery, biomedical devices, and more. Fairly powerful processors live inside printers.

All of these not-readily-visible-to-the-naked-eye computers are examples of embedded systems. Wherever you have a "smart" device, you have an embedded system.

Embedded systems don't have keyboards and monitors that interact with us. Instead, each one is a chip that sits inside a device (like a home appliance), and the device doesn't look like a computer at all. The embedded system decides what that device should do.

If you use a system of this type, you don't get the sense of working with a computer. Instead, you're just interacting with the device. If you never know the computer chip is inside, all the better. When you're toasting a slice of bread, you don't care that an embedded computer chip is distributing the heat—you just want your bread toasted.

When you finish working with a desktop, you turn it off. An embedded system doesn't usually have that luxury. After it's in place, an embedded system has to go on working for days or even years (as in a pacemaker, for example).

If a word processor or a spreadsheet has a glitch and crashes your desktop, you reboot. If the software in an embedded system fails, the results can be disastrous.

So an embedded system doesn't do computing in the usual sense. It's in place to help some other type of device do its work. The other device is the one that interfaces with the user and with the environment.

As you might imagine, programming an embedded system is not for the squeamish. It requires a lot of knowledge about the device the system will live in—what kinds of signals it sends out, what kind of timing parameters it has, and more.

Embedded Systems Concepts

Let's take a closer look at embedded systems and what they typically have to do. In the subsections that follow, we'll examine some of the more important embedded system concepts.

Time

If you go back over the discussion thus far, you'll see that time figures prominently in the embedded systems world. In fact, time is the basis of categorizing embedded systems as either *soft* or *hard*.

A soft system does its work as quickly as possible without having to meet specific deadlines. A hard system also has to work as quickly as possible, as well as finish its tasks according to strict deadlines.

Threads

In the embedded systems world, a thread (also called a *task*) is a simple program. It's a piece of an application, and it performs some meaningful job within that application. It tries to get the full attention of the CPU. *Multitasking* is the process of scheduling the CPU to work with many threads and switching its attention from one to the other.

Each thread has a number that denotes its priority within the application program, and it is usually in one of six states:

- *dormant*—it's in memory and hasn't been made available to the operating system
- *ready*—it can run, but the thread that's running has a higher priority
- *delayed*—it has suspended itself for a specified amount of time
- *waiting for an event*—some event has to happen for it to run
- *running*—when it has the attention of the CPU
- *interrupted*—because the CPU is taking care of an *interrupt*

Figure 23.2 shows a UML state diagram that presents these states and the interstate transitions. Notice the absence of a start symbol and a termination symbol. This tells you the thread moves from state to state in an infinite loop.

FIGURE 23.2

States of a thread in an embedded system application.

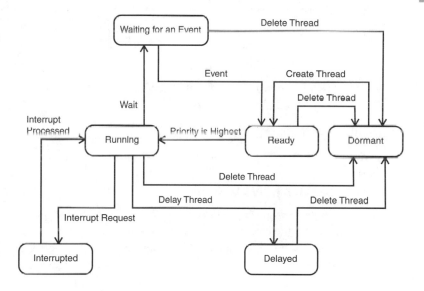

By the way, what's an "interrupt?" Read on.

Interrupts

An *interrupt* is an important little item in an embedded system. It's a hardware-based mechanism that tells the CPU an asynchronous event has happened. An event is asynchronous if it appears unpredictably (that is, out of "sync"). In the GetAGrip, for example, EMG signals arrive asynchronously.

When the CPU recognizes an interrupt, it saves what it was doing and then invokes an ISR (Interrupt Service Routine) that processes the event. When the ISR finishes its job, the CPU goes back to what it was doing when the interrupt happened.

After processing an interrupt, what the CPU goes back to is determined by the type of operating system that runs the CPU, as you'll see.

Interrupts are important because they enable a CPU to disengage from whatever thread it's working on and process events as they happen. This is tremendously significant for a real-time system that has to respond to environmental events in a timely fashion.

Because timeliness is so crucial, embedded systems have to worry about the time course of an interrupt and its processing, even though that time might seem infinitesimal. The CPU has to take some time from when it's notified about an interrupt until it starts saving what it was doing (that is, its *context*). That's called the *interrupt latency*. The *interrupt response* is the time between the arrival of the interrupt request and when the CPU starts the ISR. After the ISR finishes, the *interrupt recovery* is the time it takes the CPU to get back to where it was—to its context—when the interrupt occurred.

One type of interrupt is special: the *clock tick*. A sort of system "heartbeat," the clock tick occurs at regular intervals specific to an application (typically between 10 and 200 microseconds). Clock ticks determine an embedded system's time constraints. For example, a thread in the delayed state remains in that state for a specified number of clock ticks.

Operating System

A real-time operating system (RTOS) acts as a traffic cop among threads and interrupts, and mediates the communication between threads and between an interrupt and a thread. The *kernel* is the part of the RTOS that manages the time the CPU spends on individual threads. The kernel's *scheduler* determines which thread will execute next. As I mentioned before, each thread has a priority assigned to it.

Kernels might be either *pre-emptive* or *non-pre-emptive*, depending on how they deal with interrupts. In a non-pre-emptive kernel, when an ISR finishes executing, the CPU goes back to the thread it was working on when the interrupt request arrived. A non-pre-emptive kernel is said to engage in *cooperative multitasking*. Figure 23.2 applies to a non-pre-emptive kernel.

In a pre-emptive kernel, on the other hand, when an ISR finishes, the CPU notes the priority of threads in the ready state. If a thread in the ready state has a higher priority than the interrupted thread, the CPU executes the higher priority task rather than the one it was working on when the interrupt request arrived. Thus, the higher priority task *pre-empts* the interrupted task. Figure 23.3 shows the modification to two of the states in Figure 23.2, in order to model the pre-emptive kernel.

FIGURE 23.3

Modification of transitions between two states in Figure 23.2 to reflect what happens in a pre-emptive kernel.

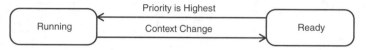

Figure 23.4 models the non-pre-emptive kernel as a sequence diagram, and Figure 23.5 does the same for the preemptive kernel.

FIGURE 23.4

Sequence diagram for the non-pre-emptive kernel.

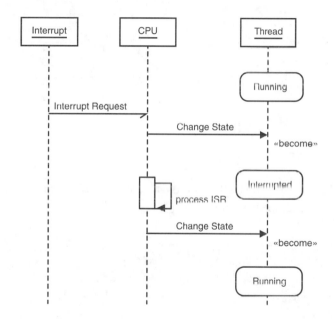

 Microsoft is starting to cut a wide path through the embedded systems domain. It's marketing Windows CE, the operating system for handheld devices and pocket PCs, as an operating system for embedded systems. Windows CE is built in modules. To fit a particular CPU and a particular embedded application, you use just the modules you need and thus keep your application lean.

The advantage of using Windows CE is that you can use Microsoft's popular toolset along with Visual C++ to build an embedded system.

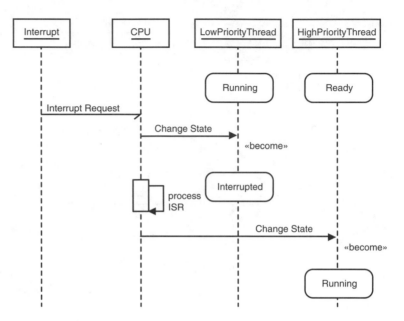

FIGURE 23.5
Sequence diagram for the pre-emptive kernel.

Although we've covered a lot of ground here, bear in mind that we've just scratched the surface of embedded systems.

Modeling the GetAGrip

Back to the task (thread?) at hand, to start creating a model of the GetAGrip. Although it's not the case that all embedded systems are object-oriented, we can still use object-orientation to model the system and its interactions with the outside world.

From our discussion of embedded systems, it's clear that we have to consider timing, events, state changes, and sequences.

Classes

As is the case with any other type of system, we'll begin with classes. To understand the class structure, we'll start with a summary description of the GetAGrip and how it works. This summary would have resulted from a domain analysis.

Here's the description. The GetAGrip consists of a surface electrode, a CPU, an actuator (to carry out the CPU's adjustment commands), and a set of five springs. The actuator connects to the springs via a mechanical interface. The GetAGrip receives asynchronous EMG signals from a surface electrode and passes them to a CPU. Each EMG causes an interrupt request, which the CPU services with an ISR. Software in the CPU analyzes the signals. When the analysis is complete, the CPU sends a signal to an actuator to adjust the tension in the springs. The actuator makes the adjustment by manipulating the mechanical interface with the springs.

Figure 23.6 shows a class structure that summarizes the preceding paragraph. Note the bold outline for the CPU, indicating that it's an active class. The idea is that the CPU is always in control—receiving and analyzing signals, and directing adjustments. It also performs general housekeeping duties within the system. Note also the use of an association class for AdjustMessage, which allows us to specify parameters for the message.

23

FIGURE 23.6

Class structure for the GetAGrip.

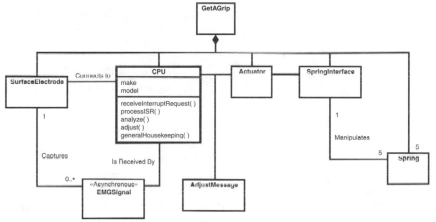

The EMGSignal and the AdjustMessage are important, so let's focus on them. The system will be interested in when a signal arrives and how strong it is, so arrivalTime and amplitude would seem to be reasonable attributes for the EMGSignal. Also, the EMGSignal will undoubtedly have complex characteristics that are beyond the scope of this discussion.

For AdjustMessage, generationTime and adjustmentAmount seem like reasonable attributes.

Figure 23.7 shows the attributes for these classes.

FIGURE 23.7

A closer look at EMGSignal and AdjustMessage.

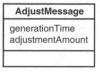

Use Cases

The JAD session I referred to earlier (which resulted in the design decision for an embedded system rather than a desktop) also resulted in a number of use cases, as depicted in Figure 23.8.

FIGURE 23.8

Use cases for GetAGrip.

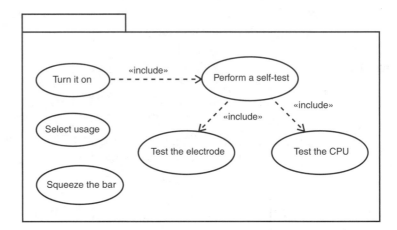

These use cases determine the capabilities to build into the system. "Turn it on" includes "Perform a self-test" which, in turn, includes "Test the electrode" and "Test the CPU."

"Select usage" refers to a number of different ways to set up the GetAGrip—ways that never occurred to Mr. Nar when he dreamed up this device. For example, the JAD participants said they'd like the option of setting "negative" repetitions—limited resistance when they squeeze the bars together, maximal resistance as they "unsqueeze."

This means we have to add an attribute to AdjustMessage to reflect the system usage. We can call it usageAlgorithm and give it the possible values increasingTension and negativeRep. Figure 23.9 shows the modified AdjustMessage class.

FIGURE 23.9

The modified AdjustMessage class.

Interactions

Let's direct our attention to "Squeeze the bar," and let's assume that the exerciser has selected the originally conceived mode—increasing resistance with increasing muscular activity. In this part of the model, we have to make sure that we consider time constraints and state changes. Assume that a clock tick interval is 20 microseconds, and that the time from receiving a signal to sending an adjustment message must take no longer than 10 clock ticks.

One more assumption: let's suppose that the RTOS kernel works pre-emptively. This necessitates a few modeling decisions. First, in order to reflect the kernel's operation, we'll treat the CPU's analyze(), adjust(), and generalHousekeeping() operations as threads, and assign them priorities.

To show them this way in our model, we have to treat them as classes—something we don't usually do with operations. This is an example of an advanced UML concept called *reification*—treating something as a class (or an object) that isn't usually treated that way. When you do that, you add richness to your model because your reified classes have relationships with other classes, have attributes of their own, and become structures that you can manipulate and store. In this case, reification allows us to show thread priorities as attributes and use the threads in our interaction diagrams.

Figure 23.10 shows the class structure for the GetAGrip threads.

FIGURE 23.10

Class structure for the GetAGrip threads

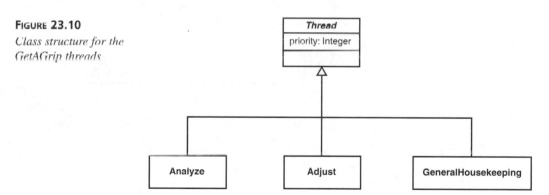

How should we prioritize the threads? When an interrupt request arrives, the CPU has to stop what it's doing, remember its context, and service the interrupt with an ISR. Our processISR() operation grabs the EMGSignal's amplitude and the other complex signal characteristics and places them in memory for analyze() to work on. The analyze() operation, then, has to have the highest priority. The adjust() operation should follow. The generalHousekeeping() operation should have the lowest priority.

Here's an example of how all this would play together preemptively. If the CPU is in the middle of carrying out some general housekeeping operations and a signal arrives, it interrupts what the CPU is doing. The CPU executes processISR() and extracts the appropriate values from the signal. What happens next? Going back to the general housekeeping would be unproductive. Instead, the CPU executes the highest priority operation, analyze(), followed by adjust().

Figure 23.11 shows a sequence diagram for "Squeeze the bar." Figure 23.12 shows a collaboration diagram for this use case. In both diagrams, we use curly brackets to indicate time constraints (as measured by clock ticks).

FIGURE 23.11

Sequence diagram for "Squeeze the bar."

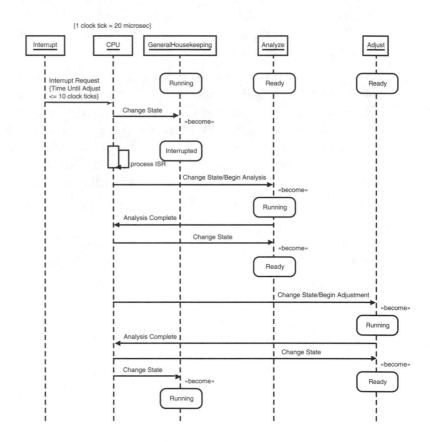

FIGURE 23.12

Collaboration diagram for "Squeeze the bar."

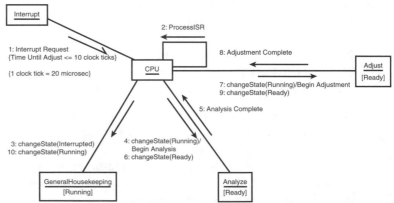

General State Changes

In addition to changes of state within an interaction, we can examine systemwide state changes. Generally, we expect that the GetAGrip will be either in the Working state or the Waiting state (between sets of an exercise, for example). It can also be in the Off state. As you might imagine, the Working state is a composite. Figure 23.13 presents the details.

FIGURE 23.13
GetAGrip state changes.

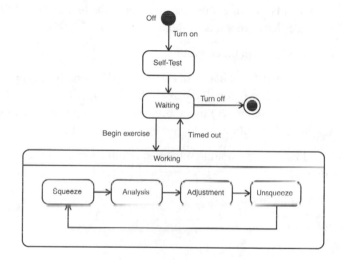

Deployment

How will GetAGrip look once it's implemented? Figure 23.14 is a deployment diagram that shows the parts of the system, along with a battery that supplies the power.

FIGURE 23.14
A deployment diagram for GetAGrip.

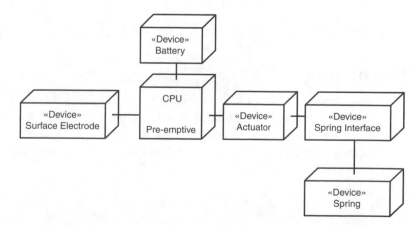

Flexing Their Muscles

When the partners received the UML diagrams for the GetAGrip, the wheels started turning.

"This is a concept we can expand on," said Goniff.

"How so?" asked Nar.

"Think about it. How many muscles are there in the human body? We can build a smart exercise device that covers lots of them."

"Really?" asked Nar again, enthralled.

"Sure," said Goniff. "If we take the electrode-CPU-springs concept a step or two further, we can develop a smart, portable barbell that people could take with them when they travel. It wouldn't weigh very much because lightweight springs would provide the resistance and the CPU would provide the smarts. We could call it 'GetABuild.'"

"Yeah," said Nar, "or we could go in another direction and make a separate machine for each body part."

"Sure. Something like 'GetAChest'."

"Or 'GetAnArm'."

"Or 'GetALeg'."

"How about 'GetALegUp'!"

At this point, LaHudra couldn't take it anymore.

"I've got one for the both of you," he said to his partners.

"What's that?" they asked in unison.

"Get a life."

Summary

An embedded system is a computer that lives inside another type of device, like an appliance. Programming an embedded system requires a great deal of knowledge about the characteristics of the device the system resides in. An embedded system can be *soft*, meaning that it doesn't have to meet deadlines, or *hard*, meaning that it does.

23

Time, threads (simple programs that are parts of an application), and interrupts (hardware devices that let a CPU know an event has occurred) are important embedded system concepts. One particular interrupt, the clock tick, occurs at regular intervals and acts as a system "heartbeat."

A real-time operating system (RTOS) directs traffic among threads and interrupts. The kernel is the part of the RTOS that manages the time the CPU spends on individual threads. The kernel's scheduler determines which thread will execute next. A kernel might be pre-emptive (in which a higher-priority thread preempts an interrupted lower-priority thread when an interrupt service routine finishes) or non-pre-emptive (in which the interrupted thread resumes after the interrupt service routine finishes).

We applied these concepts by modeling a "smart" exercise device that varies its resistance as a function of how hard a muscle is working.

Q&A

Q You mentioned "smart" systems. Do these embedded systems ever include anything like Artificial Intelligence?

A Absolutely. One subfield of AI, called "fuzzy logic," is at the heart of numerous kinds of embedded systems.

Q Is one type of RTOS more appropriate than another for certain types of embedded systems applications?

A Yes. One type we didn't elaborate on, the superloop, is the simplest RTOS. It's often embedded in high-volume applications like toys. The pre-emptive kernel is the RTOS of choice for hard systems.

Workshop

I've embedded some questions here to test your newfound knowledge, and I've embedded the answers in Appendix A, "Quiz Answers."

Quiz

1. What is an embedded system?
2. What is an asynchronous event?
3. In terms of embedded systems, what is a "hard" system? What is a "soft" system?
4. What happens in a "pre-emptive kernel"?

Exercises

1. Imagine an embedded system for a toaster. Assume that the toaster has a sensor that looks at a slice of bread as it's toasting and can sense how dark it is. Assume also that you can set how dark you want the toast. Draw a class diagram of this system. Include the sensor, CPU, and heating element (and the slice of bread!).

2. Draw a sequence diagram for the embedded toaster system. Justify your choice of a pre-emptive or a non-pre-emptive kernel. Just for the heck of it, draw a deployment diagram too.

Hour **24**

Shaping the Future of the UML

In this hour, we wrap up with a look at some current extensions to the UML and some potential extensions. You'll cover

- Extensions for business
- Lessons from the business extensions
- Modeling GUIs
- Modeling expert systems

Here we are in the final hour. It's been a long haul, but in the process you've seen a lot of the UML. In the last two hours, you've looked at applications in hot areas. In this hour, we wrap it all up with a current UML extension and a look at some other areas for applying the UML.

We discussed UML extensions in Hour 14, "Understanding the Foundations of the UML." As we noted then, you can extend the UML by adding stereotypes that customize your model to your domain. You can also add graphic stereotypes that clarify the information your model conveys. Deployment diagrams are great examples of this because clip art often substitutes for the UML cube icons.

The goal of this hour is to start you thinking about how you would apply the UML in your domain. Like any language, the UML is evolving. Its future depends on how modelers like you use and extend it.

Extensions for Business

One popular extension is a set of stereotypes designed to model a business. The stereotypes abstract some of the major ideas of what a business is all about. You can visualize them in terms of UML symbols you already know or as specialized icons (created by UML Amigo Ivar Jacobson). The intent is to model business-world situations, rather than to serve as the basis for software construction.

NEW TERM   Within a business, one obvious class is a *worker*. In the context of this UML extension, a worker acts within the business, interacts with other workers, and participates in use cases. A worker can either be an *internal worker* or a *case worker*. An internal worker interacts with other workers inside the business, and a case worker interacts with actors outside the business. An *entity* doesn't initiate any interactions, but it does participate in use cases. Workers interact with entities.

Figure 24.1 shows the customary UML notation for these stereotypes, along with the specialized icons. For each one, I've included an example from the restaurant domain.

FIGURE **24.1**

Stereotypes for business modeling.

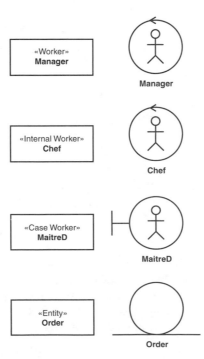

NEW TERM   The business extensions include two association stereotypes—*communicates and subscribes*. The first stereotype is for interactions between objects. The second describes an association between a source (called a *subscriber*) and a target (called a *publisher*). The source specifies a set of events. When one of those events occurs in the target, the source receives a notification.

NEW TERM   Entities combine to form *work units*, which are task-oriented sets of objects. Work units, classes, and associations combine to form *organization units*. An organization unit (which can include other organization units) corresponds to an organization unit of the business.

For another take on UML extensions for modeling businesses and business processes, see *Business Modeling with UML* by Hans-Erik Eriksson and Magnus Penker (John Wiley & Sons, 2000).

Lessons from the Business Extensions

The business extensions teach us some valuable lessons. First, it's apparent that with a little imagination, it's possible to come up with simple icons and representations that capture fundamental aspects of a domain. The operative word is "simple." Second, the representations help us think about, and create solutions in, a domain.

We'll consider these lessons as we try and move the UML into two important modeling efforts—graphic user interfaces and expert systems.

Graphic User Interfaces

A hallmark of contemporary software packages, the graphic user interface (GUI) is here to stay. GRAPPLE and other development processes and methodologies devote a JAD session to the development of an application's GUI.

In a design document, you typically include screen shots to show your client and your developers what the GUI will look like to the users. For several reasons, you still might want a specialized diagram to model a GUI.

Connecting to Use Cases

The primary reason has to do with use cases. Like most parts of a development effort, GUI development is use case–driven. In fact, the GUI connects directly to use cases because it's the window (pardon the pun) through which the end-user initiates and completes use cases. It might be difficult to use screen shots to capture the relationship between screens and use cases.

Another reason is that we might want to capture the evolution in the thought process as the GUI takes shape. In GRAPPLE, GUI development starts when end-users participating in the JAD session manipulate post-it sticky notes (which represent onscreen controls) on large sheets of paper (which represent screens). It would be helpful to have a type of diagram that captures the results of these manipulations directly—one that a modeler could easily change when the JAD participants modify the design.

A diagram that shows the connections of the screens to the use cases will help the JAD participants remember what each screen is supposed to do when they're laying out the screen components. Showing the use case connections will also help ensure that all use cases are implemented in the final design.

Modeling the GUI

A typical UML model would present a particular application's window as a composite of a number of controls, as in Figure 24.2.

FIGURE 24.2
A UML model of a window.

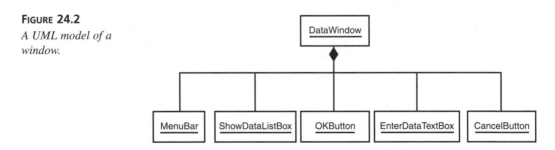

We can use attributes to add the spatial location of each component—a horizontal location and a vertical location both measured in pixels. Another pair of attributes could represent the component's size (height and width). It's easier to comprehend those parameters, however, if we visualize them. We can specify that a package will represent a window, and that the location and size of objects within the package reflects their location and size in the window. Figure 24.3 does this.

Figure 24.4 is the hybrid diagram that adds the finishing touch by showing the connections with use cases.

This type of modeling doesn't preclude showing screen shots. Instead, it can be a helpful addition—a schematic diagram that keeps the big picture in view.

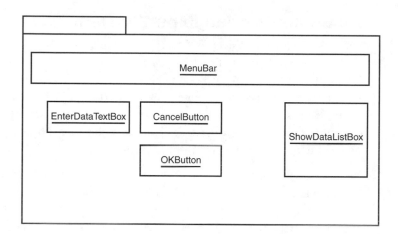

FIGURE 24.3
A model of a window that shows the locations of components.

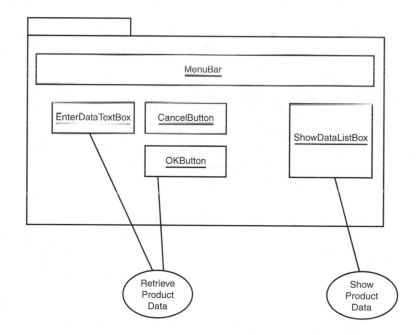

FIGURE 24.4
Modeling a window and showing how onscreen components connect to use cases.

Expert Systems

Expert systems experienced a surge in popularity in the 1980s. Something of a curiosity when they first appeared, today they're part of the mainstream of computing.

An expert system is designed to capture the insights and expertise of a human expert in a specific domain. It stores that expertise in a computer program. The intent is to use the expert system to answer repetitive questions so the human expert doesn't have to, or to store the expertise so that it's available when the expert is not.

Components of an Expert System

NEW TERM The expertise resides in the expert system's *knowledge base*, as a set of *if-then* rules. The *if-part* of each rule describes some real-world situation in the expert's domain. The *then-part* of each rule indicates the course of action to take in that situation. How does the expertise get into the knowledge base? A *knowledge engineer* holds extensive interviews with an expert, records the results, and represents the results in software. It's similar to the interview that takes place in a domain analysis, although knowledge engineering sessions are typically more extensive.

The knowledge base isn't the only component in an expert system. If it were, an expert system would merely be a laundry list of *if-then* rules. What's needed is a mechanism for working through the knowledge base to solve a problem. That mechanism is called an *inference engine*. Another necessary piece of the puzzle is a *work area* that holds the conditions of a problem the system has to solve. One more component, of course, is the user interface for entering the problem conditions. Condition entry may proceed via checklist, question-and-multiple-choice-answer, or in extremely sophisticated systems via natural language. Figure 24.5 shows a UML class diagram of an expert system.

FIGURE 24.5

A class diagram of an expert system.

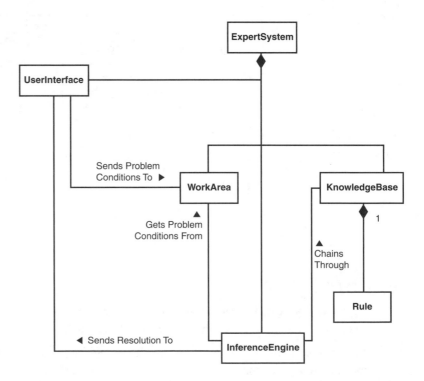

To interact with an expert system, a user enters the conditions of a problem into the user interface, which stores them in the work area. The inference engine uses those conditions to go through the knowledge base and find a solution. Figure 24.6 presents a sequence diagram for this process.

FIGURE 24.6

Interacting with an expert system.

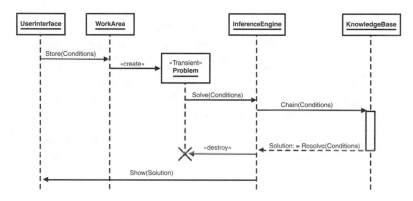

If you can form an analogy between an expert system and a human, you've pretty much got it: The work area is roughly analogous to a person's short term memory, the knowledge base is like the long term memory, and the inference engine is the problem-solving process. When you "rack your brain" to come up with an answer to a sticky problem, you're doing something like what an expert system does.

An Example

An inference engine usually goes through its knowledge base ("racks its brain") in one of two ways, and the best way to explain is with an example. Suppose we have an expert system that captures the expertise of a plumber. If you had a leaky faucet, you'd use the expert system by entering the details of the leak into the system. The inference engine would do the rest.

Two of the rules in the knowledge base might look like this:

Rule 1:

IF you have a leaky faucet

AND the faucet is a compression faucet

AND the leak is in the handle

THEN tighten the packing nut

Rule 2:

IF the packing nut is tight

AND the leak persists

THEN replace the packing

Without getting into the specifics of the plumbing world, suffice it to say that these two rules are obviously related—notice the similarity between the then-part of Rule 1 and the if-part of Rule 2. That similarity is the basis for working through the knowledge base (which typically has many, many more than two rules). The inference engine might start with a potential solution, like "replace the packing" from Rule 2, and work backward to see whether the specifics of the problem demand that solution.

How does the inference engine work backward? It looks at the if-part of the rule that has the solution and tries to find a rule whose then-part matches. In our two-rule example, that's easy—Rule 1 has a matching then-part. In industrial-strength applications, it's not so easy because a knowledge base might store hundreds, even thousands, of rules.

After the inference engine has found a rule, it checks to see whether the conditions in the if-part match the conditions of the problem. If they do, the engine keeps moving in the same direction—a matching if-part, check the if-part, another matching if-part, and so forth. When the inference engine runs out of rules, it asks the user for more information. The point of all this is that if the path through the rules is successful (that is, matches the conditions of the problem), the expert system offers the original potential solution as the solution to the problem. If not, the system tries a new path.

NEW TERM This technique of trying a solution and seeing whether the associated conditions match the conditions of the problem is called *backward chaining*—"backward" because it starts with then-parts and proceeds to examine if-parts.

NEW TERM As you can imagine, another technique starts with if-parts and matches then-parts, and it's called *forward chaining*. Here's how it works. The user enters the conditions of the problem, and the inference engine finds a rule whose if-part matches the conditions. It checks that rule's then-part and looks for a rule whose if-part matches that then-part. In our example, suppose Rule 1's if-part matches the problem conditions. The inference engine checks Rule 1's then-part and then looks for a rule with a matching if-part. Again, this is easy in our case with only two rules. When the system runs out of rules to match, it offers the then-part of the final rule as the solution. The "forward" in "forward chaining" refers to this movement from if-parts to then-parts.

If we were to model an expert system as in Figure 24.5, it would be helpful to add a stereotype that indicates the type of chaining the inference engine performs. We would add either «forward chaining» or «backward chaining» to the composite ExpertSystem class.

Both kinds of chaining are examples of the Chain of Responsibility design pattern you saw earlier. In each one, the system searches for a rule's successor.

Just as the Chain of Responsibility sometimes ends without finding a successor, an expert system doesn't always come up with a solution.

Modeling the Knowledge Base

What can the UML add to all this, and why would we want it to? One of the sticking points in expert system development is the lack of a solid standard for a visual representation of the knowledge base rules. A UML-based representation would go a long way toward standardizing the field and toward encouraging good documentation practices. It's not enough for the knowledge to reside in a software representation in a knowledge base—the rules should all be in a document as well.

Another sticking point is that use case analyses are rarely done in the course of developing an expert system. A use case analysis, complete with UML use case diagrams, might help determine the best type of inference engine to use in an expert system implementation. The deployment diagram is still another possible point of UML applicability to expert system development. Although they were once standalone devices, expert systems today typically have to fit into a corporate computing structure and interact smoothly with other systems. Deployment diagrams can be used to show where an expert system resides and how it depends on (and feeds into) other areas of information technology. Given that an actor in a use case diagram can be another system, the deployment diagram and the use case diagram can work together to provide views of an expert system in a corporate context.

Let's focus on the knowledge base. How can we represent a knowledge base in the spirit of the UML? One possibility, of course, is to represent each rule as an object. Have one of the attributes be the if-part, another be the then-part, and add attributes as necessary. Figure 24.7 shows this arrangement.

Although this is eminently doable (and many developers do it), I believe rules are important enough to warrant their own representation—and not only because they serve as the foundation of knowledge bases in expert systems. The growing emphasis on knowledge management within organizations and institutions calls out for a unique way to represent rules.

FIGURE 24.7

Representing rules as objects.

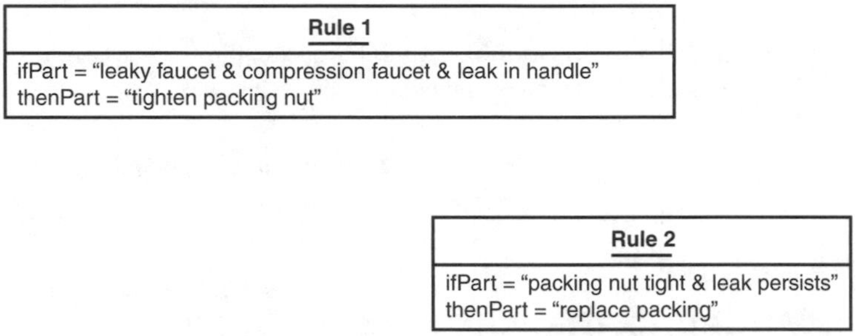

Rule 1
ifPart = "leaky faucet & compression faucet & leak in handle" thenPart = "tighten packing nut"

Rule 2
ifPart = "packing nut tight & leak persists" thenPart = "replace packing"

What would that unique representation look like? First, we'd want to make sure we show something that gives the contents of a rule's if-part, and the contents of its then-part. In order to make this representation useful, we'd also want to somehow visualize the interconnections among rules.

This can all get very thorny very quickly. Industrial-strength rules tend to have a lot more information than the two plumbing rules I showed you, and the rules tend to proliferate. We have to balance the proliferations against the need for simplicity.

Let's first create a simple icon to represent a rule. We'll begin with a box divided by a centered vertical line. The left half of the box represents the if-part and the right half the then-part. Within each part, we'll write a meaningful summary of the contents. Figure 24.8 shows what I mean, using the two plumbing rules as an example.

FIGURE 24.8

The two plumbing rules cast into a visual representation.

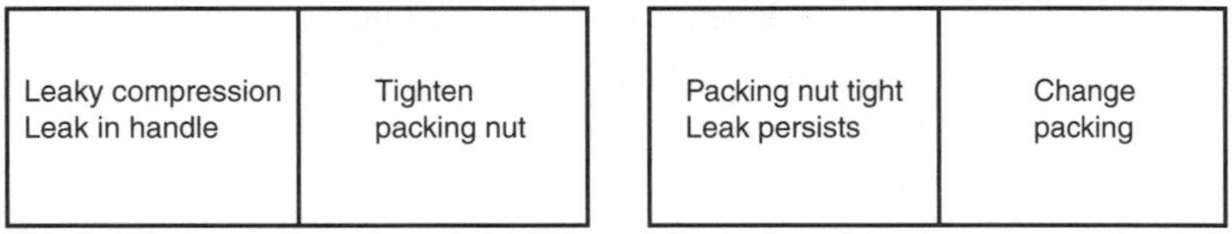

Leaky compression Leak in handle	Tighten packing nut

Packing nut tight Leak persists	Change packing

Now we have to incorporate some identification information for each rule. Let's add a compartment across the top of each box that holds a numerical identifier. This accomplishes two things: (1) It makes each rule unique, and (2) It shows where to go in a rules catalog for a complete description and explanation of the rule. If a rule is part of a subgroup of rules (as in a "faucet" subset of our plumbing knowledge base), we can treat the subgroup as a package. Then we add the package information to the identifier in the UML's usual way—have the package name precede a pair of colons that precede the identifier. Figure 24.9 shows this addition.

Now, we'll represent the relation between the two as a line between the then-part of Rule 1 and the if-part of Rule 2. Figure 24.10 shows the connection.

FIGURE 24.9

Adding an identifier to each rule.

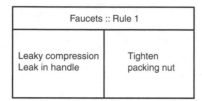
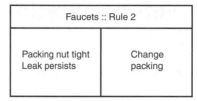

Faucets :: Rule 1	
Leaky compression Leak in handle	Tighten packing nut

Faucets :: Rule 2	
Packing nut tight Leak persists	Change packing

FIGURE 24.10

Connecting the then-part of one rule to the if-part of the other.

Faucets :: Rule 1	
Leaky compression Leak in handle	Tighten packing nut

Faucets :: Rule 2	
Packing nut tight Leak persists	Change packing

Unlike the two-rule set in our example, a rule in a real expert system is usually related to more than one other rule. If the related rules aren't nearby—either in the knowledge base or in the documentation—it will be helpful to have a way of showing the relationship even when we can't draw connecting lines.

Compartments at the bottom of the icon will do the trick. If we put them below the compartments we already have, we can show identifiers for other rules, as in Figure 24.11. The lower compartment on the left identifies rules whose then-parts connect to this rule's if-part. The lower compartment on the right identifies rules whose if-parts connect to this rule's then-part.

FIGURE 24.11

Compartments at the bottom of the rule icon identify related rules.

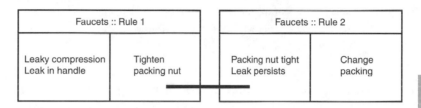

Faucet :: Rule 1	
Leaky compression Leak in handle	Tighten packing nut
10, 11, 15, Pipe ::22	2, 6, Washer ::22

Faucet :: Rule 2	
Packing nut tight Leak persists	Change packing
2, 13, Pipe ::15	17, 18, 31

As is the case with class diagrams, compartments within the rule icon could be elided depending on the purpose of the diagram. The idea is to concisely show the interconnections among rules as well as their content, and thus clearly communicate the nature of the knowledge base.

The model for the expert system is more "drastic" than the model for the GUI, in that it proposes a new "view element" (the rule icon) for the UML. The model for the GUI, on the other hand, is a hybrid diagram that consists of current UML elements.

24

Web Applications

Since the first edition of this book was published, a number of analysts have created sets of UML extensions for important domains. In this section, we examine one for Web application development.

Simply put, a Web-based system allows an end-user with a browser (a software application on a client computer) to access and view a document that resides on a host computer (a server). A *Web application* augments a Web-based system by adding business functionality, like the ability to add selections to a shopping cart and to complete transactions via credit card.

The Web Application Extension (WAE) to the UML is the brainchild of Rational's Jim Conallen. The WAE includes about a dozen graphic stereotype icons, additional stereotyped associations, attributes, and some "well-formedness" rules for combining all these elements to create a model.

Each element is associated with zero or more tagged values. Recall from Hour 14 that a tagged value is a bracketed string consisting of a tag, an equal sign (=), and a value. Its purpose is to provide important information about an element. In the WAE, for example, the tagged value for a Web page shows the path that specifies the Web page on the Web server.

While we're on the subject, Figure 24.12 shows the WAE icon for a Web page.

FIGURE 24.12

The WAE icon for a Web page.

Notice the similarity between this icon and the UML icon for a note. The folded corner is designed to reinforce the notion of a "page." Keep in mind that conceptually a Web page is a class with attributes and operations, and a specific Web page is an object. (See Exercise 1.)

Figure 24.13 shows WAE icons for three types of pages that can appear in a Web application: a server page, a JavaServer Pages (JSP) page, and an Active Server Page. Figure 24.14 shows three more: client page, frameset, and servlet.

The WAE has icons for structures other than pages. For example, when you surf the Web you often see pages whose components allow you to enter information into the page (check boxes, radio buttons, combo boxes, and more). A collection of these components for a particular page is called a *form*, and Figure 24.15 shows the WAE icon for a form.

FIGURE 24.13

The WAE icons for (left to right) server page, JSP page, and Active Server Page.

FIGURE 24.14

The WAE icons for (left to right) client page, frameset, and servlet.

FIGURE 24.15

The WAE icon for a form.

The WAE is much richer than the description in this section. For further details, see Jim Conallen's *Building Web Applications with UML* (Addison-Wesley, 2000).

You'll find a growing library of stereotype icons at www.rationalrose.com/stereotypes.

That's All, Folks

We've come to the end of the road. Now that you have a bag full of UML tricks, you're ready to go out on your own and apply them to your domain. You'll find that as you gain experience, you'll add to that bag of tricks. You might even come up with some suggestions for adding to the UML. If you do, you'll be carrying on a grand tradition.

Just after the beginning of the twentieth century, the renowned mathematician Alfred North Whitehead pointed out the importance of symbols and their use. A symbol, he said, stands for the presentation of an idea: The importance of a symbol is that it quickly and concisely shows how an idea fits together with a complex set of other ideas.

Just after the beginning of the twenty-first century, Whitehead's observations still ring true for the world of system development. Carefully crafted symbols show us the thought processes and complexities behind the wonderful systems we propose to build, and help us ensure their efficient performance when we build them.

Summary

As modelers extend and mold the UML to fit their needs, they'll shape its future. In this hour, we looked at an extension for business modeling and suggested some ways of applying the UML to other areas. We also examined the Web Application Extension (WAE), which is a UML extension for modeling Web applications.

Taking a lesson from the business extension's simplicity, we explored ways for modeling GUIs and expert systems. To model a GUI, we set up a hybrid diagram that shows the spatial relationships of screen components and their connections with use cases. This has the advantage of showing the evolution of a GUI as it takes shape, and keeping the appropriate use cases within the focus of attention.

In an expert system the *if-then* rule is the building block of the knowledge base, the component that contains the knowledge of a human domain expert. We suggested a diagram that visualizes the rules and their interrelationships. In this diagram, a box divided into compartments models the rule. One compartment contains the rule identifier, another summarizes the if-part, another the then-part, and two others show related rules. Links to nearby rules appear as connecting lines between appropriate parts of the rules.

The WAE encompasses a set of stereotyped icons, stereotyped associations, attributes, and rules for modeling a Web application. Many of the icons are designed to reinforce the idea of a page.

Q&A

Q Although in principle it looks like an expert system isn't particularly difficult to model, it seems like it would be an extremely hard program to write.

A It would be if you had to create one from scratch. Fortunately, most of the programming is done for you in a package called an *expert system shell*. All the components are ready-made. You just add the knowledge. Extracting the knowledge from a human expert is not always an easy task, however.

Q Haven't vendors of expert system shells come up with a notation for representing rules?

A Yes, and that's the problem. No single notation is standard. This field typifies the statement (attributed, I think, to famed computer scientist Edsger Dijkstra): "The great thing about standards is that there are so many of them."

Workshop

The questions in this workshop test your knowledge about applying the UML to GUIs and expert systems. The answers to the quiz questions are in Appendix A, "Quiz Answers."

Quiz

1. What are the advantages of our model of a GUI?
2. What are the components of an expert system?
3. What expert system features does our diagram encompass?

Exercises

1. Visit the home page of Sams Publishing (www.samspublishing.com) and use the WAE Web page icon to model that page. Next, model the page without using the WAE icon—that is, with a standard UML icon.

2. Imagine that an appliance manufacturer wants to create a Web-based expert system that provides troubleshooting information. When something goes wrong, an appliance owner would be able to go to this Web site, enter the symptoms, and receive advice on how to proceed. Perform a use case analysis, and use the information on expert systems and the WAE from this hour to create a rudimentary model of the Web site.

   Hints: Treat this as a class diagram. To show one page linking to another, use a simple message arrow (see Hour 9, "Working with Sequence Diagrams") that starts from the originating page and points to the target page. Then place a *Links to* stereotype near the arrow.

24

PART IV

Appendixes

APPENDIX A

Quiz Answers

Hour 1

1. Why is it necessary to have a variety of diagrams in a model of a system?

   Any system has a variety of stakeholders. Each type of UML diagram presents a view that speaks to one or more of these stakeholders.

2. Which diagrams give a static view of a system?

   These diagrams provide a static view: class, object, component, and deployment.

3. Which diagrams provide a dynamic view of a system (that is, show change over time)?

   These diagrams provide a dynamic view: use case, state, sequence, activity, and collaboration.

Hour 2

1. What is an object?

    An object is an instance of a class.

2. How do objects work together?

    Objects work together by sending messages to one another.

3. What does multiplicity indicate?

    Multiplicity indicates the number of objects of one class that relate to one object of an associated class.

4. Can two objects associate with one another in more than one way?

    Yes. Two persons, for example, can be associated as friends and as co-workers.

Hour 3

1. How do you represent a class in the UML?

    You use a rectangle to represent a class. The class's name is inside the rectangle, near the top.

2. What information can you show on a class icon?

    You can show the class's attributes, operations, and responsibilities.

3. What is a constraint?

    Represented by text enclosed in curly brackets, a constraint is a set of one or more rules that a class follows.

4. Why would you attach a note to a class icon?

    You attach a note to a class icon to add information that's not in the attributes, operations, or responsibilities. You might, for example, want the user of the model to refer to a particular document that contains additional information about the class.

Hour 4

1. How do you represent multiplicity?

    At one end of the association line, you put the number of objects from the class at the far end that relate to one object in the near end.

2. How do you discover inheritance?

    In the list of classes in your initial model, find two or more classes that share attributes and operations. Either another class in your initial model will be the parent of these classes, or you will have to create a parent class.

3. What is an abstract class?

An abstract class is a class that serves as the basis for inheritance but provides no objects.

4. What's the effect of a qualifier?

The effect of a qualifier is to reduce a one-to-many multiplicity to a one-to-one multiplicity.

Hour 5

1. What is the difference between an aggregation and a composite?

Both an aggregation and a composite specify a part-whole association between component classes and a whole. In an aggregation, a component may be part of more than one whole. In a composite, a component can be part of only one whole.

2. What is realization? How is realization similar to inheritance? How does realization differ from inheritance?

Realization is the relationship between a class and an interface. The class is said to *realize* the operations in the interface. Realization is similar to inheritance in that a class takes operations from its interface and can inherit procedures from its parent class. Realization is different from inheritance in that a class takes no attributes from its interface but can inherit attributes from its parent class.

3. Name the three levels of visibility and describe what each one means.

If a class's attributes and operations have public visibility, another class may use them. If they have protected visibility, a child (or other descendant) class may use them. If they have private visibility, only the owning class can use them. An interface's operations have public visibility.

Hour 6

1. What do you call the entity that initiates a use case?

The entity that initiates a use case is called an *actor*.

2. What is meant by "including a use case"?

"Including a use case" means that some of the steps in a scenario in one use case are the same as the steps from another use case. Instead of listing all those same steps, we just indicate the use case they're part of.

3. What is meant by "extending a use case"?

"Extending" a use case means to add steps to an existing use case. You do that to create a new use case.

4. Is a use case the same as a scenario?

   No. A use case is a collection of scenarios.

Hour 7

1. Name two advantages to visualizing a use case.

   With visualization, you can (1) show use cases to users and get them to tell you additional information, and (2) combine them with other kinds of diagrams.

2. Describe generalization and grouping, the relationships among use cases that you learned about in this hour. Name two situations in which you would group use cases.

   In generalization, one use case inherits the meaning and behaviors of another. Grouping is the organization of a collection of use cases into packages.

3. What are the similarities between classes and use cases? What are the differences?

   Similarities: Both are structural elements. Both can inherit. Differences: The class consists of attributes and operations. The use case consists of scenarios, and each scenario consists of a sequence of steps. The class provides a static view of the parts of the system, the use case provides a dynamic view of behavior. The class shows the inside of the system. The use case shows how the system looks to an outsider.

Hour 8

1. In what important way does a state diagram differ from a class diagram, an object diagram, or a use case diagram?

   A state diagram models the states of just a single object. A class diagram, object diagram, or a use case diagram models a system, or at least part of a system.

2. Define these terms: *transition*, *event,* and *action*.

   A transition is a change from one state to another. An event is an occurrence that causes a transition to occur. An action is an executable computation that results in a state change.

3. What is a *triggerless transition*?

   A triggerless transition is a transition that occurs because of activities within a state, rather than in response to an event.

4. What is the difference between sequential substates and concurrent substates?

   Substates are states within a state. Sequential substates occur one after the other. Concurrent substates occur at the same time.

5. What is a *pseudostate*? Give examples.

   A pseudostate is a state that has no state variables and no activities. Examples are the initial state, final state, and history states.

Hour 9

1. Define *synchronous message* and *asynchronous message*.

   When an object sends a synchronous message, it waits for an answer before moving on. When it sends an asynchronous message, it doesn't wait for an answer.

2. In a generic sequence diagram, how do you represent the flow of control implied by an "if" statement?

   To represent the flow of control implied by an "if" statement, you enclose the "if" statement's condition in square brackets.

3. How do you represent the flow of control implied by a "while" statement?

   To represent the flow of control implied by a "while" statement, enclose the condition in square brackets, and precede the left bracket with an asterisk.

4. In a sequence diagram, how do you represent a newly created object?

   A newly created object is represented by an object rectangle positioned in the timeline (that is, along the top-to-bottom dimension) so that its location represents the time it was created in the sequence. Add "Create()" or «Create» to the message arrow that points to the created object.

Hour 10

1. How do you represent a message in a collaboration diagram?

   By an arrow near the association line that joins two objects. The arrow points to the receiving object.

2. How do you show sequential information in a collaboration diagram?

   By attaching a number to the label of a message arrow. The number corresponds to the sequential order of the message.

3. How do you show changes of state?

   Inside an object's rectangle, indicate its state. Add another rectangle for that object and show the changed state. Connect the two with a dashed line and label the line with a «becomes» stereotype.

4. What is meant by the "semantic equivalence" of two diagram types?

   The two types of diagrams present the same information and you can turn one into another.

Hour 11

1. What are the two ways of representing a decision point?

   One way is to show a diamond with branches coming out of it. The other is to show branches coming directly out of an activity. Either way, put a bracketed condition on each branch.

2. What is a swimlane?

   In an activity diagram, a swimlane is a segment that shows the activities a particular role performs.

3. How do you represent signal transmission and reception?

   Use a convex pentagon to show signal transmission and a concave pentagon to show signal reception.

Hour 12

1. What are the three types of components?

   The three types of components are deployment components, work product components, and execution components.

2. What do you call the relationship between a component and its interface?

   The relationship between a component and its interface is called *realization*.

3. What are the two ways of representing this relationship?

   You can represent the interface as a rectangle (like a class icon) and the connection with the component as a dashed line with an empty triangle that points to the interface (the usual realization relationship). Alternatively, you can use a small circle to represent the interface, connected by a solid line to the component. In this context, the solid line represents realization.

4. What is an *export interface*? What is an *import interface*?

   An export interface is an interface that one component makes available so that other components can use its services. When another component uses these services, it's an import interface.

Hour 13

1. How do you represent a node in a deployment diagram?

   A cube represents a node in a deployment diagram.

2. What kinds of information can appear on a node?

Information on a node can include the node name, package name, and components deployed on the node.

3. What are the two kinds of nodes?

   The two kinds of nodes are processors (which can execute components) and devices (which connect to the outside world).

4. How does a token-ring network work?

   Computers in a token-ring network connect to multistation access units (MSAUs) connected in the form of a ring. The MSAUs pass a signal called a token around the ring. The position of the token indicates the computer that can send information at any moment.

Hour 14

1. What are the four layers of the UML?

   The four layers are the user objects layer, model layer, metamodel layer, and metametamodel layer.

2. What is a classifier?

   A classifier is any element that defines structure and behavior.

3. Why is it important to be able to extend the UML?

   When you start to use the UML to model real systems, you'll run into situations that are richer and more complex than the ones you find in textbooks and references. If you can extend the UML, you'll be able to reflect the nature of those real-world situations.

4. What are the UML's extension mechanisms?

   The UML's extension mechanisms are stereotypes, constraints, and tagged values.

Hour 15

1. What are some typical concerns of a client?

   Does the development team understand the problem? Do the team members understand the client's vision of how to solve it? What work-products can the client expect from the development team? How will the project manager report to the client? How far along is the team at any point?

2. What is meant by a development *methodology*?

   A development methodology sets the structure and nature of steps in a system development effort.

A

3. What is the "waterfall" method? What are its weaknesses?

In the waterfall method analysis, design, coding, and deployment follow one another sequentially.

4. What are the segments of GRAPPLE?

The segments of GRAPPLE are Requirements gathering, Analysis, Design, Development, and Deployment.

5. What is a JAD session?

A JAD (Joint Application Development) session brings together decision-makers from the client's organization, potential end-users of the system, and members of the development team. Some GRAPPLE JAD sessions pair the development team with just the users.

Hour 16

1. Which UML diagram is appropriate for modeling a business process?

The UML activity diagram is the one for modeling business processes.

2. How can you modify this diagram to show what the different roles do?

You can use the activity diagram to create a swimlane diagram. Each role is at the top of a "swimlane."

3. What is meant by "business logic"?

Business logic is a set of rules the business follows in specific situations.

Hour 17

1. How do we make use of the nouns in the interview with an expert?

Nouns become candidates for class names and attribute names.

2. How do we use the verbs and verb phrases?

Verbs and verb phrases become candidates for operations and for names of associations.

3. What is a "ternary" association?

A ternary association involves three classes.

4. How do you model a ternary association?

You model a ternary association by linking each of the three classes to a diamond. You write the name of the association near the diamond. Multiplicities in a ternary association reflect the number of instances of any two classes associated with a constant number of instances of the third.

Hour 18

1. How are we representing system requirements?

   We're using the UML package diagram along with use cases to represent system requirements.

2. Does class modeling stop after the domain analysis?

   Class modeling continues to evolve after the domain analysis.

3. What is the "schlepp factor"?

   This is the name I whimsically applied to the server having to walk around all over the restaurant. I just wanted to see if you were paying attention.

Hour 19

1. What are the parts of a typical use case diagram?

   The parts of a typical use case diagram are the initiating actor, the use case, and the benefiting actor.

2. What does it mean for a use case to "include" (or "use") another use case?

   "Including" a use case means that one use case incorporates the steps of another use case.

A

Hour 20

1. How do you represent an object that's created during the course of a sequence diagram?

   You represent a created object by placing it below the level of the other objects. You'll increase clarity if you add a «create» stereotype to the message leading to that object.

2. How is time represented in a sequence diagram?

   Time is represented as proceeding in the downward direction.

3. What is a "lifeline"?

   The lifeline is a dashed line descending from an object. It represents the existence of an object over time.

4. In a sequence diagram, how do you show an "activation," and what does it represent?

   An activation is represented as a small narrow rectangle on an object's lifeline. It represents the time period during which the object performs an action.

Hour 21

1. What is a task analysis?

    A task analysis is an analysis that a GUI designer carries out in order to understand what the user will do with the application associated with the GUI.

2. Which analysis that we've already done is roughly equivalent to a task analysis?

    The use case analysis is roughly equivalent to the task analysis.

3. What is a "clown-pants" design?

    A clown-pants design is a GUI design that incorporates an excessive amount of colors, component sizes, and fonts.

4. Give three reasons for limiting the use of color in a GUI.

    Three reasons to limit the use of color in a GUI are (1)The association of a color with a meaning may not be as obvious to the user as it is to the designer, (2)Too many colors will distract users from the task at hand, (3)Part of the user population may have some trouble distinguishing between colors.

Hour 22

1. How do you represent a parameterized class?

    The icon for a parameterized class is the standard class icon with a small box superimposed on the upper right corner. The small box consists of dashed lines.

2. What is "binding" and what are the two types of binding?

    "Binding" is the attachment of a value to a parameter. The two types of binding are "explicit" and "implicit."

3. What is a "design pattern"?

    A design pattern is a proven solution to a design problem. It's usable in a variety of situations, and you represent it in the UML as a parameterized collaboration.

4. What is the "Chain of Responsibility" design pattern?

    In the "Chain of Responsibility" design pattern, a client object initiates a request and passes it to the first in a chain of objects. If the first object can't handle the request, it passes it to the next. If that one can't handle the request, it passes it to the next, and so forth until an object can handle the request.

Hour 23

1. What is an embedded system?

   An embedded system is a computer system that resides inside some other kind of device, like a home appliance.

2. What is an asynchronous event?

   An event is asynchronous if you can't predict its occurrence.

3. In terms of embedded systems, what is a "hard" system? What is a "soft" system?

   A hard system has to meet time deadlines, but a soft system does not.

4. What happens in a "pre-emptive kernel"?

   In a pre-emptive kernel, after an ISR executes, the CPU doesn't return to the interrupted thread if a higher priority thread is in the ready state. Instead, it executes the higher priority thread.

Hour 24

1. What are the advantages of our model of a GUI?

   Our model can capture the thought processes in the evolution of a GUI and it keeps attention on the use cases connected with each screen.

2. What are the components of an expert system?

   The components of an expert system are a knowledge base, a work area, and an inference engine.

3. What expert system features does our diagram encompass?

   Our diagram shows the parts of a rule, associated rules, and the relationships among rules.

A

APPENDIX B

Modeling Tools for the UML

As you followed along with the book's discussion and did the exercises, you probably used a pencil and paper to create your diagrams. If you had to do that in your project-related modeling efforts, you'd quickly hit a number of snags. In addition to drawing those troublesome lines, circles, ellipses, and rectangles, you'd have a difficult time when you wanted to move them around and change the layout of a finished diagram.

Fortunately, technology comes to the rescue. A number of tools are available to help you create UML models. This appendix will give you a feel for three of them—Rational Rose, Select Enterprise, and Visual UML. We won't go into all their features and options, but you'll learn enough about each one to give you an impression of how they work and what they do.

Common Features

Although they have widely differing capabilities, the three modeling tools we'll look at have some common features. Each one allows "rubber-band" diagramming: Create a link between two elements and the link adjusts accordingly when you drag those elements around the screen. Each one allows at least some code generation, producing code stubs from models. Finally, all three have extensive tools and dialog boxes for editing.

Rational Rose

The market leader in UML modeling tools, Rational Rose is a product of the company that employs the Three Amigos. The latest version (Rose Enterprise 2001) has a number of useful features. On sequence diagrams, for example, the newest Rose adds indicators for creating objects and terminating them (as we discussed in Hour 9, "Working with Sequence Diagrams"). If you're creating models for Java-based systems, you'll find support for "Gang-of-Four" patterns (the subject of Hour 22, "Understanding Design Patterns").

Enterprise 2001 adds helpful User Interface features to the "classic" Rose screens that appear in Figures B.1-B.3. For example, the new version features "dockability" so that a user can customize and arrange the Rose workspace to meet his or her specific needs.

When you open the "classic" Rose (as I like to refer to Rose 98), you see the window in Figure B.1. As you'll see, the other tools have similar windows.

FIGURE B.1

Rational Rose's "classic" opening display.

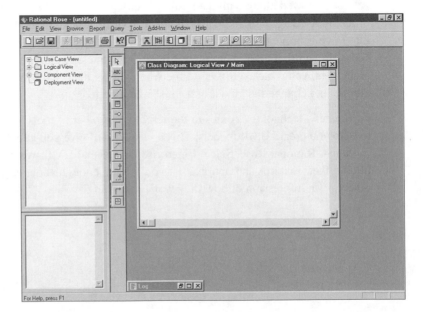

The pane on the left is the browser. The pane on the right holds the diagram window. In between is a palette of UML icons for a class diagram, which is the type of diagram that opens by default.

The browser is organized according to views—use case view, logical view, component view, and deployment view. To create a new diagram, you right-click on one of the views and the diagram choices for that view appear on a menu. Select one and a new diagram window opens. A palette of appropriate icons for that diagram also appears. Figure B.2 shows a use case diagram and its palette.

FIGURE B.2

A use case diagram and its palette in Rose.

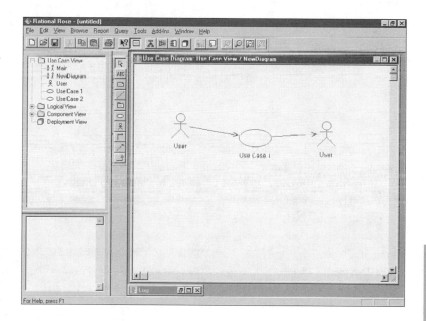

Rose adds a little pizzazz to its icons. When you want to show a class's attributes and operations as public, private, or protected, you end up with the adornments in Figure B.3.

For more information on Rational Rose (and to get a time-limited evaluation copy of Rational Rose 2001), visit http://www.rational.com.

Select Enterprise

As its name implies, Select Enterprise is designed to be a modeling tool for an entire enterprise. Toward that end, it automatically connects to a networked repository where it's accessible to modelers and model-users throughout an organization. The advantages to using a repository are that it tracks who checks the models out and back in, and it enables version control.

FIGURE B.3

Rose provides adornments for class icons.

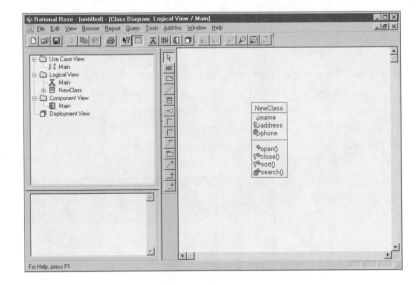

When you open a model, the Select window (see Figure B.4) bears a superficial resemblance to Rose's, but that's where the similarity ends. The two tools have decidedly different outlooks: While Rose focuses strictly on the UML, in the Select scheme of things the UML is one of several important modeling packages. Select Enterprise enables you to use non-UML symbol sets to draw data models and build business process models.

FIGURE B.4

Select Enterprise's display when you open a model.

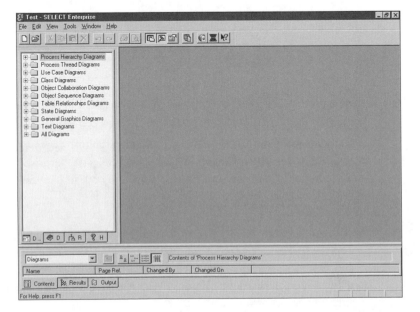

Figure B.5 shows a class diagram in Select. Note the «business» stereotypes—they appear as a default when you create a class.

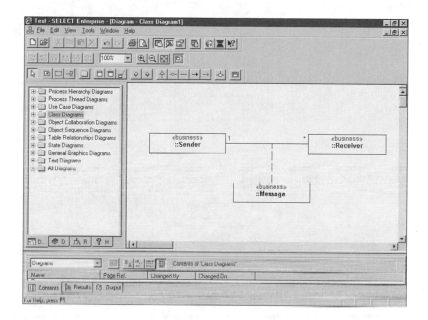

Aside from its own intrinsic contribution to a model, a Select class diagram is important for another reason. Select lets you create a state diagram only if you've already created a class to attach it to. Figure B.6 shows a state diagram. Note the name of the state diagram's class in the upper-left corner of the diagram.

To add richness to your model, you can link model items to one another. You can even link diagrams together, and you can run a report that shows which diagrams are linked to a particular diagram.

Aonix recently acquired the Select Enterprise toolset from Princeton Softech. Aonix already markets StP/UML, a UML-centric version of its popular modeling tool, Software through Pictures (StP). Having StP/UML and Select Enterprise under one corporate umbrella should result in significant changes to both in the years to come.

Visual UML

Now in Version 2.71, Visual UML continues to be a personal favorite. In fact, I used this tool to create many of the diagrams in this book.

B

FIGURE B.6

A state diagram in Select.

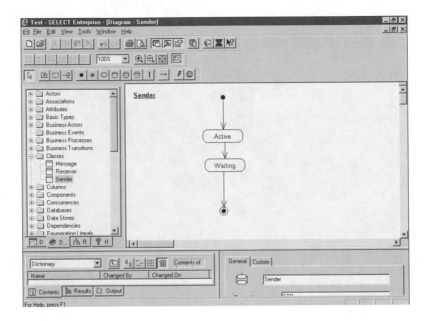

When you open Visual UML (Figure B.7 shows Version 2.71's opening screen), you see an uncluttered user interface that draws you in with its simplicity. If you know a little UML, you'll be drawing diagrams in Visual UML in no time.

FIGURE B.7

Visual UML's opening display.

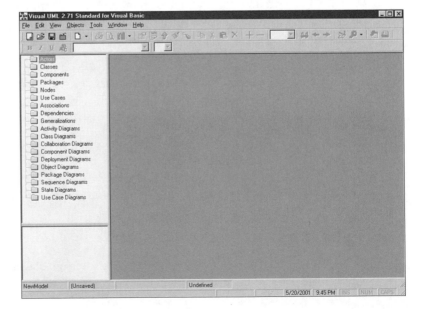

The browser/Explorer-like pane in the left side of Visual UML's window is a mechanism for creating and managing diagrams. All the diagram types (and some other UML elements) are on the top level. You're always just a couple of mouse clicks away from creating a new diagram.

Figure B.8 shows Version 2.71's palette and its window for building a class diagram. This tool's palettes provide some non-UML graphic support, as they allow you to draw boxes and lines on the diagram.

FIGURE B.8

Creating a class diagram in Visual UML.

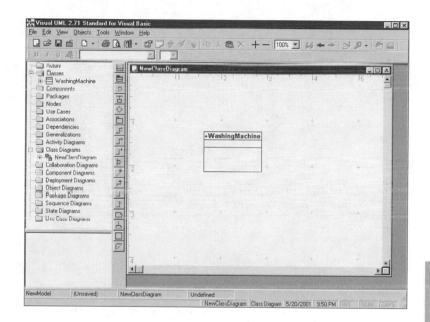

For good measure, you can link objects in one diagram to objects in another. The newest version offers expanded support for programming languages.

Go to http://www.visualuml.com to learn more about Visual UML.

The Ideal Modeling Tool

Each of the three modeling tools has a fine set of capabilities. Still, I can think of a few additional characteristics I'd like to see in a modeling tool.

One is flexibility. I'd often like to be able to use one diagram-type's icons in another to form a hybrid diagram. State icons can be helpful in the sequence diagram. The use case diagram's Actor icon can be helpful in a number of other diagrams. Microsoft acquired the Visio diagramming tool, and Visio's Enterprise edition has UML capabilities that incorporate this kind of flexibility. I look forward to ultimately seeing this in other modeling tools.

B

Another characteristic I would like to see is…more flexibility. In addition to importing icons from diagram-type to diagram-type, I'd be happy to see the ability to import clip art and use it as graphic stereotypes in diagrams. Perhaps some frequently used clips could be built into the tool.

Finally, a systematic semi-animated tutorial would be extremely helpful in any modeling tool. The tutorial could present elementary ideas about the UML and show how they map onto the modeling tool's capabilities. This would be a great service to people who are new to modeling.

APPENDIX C

A Summary in Pictures

This appendix presents some of the major aspects of each UML diagram.

Activity Diagram

FIGURE C.1

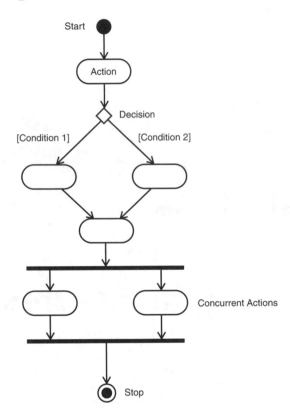

FIGURE C.2

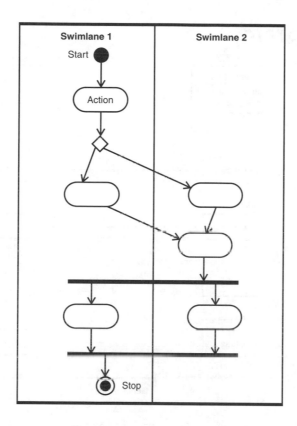

FIGURE C.3

C

Class Diagram

FIGURE C.4

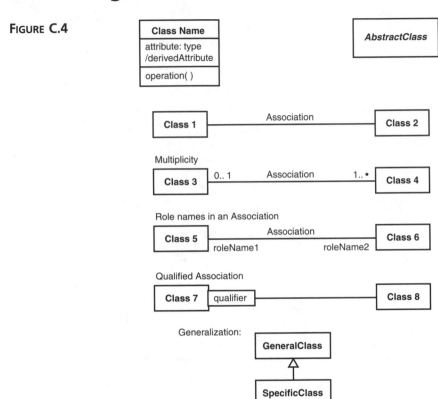

FIGURE C.5

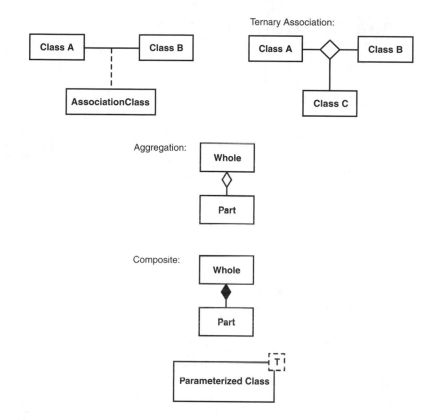

Collaboration Diagram

FIGURE C.6

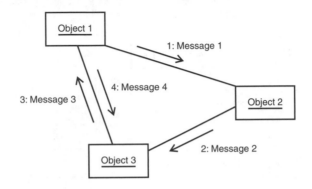

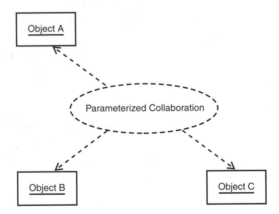

Component Diagram

FIGURE C.7

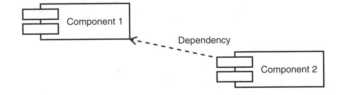

Deployment Diagram

FIGURE C.8

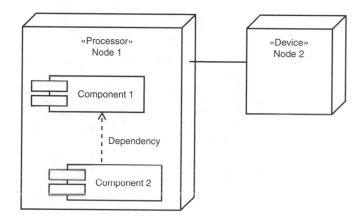

Sequence Diagram

FIGURE C.9

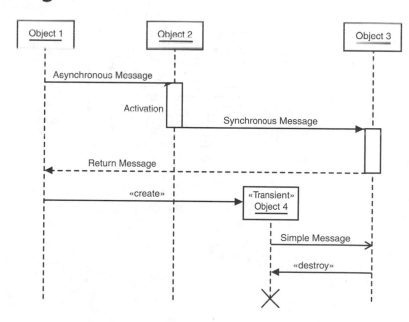

State Diagram

FIGURE C.10

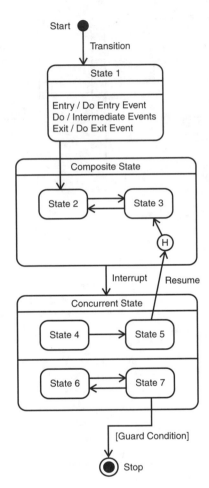

Use Case Diagram

FIGURE C.11

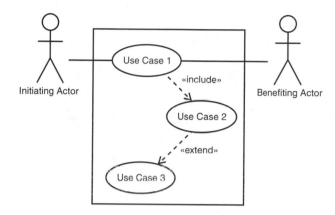

INDEX

G

Other Related Titles

Sams Teach Yourself Beginning Programming in 24 Hours
Greg Perry
ISBN: 0-672-31355-3
$19.99 US/$29.95 CAN

Sams Teach Yourself C++ for Linux in 21 Days
Jesse Liberty and David B. Horvath
ISBN: 0-672-31895-4
$39.99 US
$59.95 CAN

Sams Teach Yourself XML in 21 Days, 2nd Edition
Devan Shepherd
ISBN: 0-672-32093-2
$39.99 US
$59.95 CAN

The Object-Oriented Thought Process
Matt Weisfeld
ISBN: 0-672-31853-9
$29.99 US
$44.95 CAN

Sams Teach Yourself ASP.NET in 21 Days
Chris Payne
ISBN: 0-672-32168-8
$39.99 US
$59.95 CAN

Sams Teach Yourself C++ in 21 Days, Complete Compiler Kit, 4th Edition
Jesse Liberty
ISBN: 0-672-32207-2
$49.99 US
$74.95 CAN

Sams Teach Yourself Java 2 in 21 Days, Professional Reference Edition, 2nd Edition
Laura Lemay
ISBN: 0-672-32061-4
$49.99 US
$74.95 CAN

SAMS

www.samspublishing.com

Sams Teach Yourself Visual Basic 6 in 24 Hours
Greg Perry and Sanjaya Hettihewa
ISBN: 0-672-31533-5
$19.99 US/$29.95 CAN

Sams Teach Yourself C++ in 24 Hours, 3rd Edition
Jesse Liberty
ISBN: 0-672-32224-2
$29.99 US/$44.95 CAN

All prices are subject to change.